MUTUALITY IN EL BARRIO

Stories of the Little Sisters of the Assumption Family Health Service

Carey Kasten and Brenna Moore

EMPIRE STATE EDITIONS

AN IMPRINT OF FORDHAM UNIVERSITY PRESS

NEW YORK 2024

Fordham University Press also publishes its books in a variety of electronic formats. Some content that appears in print may not be available in electronic books.

Visit us online at www.fordhampress.com/empire-state-editions.

Library of Congress Cataloging-in-Publication Data available online at https://catalog.loc.gov.

Printed in the United States of America

26 25 24 5 4 3 2 1

First edition

To Sister Susanne Lachapelle (1938–2022)
and the families of East Harlem

CONTENTS

FOREWORD

> The world is called to be one family . . .
> —Fr. Stephen Pernet

My name is Norma Benítez Sánchez. I am originally from Veracruz, Mexico. I met the Little Sisters of the Assumption in 1991 at the LSA Family Health Service community center in East Harlem, New York, and since then they have been a light that has brightened my life.

I arrived in this country as a young newlywed, faced with new realities all around me—new culture, new language, new food—but more importantly, without a family or community. My experience as an immigrant is the story of many others who also face the same challenges I did. We come to a new land with many hopes and dreams, yet even in the midst of our powerful future goals, we experience a sense of immense loss.

Growing up in a tight-knit, loving family gave me a sense of security and deep roots. My parents were well known and loved in our hometown and the door of our home was always open to anyone who wished to enter. Our home was a beehive of life and energy. The shock of living in a very large New York City, without this kind of nurturing "family" close by, was devastating.

But all that changed in 1991. It changed because I met a woman as we both waited to see a doctor at an East Harlem clinic. She shared information about LSA's parenting class. A couple of days later I was attending those classes with women who not only spoke my language but shared a common experience. This set me on a path that would change everything.

Having a family that is present in your life to support you through thick and thin was something for which all of us in that group longed. For me, this became a reality when I met the sisters and those who would one day be my best friends and my "comadres."

I first met Sister Susanne Lachapelle in the parenting group and then other sisters who at that time worked in other programs. I was a witness to their love, caring, compassion, and solidarity, which they gave to all the families with whom they came in contact. Life was transformed for me and my small family. After a couple of years, we learned about American culture and began to celebrate every holiday at her side. As years went by, Sister Susanne had to adjust to having teenagers in the family and learn how to deal with some of the perks that accompany it. This journey has blessed me with those who have guided me into the important truth that it is not "I" who walk life's path but "we" who journey together . . .

Working for and with the Little Sisters in different capacities has fostered a deep sense of compassion in me for others as the sisters' lives have been a model for living my own. It has called me to make a "covenant" in my heart that is beautifully described in one of the LSA's international newsletters: "Today is the time to live . . . • A covenant of communion • A covenant that crosses frontiers • A covenant of encounter • An inclusive covenant • A fruitful covenant which generates blessings."

I want to thank Brenna Moore and Carey Kasten for the excellent work they did in compiling and sharing the stories of many brave women. These are powerful stories of hope in the human ability to be tender and kind even in the moments when life is hard. The process they used and the relationships they established over many years are very impressive and very "Little Sister"! It highlights the mutuality of the power of growth, which I know very personally, as the bedrock of this sacred family. LSA has always partnered with other organizations like universities and hospitals to advance their work, and this is one more example of a partnership and relationship based on trust.

Thanks to both authors for this book's spotlight on the depth of LSA's impact on immigrant and nonimmigrant families in New York City. They are giving you, its readers, a glimpse of a profound transformational process of mutuality that has affected countless families in East Harlem and beyond; a testament to the building up of a Universal Family with CARE, COMMITMENT, TRANSFORMATION, MUTUALITY, HOPE, and FAITH!

The Little Sisters are facing a critical moment in their history, with the number of sisters diminishing in the USA. The group *LSA Family in Mission* has formed with the goal of transmitting and acting on the LSA spirit with communities of need . . . into the future.

My hope is that once you have read these pages, you will catch the passion of the Little Sisters' charism, which magnifies families' inherent dignity and potential. YOU have many talents to share. I know you have creativity and energy. The world needs you. Our families need you. Come join us! Join the "we" who share the same commitments to justice and joy!

Gracias, Norma Benítez Sánchez, New York City, 2023
Member of the LSA International Laity Commission
www.lsafim.org

INTRODUCTION

Humanizing Stories

Relationships and Beginnings

THE LITTLE SISTERS of the Assumption (LSA) Family Health Service building sits on a busy block on 115th Street in East Harlem, just across from one of New York City's largest public housing complexes. A gorgeous mural right beside LSA painted by muralists Lexi Bella and Danielle Mastrion depicts two dark-skinned women with bright flowers in their hair and a magnificent red rose blooming between them. At the top, the spray-painted words "*There is a rose in . . .*" evoke the song "Spanish Harlem," the classic hit about the neighborhood.

On any given weekday, people stream into and out of LSA's bright and airy five-story structure, past the colorful mural, past the barbershop and the bodega. There are mothers, arriving often in pairs or threes, who find their way to LSA sometimes only weeks after crossing the border from Mexico, having heard, by word of mouth, of the support that *las hermanitas* ("the little sisters") offer. In the late afternoons, the children of the neighborhood, mostly from families that came from Mexico or Central America, start arriving—little girls with braided hair, boys with round faces—to complete English-language homework with tutors. There are the few religious nuns from the Little Sisters of the Assumption congregation, like Sister Susanne Lachapelle, who until her recent passing walked to the LSA agency nearly every day from her convent up the street for her ministry as a nurse. Longtime staff come in and out, like Melina Gonzalez, who has been connected with LSA for almost thirty years in so many capacities it feels like a second home. Originally from Mexico City, she first came to

LSA as a young mother in 1996 for a parenting class. With the agency's encouragement, she developed leadership skills and eventually became a valued staff member, sharing her knowledge and skills with hundreds of local families over the years.

At a time when bigger is often seen as better, LSA has kept its focus on the roughly twenty-block East Harlem neighborhood, an area that stretches from East 96th Street north to East 125th Street and from Fifth Avenue to the East River. This has long been a neglected part of the city and one of the toughest places to thrive as a child, with some of New York's highest rates of asthma, poverty, and emergency room visits. LSA is not the only place that aims to inspire change in the neighborhood; countless clinics, shelters, and food banks dot the landscape of East Harlem, some on the same block as LSA. Indeed, this part of the city has attracted social workers, government agencies, clinicians, and other activists for decades. One might see LSA as just one more social service agency, or even dismiss it as sweet or quaint (both because of the "little sisters" in the name and the daisy flower logo). But LSA is unique, part of a network of East Harlem's powerful grassroots organizations that draws from the remarkable strengths of local families in its community. LSA aims to be a place of both healing and empowerment focused on the overall holistic health of resident families. Long-term relationships are cultivated here rather than quick fixes, and it is a place that nurtures people's full potential as leaders, parents, and advocates for themselves.

This book tells the stories of the people connected to LSA Family Health Service in East Harlem. Combining oral histories from residents with in-depth archival research into the history and spirituality of the Little Sisters of the Assumption, the religious congregation that founded the LSA family health agency, these stories open a window into the world of New York's Spanish-speaking newcomers and, for the first time, into how this unique organization works with an approach it calls "mutuality." It features the personal stories of people who are rarely given voice in the public sphere, through interviews we conducted with eighteen Mexican mothers who participated in LSA's parenting programs over the past twenty-five years. In featuring their stories, this book creates a unique oral history archive we are honored to make public in English.

In contemporary public discourse in the United States, we often hear *about* undocumented Spanish-speaking immigrants as objects of fear or sympathy, but we rarely hear directly *from* them. In these chapters, we hear the stories of women, many of whom became mothers when they were very young and suffered serious challenges and traumas, who forged connections in East Harlem through the agency and went on to raise healthy children, including many who went on to college, sometimes graduate school. Several of the mothers became community leaders who helped countless other families in the neighborhood. From their narratives, we learn how these women navigated a strange city and an unfamiliar language, as new mothers in a neighborhood that has long been a site of not only formidable challenges—scarce resources, racism, and poverty—but also extraordinary strength, creativity, and cultural vitality. The stories we heard were nearly all about women who forged bonds with one another for solidarity, accompaniment, care, and neighborhood transformation.

Their accounts also shine a light on an organization that began as a small community of vowed nuns who, like these mothers in East Harlem, also trace their origins abroad. Their stories stretch back to 1891, when six Little Sisters of the Assumption nuns boarded a steamship from France to New York to begin nursing the "poor sick" in tenement houses in the Lower East Side. Unlike most of the Roman Catholic Church's efforts to minister to poor immigrants, the mission of the Little Sisters was not about service to fellow Catholics for the upbuilding of the faith in a new Protestant country.[1] Unusual for their time, the Little Sisters served and nursed the poor "regardless of creed or color or nationality."[2] In an era of virtually no health care among the poor, the demand for the Little Sisters' services in Manhattan quickly grew. To be more effective, beginning in 1958, they decided to focus their ministry on the East Harlem neighborhood. The families they worked with have represented the patterns of immigration in East Harlem: first Italian immigrants, then Black and Puerto Rican residents, and now the majority of the families involved in LSA's programming come to the agency from Mexico.

The vowed religious sisters from the Little Sisters of the Assumption congregation were highly educated women who built deep relationships with families and gained firsthand knowledge about the complexity of the challenges they faced. In the 1960s and 1970s, inspired by the Second Vatican Council and what became known as liberation theology, the sisters broadened their ministry to address larger issues affecting the health of East Harlem residents—unsafe housing, inadequate health care, isolation from the community. They hired lay staff including nurses and community health workers, as well as grandmothers from the neighborhood, social workers with master's degrees, local advocates, and many others. They partnered with major hospitals, law firms, schools, and churches. In 1970 they created LSA Family Health Service, a community-based organization legally separate from the Little Sisters religious order, but still animated by their founding spirit. This nonprofit still exists and thrives in East Harlem today.

Among the religious sisters, East Harlem mothers, and LSA lay staff that we spoke to, very few of the women used the term "feminist" to describe themselves. But they all lived their lives in disjunction from the dominant norms on offer to women—whether in France in 1891; Oaxaca, Mexico, in 1995; or East Harlem, New York, in 2022. It is an honor to share the stories of all these people and the alternative networks of care and solidarity they created.

Mutuality in El Barrio is the first book-length study of LSA's long history in New York City and of the East Harlem families that engage its services. The agency has been featured in the *New Yorker* and *National Geographic*; its work has been cited in a 1971 congressional hearing about poverty; numerous academic articles have highlighted individual projects and programs at the agency; and the organization has launched successful legislative campaigns in New York City. Yet much of its work remains unknown to people interested in issues like community empowerment, leadership development, service and justice, and immigration. It is also removed from larger nonprofits or nongovernmental organizations (NGOs) that focus on national policies and have a more prominent presence in the media and national landscape.

In our interviews and in the archival material, we encountered one particular theme again and again: what Sister Margaret Leonard, the first executive director of the East Harlem agency, called "mutuality." In a 1972 article published in the journal *Social Casework* titled "Mutuality as a Catalytic Power for Growth," Sister Margaret described mutuality as a "power-with" relational model of care that aimed to enrich the lives of both the person being served and the one serving.[3] LSA's goal was more than service. Mutuality meant the agency's vision was also focused on the development of strengths within the lives of low-income families to cultivate grassroots leadership. Given the prominence of this ideal in the work of LSA, we ask: How have mutuality practices been infused into the fiber of LSA's partnerships with families? How does mutuality equip clients with skills to tell their own stories as they move from addressing immediate needs toward independence, self-fulfillment, and, ultimately, leadership within their community? And how do these relationships enrich the lives not only of LSA clients but also of staff and volunteers?

In addition, "mutuality" prompted changes in the way LSA interprets its religious identity. When the organization arrived in East Harlem, it was staffed by nuns dressed in habit, compelled to live out the ideals of the gospel. In the following decades, LSA's staff came to include people of diverse faiths and people with no religious affiliation, from a range of racial and ethnic backgrounds. Gradually, the language of "mutuality" replaced LSA's Christian-specific messaging, allowing LSA to take Catholic particularity out of its literature. How has this recasting of religion affected the agency's work?

How the Project Came to Be: Mutuality as Research Practice

Scholarly projects with marginalized communities can perpetuate unequal relationships of power. East Harlem, like many low-income parts of New York City, has often been the subject of this so-called extractive research, where elite and well-funded scholars swoop into a community to collect data and leave, perhaps earning a publication for tenure or promotion but contributing nothing to the community in return.[4] As scholars, we are mindful of these colonial patterns of research. We have been attentive to these histories and have consciously engaged in a different kind of project, one that moved from research as extraction to a model more grounded in LSA's own principles of mutuality and cocreation. This book is the result of more than ten years of relationship building and trust between the authors and the community at LSA, relationships that grew with patience and commitment. These relationships operate on a different sense of time than research that is rushed by the tenure clock. The relationships between the authors and people connected to LSA are the context for the research, the heart of the project, and its moral center of gravity. The connection is worth explaining in more detail.

Brenna first came to LSA in 2010 when she was interested in connecting her family with a grassroots organization for volunteer work. At the time, Brenna, overwhelmed as a new faculty member and a young parent, was missing the civic engagement and connections to public life that she had known as a graduate student. As part of her fieldwork for her master's in divinity, she worked with the Greater Boston Interfaith Organization, an affiliate of the Industrial Areas Foundation (IAF), a community organizing network that trains people to have more agency in public life and centers the importance of relationship building for power. She missed the joy that comes from connecting with the larger community, meeting different kinds of people, and working on concrete goals that are mutually beneficial. Given her personal connections to Catholicism and her work as a professor of theology at a Jesuit university, she was initially drawn to LSA Family Health Service because of its Catholic roots, even though she sensed that religion was more in the background now. She knew only that LSA was a family health agency serving the low-income, mostly Spanish-speaking community of East Harlem. She contacted Trish Gough, LSA's director of volunteer services, who replied with generosity and welcome and invited Brenna to East Harlem.

Brenna remembers vividly the first afternoon that she and her children visited the agency on East 115th Street. The building was filled with people; walls were decorated with colorful homemade art (art, we would later learn, that came from the Building Bridges of Hope program to help recently arrived mothers process the traumas experienced crossing the border). Spanish and English could be heard everywhere. Brenna was most struck by how hard it was to tell the clients from the staff and volunteers. For example, she met two people working side by side. One was a teenage boy, a recently arrived immigrant, who volunteered at the food pantry while he was waiting for his asylum case to be processed. He wasn't there for services; he was volunteering. The other was a white woman from the Upper East Side dressed, memorably, in leopard-print pants and high heels. As Brenna observed them loading up the shelves together, she remembers thinking how rarely we see two people so different working alongside one another. The hierarchies that are so entrenched in our society seemed a little more jumbled at LSA, in a good way.

Trish and Brenna figured out a way that her family could volunteer in simple ways—dropping off donated snacks for LSA's after-school program, for example, and making gift bags for mothers at Christmas with the help of Brenna's neighbors. Most importantly, Brenna and her family just kept showing up at the agency. They volunteered, came to events, and got to know staff, volunteers, and families. These initial years of building relationships were crucial. And Brenna felt firsthand the mutuality LSA often describes. Though she volunteered, she noticed that the more she came to know the organization and its people, the richer and more meaningful her life felt. She began to feel again the joy she knew from the experience of a diverse group coming together to work on projects centered on shared ideals and values.

What Brenna saw at the agency also pointed to the fact that LSA embodies and practices many of the best organizing principles of community empowerment and social change. The organization had been in the neighborhood since 1958 and had gained its trust. Much of the agency's staff was and is made up of community members who focus on the assets of East Harlem's families, not just their needs. The agency helps families nurture and develop these strengths despite the difficulties and challenges they face. And its mission goes beyond service to "strengthen and empower vulnerable families and children by meeting their basic needs for food, healthcare, education and a safe home, in the belief that affirming families in their own dignity improves the entire community."[5] LSA is committed to these values: "The uniqueness and dignity of each person. The strength of families. The power of relationships. The richness of diversity. Justice as a right for every person. The creativity of the human spirit. The importance of the spiritual search."[6]

LSA's work on multiple levels stood out. It was at once personal, attentive to emotions and relationships, focused on individual families' flourishing, while also working toward structural change and building power in the neighborhood to advocate for justice. Brenna was especially impressed with the LSA nuns who were still there, elderly women she passed in the hallways and sometimes spoke to, like Sister Susanne Lachapelle, and board member and former executive director Sister Margaret Leonard. Sister Margaret has an honorary doctorate and is an accomplished leader who has published prolifically on social change in New York City and Boston. Sister Susanne, who had been working in nursing in East Harlem since 1973, was also a published author and community leader. So modest about their accomplishments, these sisters were smart, impressive, and committed.

As Brenna's engagement with LSA grew deeper as a volunteer, she listened for opportunities for making a more meaningful contribution. At one meeting Sister Margaret spoke about an unfinished project that had been lingering for years. Inginia García, a neighborhood resident who had directed LSA's Parenting and Child Development program for twenty years, began her work at LSA making home visits to new mothers and babies in the neighborhood. Today these babies are grown. Inginia had compiled a list of mothers who had taken part in LSA's programs years ago and were eager to tell their stories, stories about their relationships with the agency and its staff and the difference those relationships made in their lives. Inginia has such deep love and care for these families and believed that sharing their stories would both document the work of LSA and provide inspiration for others. Sister Margaret thought a scholar could help the agency gather, research, and write these women's experiences in the context of LSA's history in East Harlem, a history that had never been written.

This prospect intrigued Brenna. The project fit with Fordham University's stated values: it focused on New York City, engaged issues of justice—especially immigration—and, through LSA's Catholic roots, connected with the Jesuit mission of our school. It aligned with Brenna's community organizing experiences with Greater Boston Interfaith Organization and IAF. It also fit with her research interests on the history and spirituality of Catholic social justice communities around the world. Sister Margaret, now in her eighties, was also a Fordham alum.

The research felt particularly important because Brenna knew that women like Sister Susanne and Sister Margaret are emblematic of an aging generation of nuns in this country who have done extraordinary work for social justice. Memories of their remarkable lives are at risk of being lost. Documenting their stories was urgent.

While it would be difficult for an outsider who doesn't live or work in East Harlem to conduct research in this community in a way that would be mutually beneficial, the decision that Brenna and LSA staff made to embark on this project would have been impossible without the work of Inginia García. She is a neighborhood resident and beloved former staff member who has deep, family-like bonds of trust with the women interviewed. Her role as the bridge of trust for this research project cannot be understated. At the same time, it is nearly impossible for agency staff to undertake a long-term research project like this. The urgent, day-to-day needs of East Harlem families, along with regular programming and the work of grant and report writing, take precedence. The long-term partnership and established relationship between Brenna and LSA allowed for an open, honest exchange of ideas and information without which this project would have been very different, perhaps even impossible.

One rainy evening in 2019, a small group gathered in the convent apartment of the Little Sisters on 115th Street: Brenna, Sister Susanne, Inginia, Sister Margaret, current staff member Ray López, and retired staff member Gail Gordon. They talked about the possibilities and potential beneficiaries of a research project like this. They defined central tenets of the project: centering the voices of the East Harlem families, documenting the history of the agency, and highlighting best practices for empowerment and social justice that have come out of LSA's many successes.

But one topic stood out that evening most of all: the grim atmosphere in the country at the time. Dangerous, xenophobic rhetoric was on the rise. At the highest levels of political power, Mexican families and immigrants were being dehumanized. We had learned the year before about the family separation policies at the border. This xenophobia was not an abstract problem in East Harlem, where ICE (Immigration and Customs Enforcement) was knocking on the doors of families in the middle of the night for raids.[7] Families were scared to leave their apartments, even to take their children to school. The group agreed that telling these stories in the chapters that follow could offer a counternarrative to the xenophobic rhetoric dangerously circulating in the United States that animated these raids, the violence of family separation, deportations in the middle of the night. Providing positive stories to counter the vicious propaganda was just one of the many things we could do.

Although Brenna spoke Spanish, she needed a colleague to join her who worked professionally in the language. Ideally it would be someone whose scholarship also focused on Spanish-speaking communities in New York, someone with experience in and knowledge of the issues LSA's families faced.

Several colleagues suggested Carey Kasten, a professor of Spanish literature and culture at Fordham. Carey had a strong reputation on campus for centering community engagement in her Spanish language courses. In addition, she was working actively on issues of migration at Fordham. She had just returned from a faculty immersion trip to the Kino Border Initiative at the Arizona-Mexico border and was about to lead a student trip to the border. Carey was the ideal partner.

Like Brenna, Carey had sought out relationships with community partners as a way to address a feeling of disconnection. In the classroom, her language students were often uninspired, taking a class to fulfill a requirement without seeing the practical applications of language learning. In an effort to make courses more relevant, Carey partnered with Fordham's Center for Community Engaged Learning to connect course content to local communities. By working with the rich, diverse, and complex Spanish-speaking populations surrounding Fordham's Bronx and Manhattan campuses, learning from and with community members while also practicing their Spanish, students gained real-world knowledge and applications for their Spanish skills across multiple disciplines. With the Hispanic population growing at a faster rate than any other group in the United States, and more than 25 percent of New Yorkers identifying as Hispanic, it was only natural to capitalize on those strengths in the classroom.[8]

Over the years, Carey and her students have engaged New York's immigrant neighborhoods, such as El Barrio in East Harlem and Washington Heights, a predominantly Dominican neighborhood in Upper Manhattan. Carey's students have put their Spanish to work in a variety of capacities, ranging from teaching citizenship classes to helping people with applications for residency or translating birth certificates. Through this work, Carey has also formed long-standing partnerships with organizations such as the Northern Manhattan Improvement Corporation, a nonprofit based in Washington Heights that has grown since 1979 from an organization focused primarily on housing justice to become a multiservice organization. She also spent several semesters working at the New Sanctuary Coalition's (NSC) pro se legal clinic where she and her students accompanied asylees in filling out asylum applications and filing for emergency healthcare benefits, among other things. In the spring of 2013 Carey had also worked with LSA when her language students assisted in on-site Spanish literacy classes.

In 2021, Carey started leading student groups on immersion trips to learn about migration realities on the ground with the Kino Border Initiative (KBI), a binational aid and advocacy organization in Ambos Nogales. Through these experiences, she has become increasingly familiar with the immigration system and the issues that immigrants face in New York City and at the border, but she has also gained valuable knowledge about nonprofit organizations. This work has shaped Carey's teaching and informed her personal civic life, and it has influenced the way she conducted, listened to, and read through our interviews for this book.

When Brenna emailed Carey in February 2020 asking if she would be interested in collaborating on a project about LSA and its work with a group of mothers, it seemed like a natural fit. This would open the door for Carey to bring community-based migration work into her scholarship and to think more deeply about what it means to make research relevant, just as she had done with her teaching.

Mutuality in Research and the Making of the Book

In the spring of 2020 we set out, equipped with Inginia García's lists of contacts and the guidance of many former and current LSA staff and volunteers, to collaborate on this new community-engaged research project. Many staff, like Ray López, Sister Susanne Lachapelle, Sister Margaret Leonard, Trish Gough, Yolanda Tovar, and Melina Gonzalez, have worked at LSA for decades, and were a wealth of knowledge. As our work took shape, it expanded in scope and our team grew in numbers.

Larry Farmer, a professor at Fordham's School of Social Service, joined our project. Together we hired a team of eight graduate and undergraduate students. Larry provided invaluable support in orienting us with approaches to qualitative and quantitative analysis, as well as our Institutional Review Board request, which would allow us to conduct research on human subjects. Most of the students we brought on spoke Spanish, and several felt personally connected to the topic. Three students were born abroad, in Peru, Colombia, and Kosovo. Three others were first-generation students whose families had immigrated from Latin America. Yet another had roots in New York's Puerto Rican community. Many saw this project as a way to reconnect with their roots and give back to their communities.

When we submitted our first application for funding in early spring of 2020, we imagined that we would create a tight-knit research community, leading in-person group reflection exercises to define together the parameters of our research and its outcomes. Our meetings were to be robust spaces of mutual learning over coffee and meals, and the in-person interviews would take place at LSA or in clients' homes where our team could immerse itself in the ethos of the organization and its community.

By the time our funding came through in June 2020, the pandemic had upended all our lives. LSA's doors were shuttered (although their food pantry and visiting nurse service continued offering essential services). New York City and many of the clients we were to interview were on the frontlines, ill, out of work, tending to ailing family members, adjusting to college kids moving home, supervising remote learning in impossibly close quarters. Our research team, like everyone else, was also affected. We were spread not just across the New York metropolitan area, but across the country, and many of us were experiencing isolation and anxiety as we retreated into our private worlds. Everything seemed to point to putting the project on hold. But, for some reason, we began scheduling Zoom meetings with one another. We soon realized that sticking with our efforts might help us hang on to something positive, constructive, and productive during an otherwise isolating and frightening time.

In many ways, the "pause" the pandemic brought facilitated our work. Without the hustle and bustle of commutes across three campuses, multiple boroughs, and suburbs, our over-committed schedules opened up in new ways. The isolation of the "new normal," each of us tucked away in our own little pods, made our group meetings a rare opportunity for human connection beyond our families and gave new purpose to our work.

And the sense that we were in this together, that others (the research team, LSA staff) were counting on us, made us accountable at a time when so many other personal projects and deadlines were abandoned. Rarely did anyone from our eleven-person team miss a meeting. Perhaps this human connection, to each other and to the very humanizing story we were telling, was all the more necessary because of the unique, isolating circumstances we were enduring. At the same time, the pandemic equalized access to virtual platforms: elderly religious sisters, Hispanic mothers who were not necessarily adept at navigating the internet, and college students alike all became Zoom proficient seemingly overnight, allowing for virtual meetings that would otherwise not have been possible.

To address our first order of business as a research team—familiarizing ourselves with the general contours of LSA's history and services—we met with LSA staff to discuss readings and share impressions. We then drafted a questionnaire for which we relied on the expertise of Dr. Jacqueline Shannon and Dr. Tracey Dewart, who had partnered with LSA as researchers for many years from Brooklyn College and the Department of Community Health at Mount Sinai's School of Medicine. They generously shared with us a semi-structured qualitative model that they had devised for interviewing families and helped us review their questionnaire and clarify any outstanding questions. Then our student researchers translated the questionnaire to Spanish in preparation for our interviews. Throughout this process, we walked with LSA staff, volunteers, and partners, making sure our work aligned with theirs every step of the way.

As we prepared for interviews with both LSA staff and mothers who had participated in LSA's programs, we encouraged a natural conversation flow that would allow interviewees to recall specific stories about their time with LSA. The introduction written into our questionnaire for the mothers emphasized this focus: "We are interested in hearing more details about the story of your life and your relationships with your child and family, your experiences at work and school as well as your children's experiences at school as young children and currently. Finally, we'd like to hear about your involvement with Little Sisters and how you feel their support has influenced your parenting, family relationships and your children's current state." Several times throughout the survey, we were prompted to ask the mothers about specific memories or to probe for details, especially regarding the influence that LSA had on their parenting. From the start, this project was invested in telling stories.

Next, we divided the list of mothers evenly among our Spanish-speaking group members. Other team members set out to interview former and current staff members and upload documents to create a shared drive of materials secured from the LSA archive. Although initially we felt some discomfort reaching out to people whose lives and livelihoods were possibly devastated by the pandemic (we would eventually learn that East Harlem was the Manhattan neighborhood hardest hit by COVID), the agency's staff assured us that families were prepared to talk and could navigate video interviews.

From October 2020 through January 2021, we conducted seventeen in-depth interviews over Zoom and via telephone with mothers who had participated in LSA programming in the 1990s and early 2000s. Several of the mothers we interviewed spoke Spanish as a second language (Mixteco, the Mesoamerican indigenous language, was their first), but all of them were so proficient in Spanish that this was the language they spoke at home with their children.

Sixteen of the seventeen interviews carried out with mothers were recorded and transcribed. The other interview was documented with extensive notes. All of the interviews were conducted in Spanish. We initially interviewed Melina Gonzalez, the eighteenth mother considered in our study, as a staff member. Upon learning of her history with LSA as a client and young mother, we decided to include her in our research cohort. Carey then conducted three additional interviews in English with Melina between June 2021 and April 2022. In all our conversations, the mothers reminisced about their early days as parents, navigating complex systems in the city while focusing on the challenges and basic tenderness of caregiving. In all, we created an archive with more than forty hours of stories of difficulty and trauma, but also joy, strength, and growth.

In the course of our research, we also benefited from many interviews with current and former staff, including six formal interviews and many, many hours of additional, less formal conversations with nuns from the LSA congregation and staff from the health agency. Our team also gathered stories from archival material—photos, journals, unpublished writings—that the Little Sisters of the Assumption congregation still maintains in the basement of its convent, just a block up from the agency on 115th Street. We recovered videos from the 1980s; read through retreat notes from the 1960s and 1970s; pored over the massive archive of scholarship that staff and nuns produced on best practices in nursing, social work, environmental health, and empowerment based on their experiences in East Harlem; and tracked down news articles about the agency from the *New Yorker*, the *New York Times*, the *Catholic Worker*, and other sources.

In conversations with our research team, the theme of mutuality emerged as the narrative thread that tied all of the stories we had collected together, connecting the interviews with staff, mothers, and volunteers to the stories of LSA's founding religious sisters. From its beginnings, LSA has employed a model of mutual enrichment, eschewing a binary framework of helper and helped in an effort to cocreate new realities in East Harlem that benefit all parties. Throughout our research, we experienced some of this mutuality as well. Our own lives were expanded and enriched upon hearing about the resilience of these mothers, the dedication of retired staff like Inginia García and Gail Gordon, or even the sense of humor that Sister Susanne and Sister Margaret brought to the table. Traditional academic research and writing is often solitary and isolating, but in the course of researching this book during the difficult pandemic, we felt the joy of human relationality and connection. This dialogic and interactive way of doing research centered humanity and relationships.

Our team's work culminated in a Zoom presentation on May 18, 2021, in which students shared their research from the project with LSA community members, former and current staff, and board members.[9] Staff members were touched to hear about families they had not heard of in so long and to learn the ways that their work has made a difference in East Harlem. It reminded them of the core mission of their work that can sometimes get lost in the daily grind. In subsequent meetings, Sister Margaret and Sister Susanne were moved when we shared photos we found in archives or old articles that had been written about their order in the *New York Times* as far back as 1901. At a more recent presentation of our research for Fordham's Center for Ethics Education, one Little Sister of the Assumption nun Zoomed in from France to hear our stories of her religious order.[10] Throughout the research and writing of *Mutuality in El Barrio*, we've frequently paused to share our findings with the LSA community in formal and informal ways as our central goal has always been for this research to serve the community it comes from.

In the summer of 2021, with our interviews completed and a large amount of archival data collected, we sat down to write and quickly realized that there were many strands of the story we wanted to tell: an account of how a local organization interacts with its evolving migrant community; the empowering narratives of Mexican mothers living in East Harlem whose relationship with LSA's mission shaped their independence and self-fulfillment; a remarkable story of how a group of nuns works with a community on the principles of mutuality and creates substantive change; a theological history of how LSA's mission became more capacious in practice; a cautionary tale of how organizations can become removed from their central mission. The narratives featured in this book point to larger, more universal trends in urban studies, migration, sociology, theology, and more.

Throughout the process of researching and writing this book, we have continued to deepen our personal and working relationships with LSA. Through a collaborative, transparent research and writing process, we have shared our work with the protagonists in the book and sought and responded to their feedback in an effort to foreground their voices. At the same time, Brenna carried on with her volunteer work and became a member of LSA's board of directors. On an institutional level, Carey deepened ties between Fordham and LSA. Her Spanish language students started working at the agency again, and she helped establish several year-long internship opportunities for Fordham students across LSA's Advocacy, Mental Health, and Child Development programs. We invited LSA staff leaders to campus as panelists for a Fordham conference on community engagement and as participants in a summit called Partnering for Migration Justice: Building Sustainable Collaborations between Migrant Communities and Higher Education. Our understanding of LSA's mission and place in the community was deepened considerably by simply spending time at the agency, attending events, volunteering, and having countless informal conversations with current staff and the religious sisters about their lives, and our own. We are fortunate to consider many people in the chapters that follow our friends.

Likewise, we are pleased that LSA has been able to feature some of our presentations in fundraisers. And our work inspired a group at LSA, including Brenna, to organize an agency staff retreat as we all recovered from COVID and needed to remind one another about the mission and values behind the work. Throughout, this project has engaged the same ideals of partnership and collaboration that our chapters describe. Our accounts of mutuality invigorated LSA's operations and animated a rededication to the agency's founding principles. We cannot express enough our gratitude to the current and former LSA staff, partners, and volunteers who joined our meetings and helped our research team analyze the stories we heard. Likewise, their appreciation for and encouragement of our project inspired us to write this book, which not only marks the culmination of a research project, but also points to the future of our collaborative work.

While working on the book, both of us deepened our knowledge and understanding of migration issues through visits to the US-Mexico border. In Carey's work with the Kino Border Initiative, she and her students have listened to harrowing stories from migrants: a child forced to witness her grandfather's murder, senseless gang beatings and extortion, unrelenting spousal abuse. On a 2023 trip, Brenna heard stories from countless families with young children who had been turned away at the border, while others prepared to board buses headed to distant cities like New York. Some will find their way to LSA and places like it. These experiences helped us consider what it means to listen and act in solidarity with these stories, to see them as narratives of humanity and complexity, and of empowerment and healing, both for the storyteller and for the listener.

The organization of *Mutuality in El Barrio* places the stories of the women we interviewed at the center of the narrative, framing them with the history of the Little Sisters of the Assumption religious order at the beginning of the book and current realities at the agency at the end of the book. Chapter 1 draws from Little Sisters of the Assumption archival material and oral histories with religious sisters, as well as historical records of East Harlem. It tells the story of how a group of six French nuns made their way to New York City's Lower East Side, and by 1958 transformed their work into a social justice, community health ministry in East Harlem. When they moved to East Harlem, they joined the activist spirit of the neighborhood, battling the fallout from "urban renewal" and expanding their nursing ministry to include community health with a focus on empowerment and advocacy. By the 1960s and 1970s, they had expanded their ministry by hiring neighborhood leaders and the seeds of the current organization were planted.

Chapter 2 focuses on one remarkable story, that of Melina Gonzalez, who exemplifies the radical possibilities of mutuality. Melina's story exhibits the three-phase model of mutuality that LSA employs in its programming with families. This series of steps helps clients become increasingly responsible in all areas of their life, ranging from personal and family life to their role in their community. Melina's trajectory—from English language learner, to hired staff member and award-winning civic leader in her community—embodies the results of LSA's mutuality in action.

Melina's story serves as a bridge from the agency's history to chapter 3, where the voices of the other seventeen mothers who were interviewed take center stage. This chapter identifies common themes among their stories of migration and resettlement in East Harlem to examine how they incorporated the spiritual ideals and practical skills from LSA's Parenting and Child Development program into their lives today. Our fourth and final chapter discusses LSA's shift to a mostly lay secular staff, examining how the agency developed the vision and practice of mutuality in a new context, with a changing landscape of funding and fewer religious sisters involved.

We close the book with a reflection on Sister Susanne Lachapelle's recent and sudden passing, and on her and Sister Margaret's unpublished writings on illness, death, and tragedy, the darker or shadow sides of life. These are the aspects of life that are resistant to programs and empowerment, that are inevitable. But in low-income neighborhoods like East Harlem, the shadow sides of life are intensified, baked into the many structures of our country that perpetuate inequality.

Taken together, we hope the chapters that follow will appeal to people eager to enrich our understanding of humanity by listening to voices rarely present in our public sphere. By reading these stories alongside the agency's unique history and mission, readers gain a greater understanding of ways to inspire local grassroots work that responds to community needs. This book will also prove useful to people interested in collaborative research that helps us learn and grow in ways that are meaningful to the world and to ourselves. Without romanticizing LSA's work or overlooking its shortcomings, we seek to uncover best practices. In this spirit, as scholars we are inspired by works like Rita Felski's recent *The Limits of Critique*, which asks scholars to move beyond critique and deconstruction, and reflect on possibilities revealed by the worlds we study.

In this vein, our book joins other books highlighting stories of faith-based activism and organizing in New York City, such as Angel Garcia's *The Kingdom Began in Puerto Rico: Neil Connolly's Priesthood in the South Bronx* or Susan Greenfield's *Sacred Shelter*. We dialogue with scholars exploring Mexican populations in New York, like Robert Courtney Smith, whose pioneering work as a scholar and activist engages populations beyond academia to advance substantive change in local Mexican communities. Or Alyshia Gálvez's 2009 book *Guadalupe in New York: Devotion and Struggle for Citizenship Rights among Mexican Immigrants*, which highlights the importance of religious practices in defining Mexican New Yorkers' ideas of citizenship well beyond narrow legal parameters. Our project adds to conversations advanced by Courtney Bender's *Heaven's Kitchen: Living Religion at God's Love We Deliver*, about the changing moral and religious imagination of New Yorkers involved in one of the city's best-known nonprofits. Our work also fits within scholarship on East Harlem that aims to listen as closely as possible to the voices of the community, and the worlds they have created, like Christopher Bell's *East Harlem Remembered: Oral Histories of Community and Diversity*, or Robert Orsi's beautiful classic, *The Madonna of 115th Street* (about a street festa that used to take place right up the street from LSA). *Mutuality in El Barrio* also joins studies that aim to see the story of Catholicism beyond the often-grim fixation on the patriarchal world of bishops, priests, and the like. The stories here broaden the focus to include not only the frequently overlooked contributions of religious sisters but also the many secular people and people of other faiths who have connected with a community with Catholic roots, but whose mission has expanded over time.

The heart of this book is the stories of people. Brenna and Carey are both trained as scholars in the humanities—religious studies and Spanish literature, respectively. Although these disciplines may seem removed from the community-engaged work in East Harlem, we have seen so many points of contact. For instance, Doris Sommer's book *The Work of Art in the World: Civic Agency and Public Humanities* underscores the importance of the humanities, arguing that art and the concomitant interpretation of art do real work in the real world. She writes, "At the core of human practices—from nation building to health care, from intimate relations to human rights and resources—art and interpretation affect practical interests and explore possibilities."[11] Likewise, the stories this volume tells of LSA's history and the stories of the families that interacted with the agency, as Sommer proposes, can "morph into institutional innovation" and lead to real-world change.[12]

The idea that storytelling can motivate authentic, innovative transformation foregrounds much of our work as scholars and teachers. It is through storytelling that we have found the most natural bridge between our training as scholars in the humanities and community engagement. Storytelling plays an essential role in migration studies and activism, where stories serve to document the undocumented and help us understand realities often obscured by politics and the news media. Stories also help us see beyond monolithic views of culture, whether stories of courageous nuns who have dedicated their lives to service and justice, or stories of resilient, remarkable women who crossed the border only to discover personal reservoirs of strength and joy. These humanizing stories bridge the divide between us/them, US/Mexico, cocreating a narrative of us, together.

As Mexican author Valeria Luiselli explains in her 2017 book *Tell Me How It Ends: An Essay in Forty Questions* about the 2014 wave of unaccompanied minors entering the United States: "Perhaps the only way to begin to understand how dark these years are for migrants who cross borders from Central America, Mexico, and the United States is to record as many individual stories as possible. Listen to them over and over again.

Write them down, over and over again. So they won't be forgotten, so they remain in the annals of our shared history and in the deepest part of our conscience."[13]

Stories humanize the complex and harrowing situations surrounding migration that can feel distant from our daily lives and that all too often are reduced to case numbers or legalistic jargon. The moving accounts that migrants tell of atrocities and horror but more importantly of love, tenderness, and strength provoke reactions that ideally motivate action.

Similar questions arise in the *testimonio* genre, where power dynamics are at the very least questioned and, at best, turned on their heads. This traditionally Latin American literary genre—which sparked revolutions in Spanish departments at universities throughout the United States—centers voices of those customarily excluded from academia to recount personal experiences that communicate struggle and resistance. As Tobin Hansen, who teaches anthropology at the University of Oregon, reminds us in the book he coedited with María Engracia Robles Robles from Kino, *Voices of the Border: Testimonios of Migration, Deportation, and Asylum*, testimonios are made to circulate, to travel from person to person and place to place. As they do, their potential increases: "Knowledge is produced through testimonios over time as events are lived, recounted, and retold, and across place, as new considerations of various aspects of life in and between places are revealed and themselves travel."[14]

Like Sommer's argument for the revolutionary potential of the humanities, testimonios offer a potential for transformation. In the words of literary critic John Beverley, "testimonio aspires not only to interpret the world, but also to change it. Nevertheless, how one interprets the world also has to do with how one seeks, and is able, to change it."[15] In this book, we have worked together to document and interpret the testimonios of the LSA community as one way to realize the potential of our own community engagement.

The stories we tell here are only made real in the context of relationships of mutual trust between speakers and listeners, between authors and staff, staff and families, families and authors, and now, authors and readers. While this book project is finally complete, we are not "done." The LSA community is now part of our lives, and our lives are richer for it. We will continue to work together to cocreate solutions for the flourishing of the families who are so often demonized, misrepresented, or simply ignored in our country. There are many more stories to tell, and more relationships to cultivate. Like stories told in *testimonios*, the stories of LSA and its families bring to life and celebrate the beauty and resilience of a community. And the greatest honor you can do to these voices is to act on them, to tell and retell them "una y otra vez" (over and over again), as Valeria Luiselli says. Personally, we are grateful for the experiences and relationships that LSA has made possible. It is an honor and a privilege to share their stories.

1

"The Power of Growth Is in Relationship"

The History of the Little Sisters of the Assumption Nuns in East Harlem, 1865–1970

SISTER SUSANNE LACHAPELLE, a nun with the Little Sisters of the Assumption, lived in East Harlem for fifty years until she was eighty-four years old. She worked there as a home nurse and advocate for hundreds of low-income neighborhood families. The Little Sisters convent is located on 115th Street, just a block up from the LSA health agency. In a conversation about her life's work, Susanne's blue eyes stood out from beneath her glasses, and she spoke in a soft voice that carried a faint accent from her native Worcester, Massachusetts, the city outside Boston where she was raised. Susanne's mother died when she and her twin sister were twelve. "It was a difficult time," she said of those years.[1]

Sister Susanne was drawn to caretaking at a young age, and nursing as a profession was a natural fit. She had known about the Little Sisters of the Assumption since she was fourteen because the order had a convent near her house, and she had volunteered with them. At first, she became a hospital nurse, but although she liked nursing, she did not like the hospital setting. The Little Sisters' work of home nursing was a perfect alternative.

Susanne made her vows with the Little Sisters of the Assumption in 1962, when she was twenty-four. Almost sixty years later, speaking to us and still living in East Harlem, she remembered vividly her first assignment in Charlotte, North Carolina. By then, the Little Sisters had set up home nursing ministries to the poor not only in New York, but in Charlotte, Boston, Philadelphia, and Walden, Massachusetts. Susanne shared some of the informal, unpublished writings she had kept over the years. She described her experiences in Charlotte as a new sister and nurse:

> I was asked to visit a new referral from the hospital, an elderly woman just discharged, who needed daily visits for a leg wound. I found my way up a dirt road, with many shacks, housing several families and children everywhere. Mrs. T hobbled to the door to let me in. Not only did she have a large wound that covered the lower part of her leg, but the inflammation extended above the knee as well. She related the story of what happened. A man tried to rob her the day after her social security check came. When she resisted him, he dragged her across the floor, and her leg was caught under the frame of the door. He took her check and fled, leaving her pinned under the door frame where she remained until a neighbor came a few hours later, to rescue her and send her to the hospital. Mrs. T is caring for her three young grandchildren as their mother is gone. It was summer where the 8am temperature in Charlotte is 100 degrees and continues to climb during the day.[2]

Even as she described that scene—the wounds, the robbery, the sweltering heat—Susanne emphasized something she always stressed about the families she came to know over the many decades of her work, first in Charlotte, then Boston, then East Harlem, where she worked for a half a century. She described Mrs. T's resourcefulness, her commitment to her grandchildren, her resilience, her *assets*. Susanne's ability to see the strengths of the low-income families she has worked with exhibits something of the distinctive sensibility she shared with many of the people in this book. We will explore the meaning of mutuality in the chapters that follow. At its core, mutuality focuses on the inherent strengths within vulnerable families and how these strengths can be developed in the context of relationships through practices that recognize and develop people's capacities, even in the midst of crises.

Through her job as a home nurse for fifty years in East Harlem, Susanne grew very close with families there and was present for much sickness and death in the neighborhood, where poverty exacerbates health issues. She stood at the bedside of mothers, children, and grandparents suffering from poverty that in East Harlem has been combined with epidemics like AIDS, crack cocaine, and now COVID. Despite these difficulties, Susanne worked to develop the considerable assets of the hundreds of families with whom she was involved over the years. She wrote movingly about many of these patients who touched her life.

Sister Margaret Leonard is also a member of the Little Sisters of the Assumption congregation. Margaret is also in her eighties. A tall woman who now walks with the aid of a cane, she has a commanding presence. She speaks fluently about issues such as empowerment and the development of the strengths of low-income families in an accent recalling Everett, Massachusetts, the industrial suburb just north of Boston where she grew up. "Justice," she often says, "is a constitutive dimension of the preaching of the gospel."[3] The sentence comes from a 1971 Bishops statement, when many in the church—nuns like Margaret and Susanne and priests like Oscar Romero and Gustavo Gutiérrez—helped shift the pastoral atmosphere of the church and put justice work with the poor at the center of their understanding of mission and ministry.

Though Margaret now lives in Boston, where she helped lead another remarkable agency called Project HOPE supporting women struggling with housing stability, she returns regularly to East Harlem. She served as an executive director of LSA from 1967 to 1975 and today sits on its board of directors. Under her leadership, LSA was transformed from a small ministry run exclusively by religious sisters into an extraordinarily effective grassroots organization staffed primarily by laypeople of all faiths and no faith, with formidable ties to hospitals, government agencies, academic institutions, and foundations. These partnerships remain at the core of LSA's work to this day. Through her work, Margaret also helped develop the capacity and leadership of hundreds of families in East Harlem, especially young mothers.

Sister Margaret communicates in a way that suggests she is used to speaking truth to power. Despite her gentle tone, she advocates for and with families, promoting structural change in society. Like Sister Susanne, she has been engaged in this work for sixty years, and it comes naturally to her. From a young age Margaret felt "inclined to the poor," as she put it.[4] She learned about the Little Sisters of the Assumption as a teenager when the sister of a friend joined the religious order. Sister Margaret was attracted to its ministry of going into homes. The direct encounter and long-term relationship building with families felt more personal than regular Christian charity or the secular state-run social service and welfare agencies she was familiar with in Boston.

Sister Margaret took her vows in 1959 and moved to East Harlem that same year. From 1965 to 1967, Margaret was a student at Fordham University's Graduate School of Social Work in New York. She served as executive director of LSA from 1967 to 1975. She also served as provincial superior of the U.S. Province of the congregation, making her the de facto head of the national branch of the international Little Sisters of the Assumption order.

The name Little Sisters of the Assumption points to a central paradox that women like Margaret and Susanne embody. The word "assumption" refers to the Assumption of the Virgin Mary, the popular religious devotion celebrating Mary's ascending into heaven after her death in a bodily way, flesh and bones, like Jesus. The Assumption is a devotional signal that radical reversals can happen, symbolizing newness, utter transformation.

The sisters have engaged in transformative work for decades. To outsiders, the diminutive language of *smallness* ("Little Sisters") can obscure the scale and power of their accomplishments. But this is the intentional paradox, stemming from the reversal of expectations of the gospel, the power and holiness of the gentle ones, those who have divested themselves of our standard models of strength and dominance.

Both Sister Margaret and Sister Susanne embody this paradox; they are unassuming and deflect their considerable accomplishments. But in East Harlem when they were young women in the 1960s and 1970s, they engaged in direct political action that brought them face to face with structures of power in solidarity with neighborhood families. They entered rat- and roach-infested buildings to work with victims of domestic violence. A woman named Sonia Singh, with whom the Little Sisters began working when she was a teenage mother in an abusive relationship in the late 1960s, remembers that in working with her "they could have been killed."[5] Susanne and Margaret have dealt with the Mafia, gang members, families struggling with immense challenges like domestic violence or HIV/AIDS diagnoses. They have both published widely in academic journals in their respective fields, and Margaret has honorary degrees from Seton Hall, Tufts, and the University of Massachusetts in Boston.

"These are smart, smart women," said Trish Gough, a longtime LSA staff member and friend of Sisters Margaret and Susanne.[6] Sonia added: "They are fearless. The nuns in East Harlem were young women when I knew them, but they were so courageous, more courageous than a man, more fearless than a six-foot-ten basketball player. I run out of words to describe them."[7]

Indeed, the nuns are remarkable by all accounts, but they are likely to downplay their accomplishments and instead focus on the stories of the families, especially the young mothers, the grandmothers, and the countless children with whom they built relationships over the course of their life's work. Piecing together their stories requires some digging, and builds on recent historical studies of the histories of Catholic nuns, especially Margaret McGuinness's award-winning and groundbreaking *Called to Serve: A History of Nuns in America*.[8]

This chapter is the result of that digging. It draws on oral histories with families who knew the Little Sisters when they established themselves in East Harlem in the late 1950s and 1960s, interviews with the nuns and early staff members, and newspaper and magazine articles about their work stretching back to the formation of their religious order in 1865, along with published and unpublished writings from members of the community. Taken together, these materials tell the story of the Little Sisters of the Assumption in East Harlem.[9] What ideals, histories, and spiritualities brought them to East Harlem? What relationships helped them work effectively for social change in this twenty-square-block neighborhood, and how did the neighborhood change the religious community itself? How did the Little Sisters of the Assumption nuns formulate the ideals and practices around the theme of mutuality that still anchor and animate the agency now, nearly seven decades later?

The Journey from Paris to East Harlem

The story of the Little Sisters of the Assumption Family Health Service begins in 1865 in Paris, where the Congregation of the Little Sisters of the Assumption, a Catholic order of nuns, was born. Readers are likely familiar with popularized portraits of impoverished, industrialized Paris from novels like Victor Hugo's *Les Misérables*. But scholarly historical accounts also describe nineteenth-century urban France as a place where families were fighting to keep the "wolf from the door" while facing impoverishment, hunger, and disease after decades of upheavals from revolution, war, and industrialization.[10]

In this setting, a forty-one-year-old French priest of the Assumptionist order, Father Étienne Pernet, partnered with a young woman named Marie Antoinette Fage to reimagine what religious service to the poor could look like. Within the symbolic universe of Roman Catholicism, Father Pernet and Antoinette Fage made the ultimate power pair: Fage had been orphaned as a teenager, was impoverished, and lived with a disability, a curvature of the spine. Much like St. Ignatius of Loyola, who limped from a battle wound, or Teresa of Avila, who suffered from migraines, Fage was also known for her piety and dedication despite her challenges.

Fage's physical precariousness endowed her with a certain spiritual charisma, enough to fuel a new religious order, much like Ignatius and Teresa. "Destined to accomplish a great and noble mission on behalf of suffering humanity," one of her early hagiographers proclaimed, "she was being tried like gold in the furnace, so that she might learn by bitter experience the hardships and miseries of the poor and sick, to whom her life was to be devoted."[11]

Though Father Pernet too had endured a difficult childhood, he grew up to be a charismatic, well-connected priest with the Assumptionist order. He had the relationships and resources to make things happen. As a priest, he worked closely with youth groups, children from families suffering from extreme poverty. He learned about their lives and wanted to do something different. Together, he and Fage created a new and experimental community of nuns who were trained as nurses and went directly into the homes of poor families in the midst of medical crises. They offered emergency nursing, homemaking, and spiritual assistance. Fage took her vows in this religious order in 1878. It was a remarkable success—within just a few decades, there would be outposts all over the world.

From one perspective, an order of nuns dedicated to the poor and sick was not necessarily an innovation in late-nineteenth-century Europe. During the Industrial Revolution in Europe, many other Catholic religious orders were already dedicated to serving the needs of the vulnerable, and on a massive scale. But these orders typically did so by strengthening existing Roman Catholic institutions, such as orphanages, hospitals, homes for unwed mothers, and homes for the elderly, institutions in which priests and nuns held considerable, almost uncontested power over those under their care.[12]

At the time most countries in Europe, and especially France, had undergone processes of liberalization, and state-funded institutions like schools and hospitals became secularized. Catholic religious orders responded with the robust, even triumphalist construction of alternative Catholic institutions, notably schools and hospitals, as a rebuke and counter to those run by the state.[13] They saw their ministry as a response to the perceived inadequacies of state institutions. We see some of this skepticism about state care in the early vision of Pernet and Fage.

"The hospital," Pernet wrote, "is repugnant to the poor, on account of the separation it imposes. They feel terrible loneliness and longing for home. . . . Numbers of the sick poor are utterly neglected and reduced to a condition of most distressing misery."[14] Pernet's intentions for this new community highlight a concern that many other religious orders would have shared for the "working-man and his family. For they, in this age of liberalism and independence, had been completely forgotten and neglected."[15]

Offering alternative networks of Catholic care was a way to address the issue of faith among the working classes and a prime opportunity for evangelization, an issue of urgent concern for the church in the age of Karl Marx. For priests like Pernet, addressing the medical and physical needs of poor families was an end in itself, a Christlike act of service. But the early work of the Little Sisters was also thoroughly energized with missionary zeal. While the order would later distance itself from these explicitly missionary goals, the early literature described a new order of nuns who "would alone be capable of penetrating into those hovels of the poor," offer medical care and consolation, and "gain their hearts and rekindle their faith."[16]

But there were some key differences in this new religious congregation Pernet and Fage envisioned. The Rule of the order stated that the poor must be served in their own homes; the order would not be involved in building hospitals or other Catholic institutions. The Rule stated that only the poorest of the poor could be nursed—the sisters were forbidden from offering services to any who could otherwise pay. And unlike other religious orders or nurses, they could accept no donations from the families they served—no money, no food, not even a sip of water. They had to live on the alms of supporters alone—no convents or mother houses were given to them by the church. They were also instructed not to preach or proselytize with words; the actions of service alone were meant to communicate the gospel. They sometimes ate at the same charity soup kitchens as the poor families they served.[17]

One might expect that the Catholic literature about the Little Sisters would emphasize the extremity of their vows of poverty, but even the secular press seemed shocked at their commitments. One 1920 newspaper article about the origins of the Little Sisters described them as nuns who committed themselves to "all that poverty can bring, suffering, cold and hunger." The article added, "They were not deemed practical even by other priests and nuns. They were without capital, without credit. People refused to believe in the future of a work that the wisdom of the age condemned. They did not even hesitate to call the attempt a folly."[18]

Despite the undertaking's reputation as a foolish experiment, in 1865 Pernet and Fage gathered six young women who signed up for the new order.[19] Instead of serving the boundaries of a particular parish, they chose the Gros-Caillou district of Paris (near the center of the city) because of what one nun described as "the countless number of poor people living there."[20] The new sisters took vows of poverty themselves, lived off alms, and furnished their humble apartment with "six old chairs, which they were obliged to carry from room to room as the occasion required, a few cooking utensils, two wooden tables, and a chest of drawers without a lock. These things were all that the house contained."[21] The nurses called one another "sister" and regarded Fage as the superior, "the Mother," who later took the religious name of Marie of Jesus.

They began their work. The rhythms of the nuns' lives were similar to those of other religious orders. The new sisters divided their days into thirds: eight hours for sleep, eight for work, and eight for prayer, devotion, and contemplation. But the work itself was arduous, especially compared to that undertaken by other French orders of nuns. Fage's early journals from 1885 describe nuns catching the illnesses of the families they served (two of the first six members of the community died of cholera); the nuns had to beg for the most basic items, including their own food; and they were not always prepared for how difficult the work was. Unsurprisingly, some of the first members left the new order for more comfortable ones.

In Fage's published journals, she describes the young French sisters going into the homes of the poor as trained nurses but helping with tasks for which they had little preparation, like keeping a fire safely lit or dealing with vermin.[22] One can imagine disasters. Yet for the most part, they apparently did what they set out to do: they nursed poor families in their homes through health crises, they provided childcare, homemaking, and caretaking when a parent was ill, sometimes for days in a row, and sometimes seeing the family through a death. They filled an important gap that no other religious order addressed at the time or for decades to come.

This first year, members of the order informally called themselves "*gardes-malades des pauvres à domicile*" (nurses for the poor at home). A year later they took the name Les Petites Sœurs de l'Assomption after the popular devotion celebrating the Virgin Mary's assumption into heaven after her death.[23] Pernet was also an Assumptionist priest, and this new community became part of the larger global Assumptionist family.[24] Father Pernet encouraged the "little" sister symbolism, tapping into long-standing Biblical imagery about the paradoxical power of weakness and humility. The nuns in this order, Pernet wrote, should "make themselves little, with the little ones, humble with the humble, the weak, the poor, the abandoned, with all those whom the world sets aside and abandons."[25]

Though Mary's Assumption holds theological prominence as the congregation's name, the early devotional material of the Little Sisters centered more significantly on Jesus. A glimpse into the sisters' spirituality helps us make sense of the inner sensibilities that animated their work.[26] In the first Rule Pernet created, during their time of devotion and prayer the nuns were encouraged to imagine themselves as Christ himself, much more than merely Christian nurses or servants.

This was not just an idea they were taught. It was meant to be felt, sensed, and internalized. Pernet described his Rule as the words he wanted the Little Sisters to "breathe into the depths of your hearts and into the marrow of your bones." He continued, "May your actions speak Jesus Christ. If you are not another Jesus Christ, you cannot be a Little Sister of the Assumption." He told them, "Go and preach the Kingdom of God," but added,

> It is not enough to speak. You must bear witness to God by your actions. I can well imagine that when you go into a house where there is poverty and you begin sweeping up and doing the cooking, I can well imagine that you might find all of that uninteresting and, at the same time, not very stimulating for your zeal, and that you might be tempted at first not to see the link between that sort of work and the sublime purpose of your apostolate. However, my daughters, you must accept to use the broom and wash the dishes, and you must serve the poor, not as servants but as apostles. That is how you must preach Jesus Christ.[27]

In 1876, echoing the gospel of Matthew 11:5, Pernet added, "You will be the eye of the blind, the feet of the lame, the ear of the deaf; you will be the mothers of the poor. There is a royal dignity in the poor. The more destitute they are, the more worthy they are of the attention of the Son of God and consequently of your own."[28] The story of the Little Sisters begins to make sense only if we enter into the religious imagination that recast the work of home nursing as something other than what must have been at times frightening, exhausting, or even repugnant. Touching wounds, washing and bandaging those who could not afford hospital stays were recast as sacred, royal, and holy actions. This devotional material formed the inner sensibilities of the sisters and compelled them toward a life of radical service.[29]

By 1875, just ten years after the founding of the order, the original six had grown to forty-eight nuns, all dedicated to home nursing of the poor in Paris.[30] By 1883, the new congregation counted 119 sisters and fifteen communities in France, and now England too.[31] In these first two decades they had endured massive outbreaks of cholera and smallpox, the 1870 siege of Paris in the Franco-Prussian War, and the death of several of members of their order.

As their dramatic reputations grew, the nuns began attracting the admiration of wealthy Catholic patrons eager to support their work. But here, the Little Sisters were different from other orders. They realized how great the needs were but how limited their scope would be if they worked alone. Fage's journals also note that poor families in the neighborhood requested far more help than the nuns could offer: "The impossibility of nursing more than a small number of patients is one of my greatest sorrows," she wrote just a few months into their experiment.[32] Rather than simply requesting alms from the rich to support their work, as had been customary for Catholic religious orders, they expanded their vision.

They wanted the rich to be "personally," as they put it, invested in their work, beyond just donating money. Pernet and Fage wrote in one of the earliest Les Petites Sœurs documents, "The rich should take part in the work of the sisters, they must come near to the poor and help them."[33] They began advocating for what they called the "mixing of classes in society." They envisioned a community of wealthy and sympathetic patrons who would offer the "same services as the Sisters," serve the sick poor in their homes as assistants, and build personal relationships with them under the direction of members of the order.

In 1876, an association of lay women called Les Dames Servantes (Lady Servants) was formed to assist the Little Sisters. Each year these women, mostly well-off mothers and wives, vowed to "dedicate themselves alongside the Little Sisters of the Assumption, and in the same spirit and under the same guidance, to the care of the sick poor in their homes and to the renewal of the working-class family through the Catholic religion."[34] The male counterpart of the lay group was formed in 1881.

Some of the early literature about these lay associations reflects paternalistic assumptions about the rich simply serving the desperate poor while keeping social and economic hierarchies intact. But for the nineteenth century, the community was prescient in thinking more creatively and equitably about these new relationships among different classes. This approach reflected larger late-nineteenth-century currents about justice and worker rights. Pernet advised the new lay associates: "You who are accustomed to giving orders, I would ask you to forget at times that you are in charge in order to give of your person when you are among the poor."[35] This sense of meeting the poor where they are and resisting temptations to control was later developed further by the order and, in East Harlem, became central to LSA's founding and self-understanding.

Gradually, there developed an awareness that these new relationships could do much more than help heal the sick in their homes: they could change the entrenched structures of society. "We study together—the rich and the poor—social and economic problems," Pernet said in a talk to the lay associates in 1885, "with a view towards the true happiness and well-being of the working man."[36] This way of thinking about larger social and economic issues began to stretch the Little Sisters' ministry by viewing the spiritual work of home nursing within a much broader context of societal transformation.

It was an attractive model. By 1890, the *Catholic Telegraph* reported that there were seventeen branches of Little Sisters of the Assumption in Paris and London. In each new location, communities of laypeople who supported them ("confraternities") "sprang up around them."[37]

By 1891, the Little Sisters crossed the Atlantic to the United States. Unlike most religious orders who came to the Americas at the invitation of bishops to educate Catholic immigrants and develop Catholic hospitals, the Little Sisters came to do something very different. A group of wealthy Catholic women who saw the work that the Little Sisters were doing in France wanted to replicate it at home in New York. On April 19, 1891, the New York newspaper *The Sun* reported, "Little Sisters of the Assumption Coming Here from France."[38]

> The steamer La Bourgogne of the French line, which is expected to arrive in this city today, has among her passengers six women who are to nurse the sick poor of New York irrespective of creed or nationality or color. They will receive no remuneration for their services from the people whom they will attend. The women are members of a Catholic sisterhood known as the Little Sisters of the Assumption. . . . They will go every day to perform their labor among the poverty-stricken sick in the metropolis. The Sisters will inaugurate their work by May.[39]

The women who invited them paid their fares and secured a temporary apartment for them on Second Avenue in the Lower East Side, a neighborhood that was home to poor newcomers from Ireland and Italy, as well as Jews from Russia and Eastern Europe, and included blocks occupied by Black families.[40] Soon a wealthy patron gave them their apartment located at 247 East 15th Street. It became their convent.

The six sisters began home nursing in the Lower East Side tenement buildings right away, serving as temporary home nurses and caretakers. Some of the sisters spoke only French, and some spoke German, which they used with some immigrant communities from Europe. But eventually they all learned English. Other orders of Catholic nuns who were already established in New York helped the newcomers get settled. The tenements at the time were notoriously dark, dirty, tiny, airless, vermin-ridden apartments with no indoor plumbing.

It must have been disorienting, perhaps at times traumatic. But the first nuns wrote in notebooks that they nonetheless found it thrilling. The Little Sisters archive has preserved these documents in their old handwritten script. One of the nuns, Sister Marie-Mercedes, wrote three months after her arrival: "The whole world seems to have come together in this city of steel. It's real American country in the midst of snow and ice, with glorious sunshine and the bluest of skies! Everything looks so cheerful that one would never guess the hidden misery of the poor and the sick." A fellow sister wrote that Marie-Mercedes became "attracted to those sick who were most repugnant, those whose wounds did not respond to medical treatment and therefore demanded continued and laborious care; but above all she was attracted to those unappreciative ones who did not know how to show either satisfaction or gratitude, for in those she found and loved God alone!"[41]

Just as in Paris, going into tenement buildings to nurse people suffering from communicable diseases was dangerous work. Only one month after the sisters arrived, Sister Marie Euphrasie caught typhoid fever from a family she served and died soon after. As *The Sun* reported, "Sister Marie Euphrasie, one of the six sisters who came here from Paris on April 19, 1891 for charitable work in tenement houses, died early on Wednesday morning at the home of the Little Sisters of the Assumption, 208 Second Avenue. Her round, cheerful face was familiar to the east side poor people. She was 25 years old. About two weeks ago she nursed a family stricken with typhoid fever. Nine days ago she fell ill of the same disease."[42]

Marie de Christ, the mother superior who came with them to the United States, wrote to Pernet, "I am sitting here, looking at this paper, wishing it could tell you, on its own, the terrible news that I hardly have the courage to put into words. I know I am about to cause you a great deal of suffering, so I place myself at the foot of the Cross, searching for the courage it gives. What would become of us without the strength it inspires? Our beloved Child, Marie Euphrasie, has entered into her eternal home."[43]

Another French order of nuns in New York serving the sick, the Bon

Secour sisters, donated a gravesite for her burial, where "in great sorrow" they "left our little child sleeping under the stars," as Mother Marie de Christ wrote. She mailed a lock of Marie Euphrasie's hair, her ring, and photos of her family to the mother superior in Paris to pass along to her family.[44]

The news of Sister Marie Euphrasie's death made a splash in New York—a prominent physician wrote a letter published in the *New York Times* about the nun, explaining the desperate need for the home-nursing skills the Little Sisters were bringing to New York's impoverished tenement dwellers in their own homes (fig. 1). He urged New Yorkers to donate to the newly arrived order and support their risky work.[45]

The sisters were honored when Pernet visited them from Paris in May 1892 and brought four more sisters to join them in their expanding ministry.[46] By 1896 other reports noted that the work of the Little Sisters was in such demand in the city's tenements that the financial burden could no longer be borne by the women who originally sponsored them. And so the women began serious fundraising.

They first organized card parties at home to raise money, but their efforts quickly grew to include plays, concerts, and fashion shows held at the fanciest hotels. Their efforts were successful, and the city's newspapers reported on both the high society fundraisers and the radical dedication of the nuns.[47] By 1894, a wealthy couple sold one of its homes and gave the entire proceeds to the Little Sisters.[48] In 1898, only seven years after their arrival, *The Sun* reported on a group of artists who performed songs and a play to raise money for the Little Sisters who "are forbidden from providing nursing to any but the poorest" in the city.[49]

The archbishop of New York asked them to expand their services and establish a second community uptown. In October 1900, another donor gave the Little Sisters of the Assumption a house on 125 West 130th Street in central Harlem. "When we think of those early days in 130th street," one sister wrote in an unpublished letter, "we think also of the dear friends and good neighbors who did so much to help the Sisters and their patients and who smoothed out so many of the little difficulties that necessarily attend upon a new Foundation. Among the first of these was the Farrell family whose house adjoined the Convent. How often Mrs. Farrell sent peaches from her garden or fresh-baked cakes from her kitchen. Whenever the Sisters ran out of linen or bedding for some poor patient they would always come to Mrs. Farrell who never failed them."[50] The support that laypeople offered allowed the sisters to maintain a great deal of autonomy from the church hierarchy by operating more or less outside diocesan structures.[51]

Countless articles in the *New York Times* throughout the 1920s, '30s,

A NOBLE NURSE'S DEATH.

HER PATIENT RECOVERED, BUT SHE FELL A VICTIM TO THE DISEASE.

To the Editor of the New-York Times:

The recent death of Sister Marie Euphrasie of the Little Sisters of the Assumption was surrounded by such sad and unusual conditions that I beg a little of your valuable space to give a few of the details.

Sister Euphrasie had been nursing a poor woman, who had only recently come to America with her husband and four young children, and was in extremely poor circumstances. The husband had not yet secured steady work, and when sickness came was unable to provide for the extra expense. Thereupon, as so oftens happens among the poor, friends came forward with their little savings and secured what was necessary. One of them was fortunate enough to discover the Little Sisters of the Assumption, and a competent nurse soon made her appearance.

She nursed the mother and two of the children, sick at once, with the most scrupulous fidelity. Not a single detail of treatment was neglected. It was impossible to enter that poor home, spotlessly clean, and see the sister quietly moving about, caring for her sick and encouraging all alike with her cheerful, wholesome presence, without being inspired with the greatest respect for her and admiration for the spirit that she brought to her work. She was not one of those who give a few superfluous dollars or spare a few hours from a life devoted to pleasure for the sake of their poorer sisters, but a young, healthy, intelligent woman, of cheerful disposition, who was devoting her whole life to the needs of the poor. I can honestly say that it was her intelligent, conscientious nursing which saved this poor woman to her children, for she was on the verge of the grave. She left her and the children convalescent and went home to sicken and die in ten days.

We did not hear of her death until we sent for her to nurse the husband, who had contracted the disease. On learning the sad news the poor woman truly said, "She died to save me." The husband died.

I presume that such incidents as the above are not uncommon in the lives of these sisters. They deserve to be recorded, however, for they flavor of true heroism. Many of the poor, suffering from acute disease, die from lack of just such intelligent watching and nursing as saved this poor woman. Her husband was thus lost. The worthy sister died in successfully supplying this want, and New-York has suffered a positive loss in her death. It is in appreciation of this fact, and as a poor tribute to her memory, that public attention is drawn to the facts of her death by

THE PHYSICIAN.

NEW-YORK, Friday, June 26, 1891.

Figure 1. Letter to the editor in the *New York Times* from a medical doctor extolling the work of the Little Sisters of the Assumption, following the death of Sister Marie Euphrasie in 1891. Sister Marie contracted an illness from a patient in the tenement houses in the Lower East Side just weeks after arriving from France.

and '40s describe elegant fundraisers produced by laypeople at the Commodore Hotel, next to Grand Central Station, complete with live music and card games to raise money for the order's work of "nursing the sick poor in their homes, caring for children and keeping families together while nursing the ill and destitute" (fig. 2). Many Catholic New Yorkers included the Little Sisters in their wills. By 1939, the Little Sisters had served 1,250 families in New York.[52] In 1949, the Little Sisters provided 64,760 hours of free nursing care in Manhattan.[53]

The sisters also replicated the vision of the founders by establishing lay communities of assistants. Members included both the wealthy and some of the poor families served. The sisters hosted monthly discussions in their uptown and downtown convents with the goal of, as one sister wrote, "the mixing of classes in society."[54] The Little Sisters of the Assumption in New York kept growing and moved into a larger house in central Harlem at 340 Convent Avenue at the corner of West 144th Street, a building shared with Our Lady of Lourdes parish.

An August 29, 1920, article in *The Sun* remarked that the order was thriving in New York despite the difficult lives of the nuns. "The nursing

Figure 2. Fundraiser for the Little Sisters' home health ministry at the Commodore Hotel in New York City, 1950s. (Photo courtesy of the Little Sisters of the Assumption archive)

sister may not receive any reward or remunerations whatsoever for her labors," the reporter noted. "They may not even take a glass of water or a crust of bread or an hour's sleep in the house where they are nursing. They nurse the sick poor without regard to creed or color, and the poorer the people are, the more sure they are of receiving the prompt attention of the Sisters."[55]

But what most shocked the reporter was that their work attracted the attention of wealthy patrons and earned their support—not just through donations, but through accompanying the Little Sisters into the homes of the sick poor. "These ladies regularly go out with the Sisters, wash the dirty faces of the children, wash dishes, do all the work that the Sisters themselves do," though they had, the reporter noted, "not yet reached the Sisters' state of immolation."[56] By 1920, the Little Sisters of the Assumption embodied what many Catholics in the United States were aiming to do.

What was it like to have a Little Sister of the Assumption nun, in her long black robe, white veil, and wimple (their habits were simplified in the 1950s and became optional in 1967 after Vatican II) enter your home to clean, change bandages, give medicine, feed babies, sweep up? Sometimes the families were Black and the nuns were white; sometimes they were Italian, Irish, Eastern European and spoke different languages, while some of the sisters didn't yet speak English.

And if you were a child, to have your face washed by a stranger? A stranger who goes by the name "Sister," which inevitably was confusing to some families? Or perhaps you were helped by one of the nun's wealthy female assistants? What did they say to the families? What did they talk about? Were the families embarrassed? Grateful? A combination? In later chapters we will hear from some of the families who worked with the Little Sisters once they established themselves in East Harlem, but there is a silence in the archive about the families' experiences in these earliest years.

Scholars have good reason to be skeptical about the universally sunny reports in the Catholic press about how these sisters were received, how the nuns swooped in like angels and then disappeared following a teary goodbye. In imagining white European Catholics coming into tenements filled with immigrants as any kind of savior, skepticism is understandably called for. That said, even in the secular press, evidence suggests that the Little Sisters were largely welcomed, if for no other reason than the virtual nonexistence of government health care for the poor at that time and for several decades to follow.

In 1903 the *New York Times* published an investigative report about the "servants of the poor who labor in the slums," a study of Little Sisters of the Assumption and two other religious orders from Europe who came to Manhattan and Brooklyn to nurse the poor, all with their own unique styles. The headline was clear: "Members of an Order Who Live Up to the Title of their Organization—How They Command Respect from All Classes with Whom they Come in Contact."[57]

The reporter had accompanied one of the nuns to a home visit and published a detailed account of how he witnessed the sister help a young mother who was sick and had been severely beaten by her husband. The mother was unable to care for the baby. Someone called for the nuns. The reporter wrote that the nun cheerfully cleaned the woman up, enlisted the neighbors to help, fed the baby, put new linens on the bed, and tended the mother's wounds.

Neighbors were terrified and suddenly scurried when the drunk husband returned, but the nun paid him no mind. As soon as the man sobered up, she set him to work fetching medicine, taught him how to hold the baby, and refused to leave until he tearfully apologized to his wife. "The sight of the dark robed nun," the reporter mused, "and the expression of the calm, sweet face that brings a message of hope to the sick room seems to arouse in his breast some latent spark of decency." The reporter was shocked by the whole scene.

Gradually, it wasn't just the wealthy women who became assistants and volunteers, as the Little Sisters of the Assumption aimed to cultivate the talents of the poor families they served, getting them to volunteer and contribute once they were out of crisis mode with an illness.

One famous story is that of Pope Francis, whose family were low-income Italian immigrants in Argentina; in 1930, when he was a baby, an Irish Little Sister of the Assumption nun helped his overwhelmed young mother, who was recovering from an illness. When his parents got back on their feet, they joined the lay associations and helped neighbors through sicknesses and other troubles.[58] For this reason, Pope Francis grew up with an affection for the Little Sisters of the Assumption, and he chose the Sisters' East Harlem location as a stop on his visit to the United States in 2016.[59] By 1950, there were two thousand nuns in a hundred communities around the world—in France, the United States, Argentina, Ireland, Spain, Uruguay, Belgium, Italy, and Egypt.

Other Catholic religious orders of nuns were also dedicated to the poor, some were dedicated to the sick, and a handful even did home nursing. But the Little Sisters' unique rule was singularly focused on the sick poor alone, meeting them not in the new public and private hospitals, but in their homes. They were extreme in their refusal of the wealthy client and of payment for any of their work. They were fueled by a religious imagination that saw the toughest, dullest, most frightening labor of care as the work of Christ.

They were interested in more than simply addressing medical and household emergencies. They were invested in mixing classes in hierarchical societies and thinking about structural changes in society, even early in the order's founding. Already in 1930, as the United States was plunging into the Depression, they described their work in more expansive terms: "Reaching beyond physical care," they said in one letter seeking funds, "their social service is aimed toward helping the families of the poor regain a self-sufficient footing."[60]

They avoided building institutions like schools, medical centers, and convents that would inevitably give them responsibilities, entanglements with power and money, like bishops. "Adaptability is part of our charism," as Sister Margaret once put it, "and since we've never been tied to maintaining institutions, we've been able to change with the times."[61]

That the community resisted building institutions to maintain, like hospitals and schools, together with the fact that they were independent from diocesan structures, meant that on issues of justice, they were often ahead of the Catholic mainstream. According to Mary Oates, by 1930 Catholic hospitals were far more likely than other hospitals to maintain strict racial segregation in staff and patient populations.[62] Though more research needs to be done on the topic of race and the history of the Little Sisters religious congregation in the United States, as early as 1903, the Little Sisters were known to minister in the homes of any race or religion. To be sure, religious communities working within the home nursing tradition did not face pressures for desegregation in the way schools and hospitals did.[63] Because their rule was *only* to nurse the poor who couldn't pay, and they had no expensive buildings to maintain that required placating the white majority, they were less entangled with racist dynamics of the American Roman Catholic Church. In 1956 the first Black woman, Mary Desti Thomas, was received into the Little Sisters of the Assumption community. She took her vows as Sister M. Martin de Porres.[64]

Major changes were to come again in 1958 when the Little Sisters of the Assumption expanded the focus of their ministry to include East Harlem, a Black and Puerto Rican neighborhood almost a hundred blocks north of the Lower East Side, where they had begun their work in New York City. The shift would inaugurate significant developments in their own understanding of themselves as a community.

Transformations in East Harlem

By the late 1950s, profound spiritual, political, and cultural shifts were under way for Catholics around the world, including the Little Sisters. In January 1959, when Pope John XXIII declared that he would "throw open the windows of the church," he set in motion the sweeping transformations that would become inaugurated at the Second Vatican Council (1962–65). But even before then, there were hints of changes that were to come for priests, nuns, and the laity. In 1959 a Catholic newspaper in Philadelphia published a photograph of a Little Sister of the Assumption nun wearing a new, modified, simpler religious habit with less fabric for the dress, and a smaller veil that proved easier to move around in.[65] After Vatican II, as the council came to be known, many religious orders reflected on their relationship to the contemporary world and concluded, among other things, that they no longer wanted their dress to be a visible marker of dramatic distinction between religious and laypeople. Most Little Sisters of the Assumption nuns opted for ordinary clothing by the early 1970s. But the matter of dress was a symbolic visual that communicated a deeper theological message about vowed religious presence *with* rather than separation *from* the ordinary people of the world.

With Vatican II, the Roman Catholic Church declared its deep connection with "the joys and the hopes, the griefs and the anxieties of the men of this age, especially those who are poor or in any way afflicted."[66] The word "solidarity with" as opposed to "charity for" the poor (and its assumptions of an "us" and a "them") became more common in theological literature and church documents. Many progressive Catholics began to focus less on performing good deeds and more on the systems in society that kept people disempowered.[67]

During these years in the middle of the twentieth century, the Little Sisters joined with other Catholic communities whose members were thinking along similar lines. In New York City in the 1940s and 1950s, for example, the Jesuits operated labor schools to teach union organizing, and the Catholic Worker House on the Lower East Side, led by the activist and writer Dorothy Day, ran a house of hospitality for the poor and engaged in antiwar activism. Chicago in the 1950s was the site of the celebrated collaborations between the prominent French Catholic philosopher Jacques Maritain and the community organizer Saul Alinsky, whose work several decades later would inspire a young community organizer named Barack Obama.

By the early 1970s, newly emerging liberation theologies from Latin American countries like Peru and El Salvador were advocating that the starting place for theology must be the actual experiences of the poor. In these contexts, the Kingdom of God was imagined not so much as an afterlife but as a concrete possibility that inspired hope for social change here and now, the lifting up of working classes and the poor. In these locales, Catholic laypeople, activists, priests, and nuns joined non-Catholics around the world and reimagined how the gospel could speak to issues of justice, equity, and renewal. The congregation's roots fit in with these newer ways of talking about spirituality, poverty, and justice.

When Sister Margaret Leonard, who had completed her vows in 1957, first came to New York City as a Little Sister of the Assumption in 1964, all of these ideas were in the air. The Little Sister of the Assumption order had deep connections by this point to Latin America, with communities in Argentina and Colombia, and the movements of liberation theology were reaching their communities around the world. At the time, the New York Little Sisters were living in an apartment at 1195 Lexington Avenue on the Upper East Side of Manhattan. They were given an apartment in one of the wealthiest neighborhoods in the city, while they continued to provide home health services in some of the poorest neighborhoods. This included the Lower East Side, where they had always worked, but now also the South Bronx, Central Harlem, and starting in 1958, East Harlem.[68] That year, in 1958 they established a ministry they referred to as the "Little Sisters of the Assumption Family Health Service," the organization that oversaw the home nursing programs throughout the city. Initially, it was staffed and run exclusively by the Little Sisters.

When Sister Margaret joined the Little Sisters in New York, she also enrolled as a graduate student at Fordham University's School of Social Work (fig. 3). With the social work training and the theological atmosphere of the era, Margaret began to think about the Little Sisters' mission to "the sick poor" in new ways. She began to ask," How do you really address poverty without changing the policies that perpetuate it?"[69]

Margaret explained in an interview recalling her early days in East Harlem that her faith involved a commitment to "changing the community to make the world more just and loving."[70]

In 1967, Sister Margaret became the executive director of the Little Sisters of the Assumption Family Health Service. The first major change she helped set in motion was to select just one modest part of the city to focus on so that members of the order could go small and deep and build long-term relationships with the families they worked with. She believed

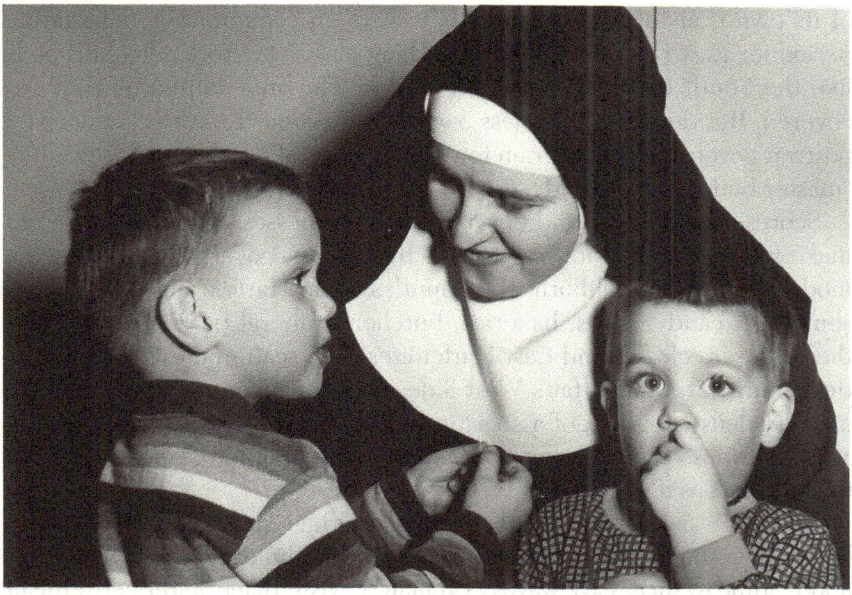

Figure 3. Sister Margaret Leonard with two boys, undated, likely early 1960s. (Photo courtesy of Sister Annette Allain)

that the sisters could be more effective if they zeroed in on a particular neighborhood rather than aiming to cover the whole city.

"It became clear to us," Margaret recalled, "that if we wanted to have an impact upon families and to create opportunities for them to obtain healing and move beyond poverty, it was important for us to focus upon a more limited geographical location with a community focus."[71]

Although the Little Sisters had relationships with families all over the city, by the 1950s they were increasingly drawn to East Harlem, the neighborhood that stretched from East 96th Street north to East 125th Street and from Fifth Avenue to the East River. First, the families they had come to know through home nursing in East Harlem invited them. "We had served many families who resided in the East Harlem community," Sister Margaret wrote in an unpublished essay, "and with force they asked us to come to be part of their community and to work together with them to gain important access to health care services. The quality of the relationship with the families there was like a gravitational pull to come, to be with them, to build the fabric of a community. The invitation was compelling."[72]

But the undertaking was tricky. At the same time the sisters began getting to know families in East Harlem, the neighborhood was in the midst of its own transformation. The 1950s were an economically devastating period for East Harlem and other working-class New York neighborhoods like the South Bronx and East New York. The area still hasn't fully recovered. Residents and business owners were subject to the ill-conceived postwar governmental program for "urban renewal" led by New York City's "master builder" Robert Moses.

Scores of tenements and thriving small businesses were demolished to make way for public housing towers that loomed over what was once a modest, low-rise neighborhood. Countless East Harlem businesses were shuttered: candy stores, bakeries, butchers, funeral parlors, and movie theaters were closed, and East Harlemites were scattered to the Bronx, to the suburbs, to Manhattan's West Side, shattering a once thriving culture of "very dense network of associations."[73] Between 1950 and 1960 nearly 1,600 businesses employing more than 4,500 people disappeared from these streets as if swept away by the wind.

While it was never an affluent or even middle-income area, East Harlem before the 1950s had been a racially and ethnically mixed neighborhood, home to successive waves of Italian, Jewish, Black, and Puerto Rican residents. But government-sponsored urban renewal wiped out working-class neighborhoods and replaced aging tenements with sleek new towers intended to house more people. Most Italian and Jewish residents fled to the Bronx and the suburbs. East Harlem became a predominantly Black and Puerto Rican neighborhood in which only the poorest remained.[74] The families that returned to East Harlem to take up residence in the neighborhood's massive new public housing towers felt that the neighborhood had been profoundly transformed. People described the streets as almost "bombed out" and eerily silent, with chain-link fences stretched around housing project lawns to keep children from playing on the grass.

By 1965 East Harlem held the distinction of having more public housing than any other neighborhood in the city. "My family tried to fight it," one local resident recalled, "but we were the little people."[75]

During these early years of economic devastation in East Harlem, there was not enough progressive leadership to represent the interests of its low-income residents. And their needs were considerable. The area was increasingly beset by poverty, mental illness, alcoholism, drug addiction—especially heroin by the 1950s—and lack of access to medical care and municipal services, not to mention poor housing and schools.

Piri Thomas's acclaimed 1967 memoir *Down These Mean Streets* depicts the extreme poverty and violence that plagued the neighborhood in the 1940s, 1950s, and 1960s. Drugs, crime, racism, gangs all populate the

East Harlem in which Thomas grew up. But he also communicates the deep attachment residents felt to the neighborhood, the sense of belonging, wonder, and homecoming that East Harlem provided. Despite the neighborhood's rough patina, the culture and community it offered for Thomas were unmatched.

> In the daytime Harlem looks kinda dirty and the people a little drab and down. But at night, man, it's a swinging place, especially Spanish Harlem. The lights transform everything into life and movement and blend the different colors into a magic cover-all that makes the drabness and garbage, wailing kids and tired people invisible. Shoes and clothes that by day look beat and worn out, at night take on a reflected splendor that the blazing multicolored lights burn on them. Everyone seems to develop a sense of urgent rhythm and you get the impression that you have to walk with a sense of timing.
>
> The daytime pain fades alongside the feeling of belonging and just being in swing with all the humming kicks going on around you.[76]

Thomas, a dark-skinned Puerto Rican man, is drawn back to El Barrio time and time again. When his family moves to Long Island, Thomas goes so far as to live on the streets of East Harlem because he feels out of place in the white suburbs. When he returns to El Barrio after a stint in prison, Thomas describes the changed landscape with its new public housing, but the neighborhood's persistent underlying spirit. "I heard all the noises I'd missed for so long—screaming broads, crying kids, hustlers, dogs yapping, and cats making holes in mountains of garbage. The stoops on 104th Street were full of people. . . . My Harlem had a somewhat different face. Big brick housing projects were all over the place, big, alien intruders. They had been mutilating my turf while I was gone, but the heart was still there. New faces and old hearts."[77]

With such deep affection for their home, residents were understandably wary of so-called white saviors who would come into the neighborhood with dreams of redemption and social transformation.

For instance, the neighborhood was initially slow to warm to an organization that called itself the East Harlem Protestant Parish, a storefront church established in 1958 by two white graduates of the nearby Union Theological Seminary. They came to the neighborhood to organize local residents and create small communities of scriptural reading and reflection. By 1959, a year in, they were making almost no headway with the neighborhood's Black and Puerto Rican families. A local resident told them with brutal honesty that this was because they were outsiders.

"I know why this isn't working," the man explained. "You guys are a bunch of phonies. The great middle-class group of white saviors out to help these poor broken-down people. And you three people are standing on the banks of East Harlem, safe and secure, throwing life jackets to these drowning people. Until you jump in and become the drowning person with the others and help them find the meaning of life nothing will happen."[78]

The leaders of the East Harlem Protestant Parish, Norm and Peg Eddy, who served as co-pastors, heeded his advice. They decided to move to an apartment on East 100th Street, immerse themselves in the neighborhood, and raise their family there. They earned the trust of their neighbors, established themselves as well-respected leaders, not outsiders, *alongside* those they aimed to empower and serve, sharing in their challenges and victories. Norm and Peg Eddy eventually held study groups for young East Harlem activists, church leaders, and community members around issues of spirituality and its relationship with social justice.

The Eddys' activism and service were directed toward long-lasting structural changes for East Harlem: they set up a credit union, marched against police brutality, demanded better municipal services. Institutions like the East Harlem Protestant Parish joined other new community organizations in the neighborhood that emphasized empowerment at the grassroots level, from the ground up, with the goal of developing leadership within the neighborhood itself and reestablishing the social fabric that had frayed thanks to urban renewal.

The Eddys were among the first important community partners with whom the Little Sisters collaborated in this part of the city. Thanks to them and other burgeoning activist groups, East Harlem by the 1960s was beginning to be known as the city's major epicenter of interfaith activism. Sister Margaret, who had befriended the Eddys, remembered, "They shared a spirituality that was sacred to us, so we got to know them. Then we worked very, very closely." Margaret and her fellow sisters joined the Eddys in their meetings, prayer groups, and the Bible studies they ran out of their apartment and storefront church in the 1960s.

The Little Sisters of the Assumption had some unique advantages as they considered putting down roots in East Harlem. Sister Ana Virginia Figuera, a Puerto Rican nun born and raised in the small southern Puerto Rican village of Yauco, worked closely with Margaret. She entered the Little Sisters religious order in the United States and made her final vows in France. She was bilingual and when she came into East Harlem as a home nurse, she became known in the neighborhood as a fellow Puerto Rican. Margaret remembers Sister Ana as "absolutely central" to building trust in

East Harlem, developing authentic, mutual relationships with local families, and eventually taking leadership to get the Little Sisters to exclusively focus their ministry there in the early 1960s.

Margaret remembers that in East Harlem everyone—shopkeepers, families, children—knew and loved Sister Ana. At the time, many nuns were opting for ordinary clothing, but "not Sister Ana. She wore a full habit." She spoke Spanish with families, communicating she was both a nun *and* a local, an insider *and* outsider at the same time. Her insistence on wearing a habit, even through the 1970s, perhaps indicated something about what she knew the people from her homeland expected piety to look like. Margaret remembers that when Ana would walk the streets of East Harlem, Puerto Rican families would cross themselves and genuflect, something they did only with her. At the time, beginning in 1960, the church had begun to send sisters to Puerto Rico to learn Spanish. The archdiocese supported this language-immersion program for any priest or nun in New York City working with Spanish-speaking communities. But with Sister Ana, the LSA congregation was several steps ahead.

From 1958 to 1968, six Little Sister of the Assumption nuns and social workers took buses and trains from their home on Lexington Avenue to East Harlem to do home nursing and family assistance. With the help of Sister Ana, in 1968 after ten years of commuting, the sisters purchased a single-residency apartment building on East 115th Street, directly across from East Harlem's Health Center. The sisters didn't live in the building, but for the first time they had an "agency," a storefront office in which their work was consolidated. They used the space to hold meetings, host study groups, and expand their ministry to include parenting groups. They referred to this new center run by the nuns as a "health agency." Sisters Ana and Margaret oversaw this transition and Ana's neighborhood connections helped facilitate the process.

Shortly after, under Margaret's executive directorship, the Little Sisters decided to untether the new health agency from the religious congregation of nuns. They established a nonprofit organization, with its own 501c3, Little Sisters of the Assumption Family Health Service, which we refer to as LSA, as the agency is commonly called. Sister Margaret installed an independent board of directors to whom the staff—still all nuns in 1970—were responsible. Now "the health agency," was separate from the "congregation," the community of nuns themselves. This was a major change. The health agency was no longer under the auspices of the religious community. It was now *staffed* by nuns but had a lay board and began hiring people outside of the religious order. Part of what guided Sister Margaret's decision was the 1965 passing of Medicaid and Medicare—now many of their clients would have health insurance but it was incredibly complicated. It would require a board with significant expertise in this changing medical and financial landscape.

This decision of creating a new nonprofit agency officially separate from the congregation ended up being one of the most prescient and strategic for the development of LSA as a community-based, neighborhood organization. The agency avoided many of the troubles that began in the 1980s for many other explicitly Catholic philanthropic organizations. In light of challenges to the church's standing on issues of gender and sexuality in the United States (which began in the 1970s and have continued unabated), public support of Catholic Church–based nonprofits began to decline.[79] LSA enjoyed some distance from the problems confronting Catholic philanthropic organizations in subsequent years.

Sisters Ana and Margaret also spearheaded the more radical change that was to come in 1971. Up until then, the Little Sisters of the Assumption nuns had been commuting to their storefront agency and people's homes in East Harlem from Lexington Avenue and 81st Street, but they knew they needed to be in East Harlem as neighbors, to make their home there. In 1971, Ana found an old convent building at 475 East 115th Street, facilitated the purchase, and five sisters moved in. "From this new abode," archival notes read, "they became involved in the community in new ways and became part of the fabric of East Harlem from the inside out." They named the new apartment Our Lady of Hope Convent. Now the Little Sisters had a nonprofit agency *and* their congregation had their home in *el Barrio*.

The health agency buzzed with activity right away. When remembering the feel of the neighborhood at the time, the Little Sisters talk about the poverty and the challenges the families faced, but also about characters who inhabited this twenty-square-block area and the neighborhood's vitality. In these different buildings in a three-block section of East Harlem, the nuns began to establish even more partnerships and relationships. In 1974, as the agency expanded, Little Sisters bought a three-story brownstone on East 118th Street that was part of Holy Rosary Parish. "It had 3 floors and a back garden, and a kitchen, and a meeting space," recalled Sister Margaret. "We stored clothing, shoes and food for those in need. It was our first community center."

Little Sisters of the Assumption nuns who lived in other parts of the United States were hearing the buzz about the activist spirit of East Harlem that had gathered around Sister Margaret, Sister Ana, and a growing

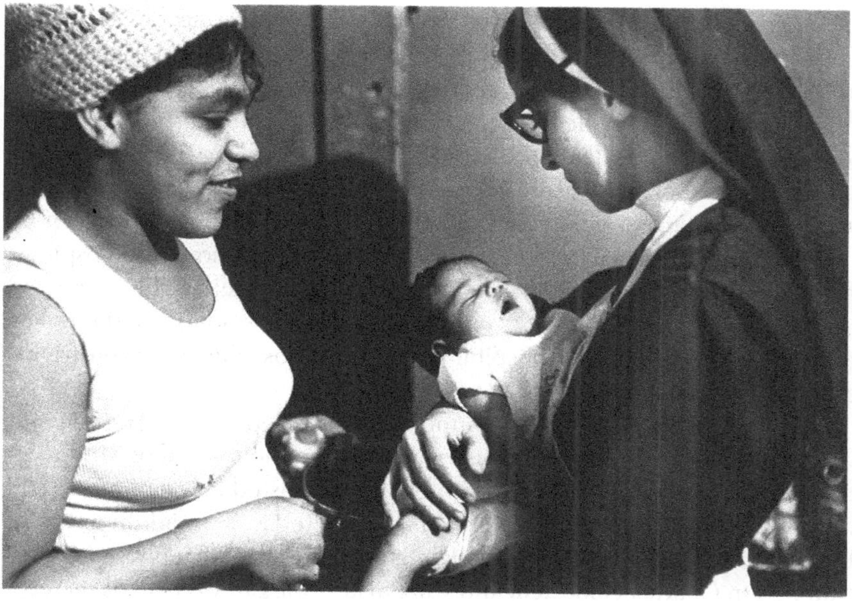

Figure 4. Sister Susanne Lachapelle, 1973. (Photo courtesy of Sister Annette Allain)

network of volunteers, families, and activists who partnered with the agency, "That attracted me," said Sister Susanne, who had been working in Charlotte, North Carolina, "the inequity, the justice challenge, the fact that we could get into social justice and demonstrate, and that we could work with the people. I told them I wanted to come to New York, and after a while, they sent me."[80] In 1973, Sister Susanne joined the Little Sisters in East Harlem.[81]

It was clear that East Harlem was turning out to be an ideal location for the Little Sisters because of their ministry's focus on health care and nursing. While the French Little Sisters saw themselves as a counterweight to state-run hospitals, in New York City the sisters worked with local hospitals. Under Sister Margaret's leadership, partnership with hospitals—their research, their medical teams, their facilities—became central to the agency's mission of health care for the poor.

Most notably, they partnered with Mount Sinai, one of New York City's major hospitals and medical schools, located in East Harlem. In 1968, Mount Sinai hired a pioneering physician, Dr. Kurt W. Deuschle, to create a community health program to focus on the needs of East Harlem residents and address the neighborhood's daunting health issues in more creative, effective ways. To do this successfully, the hospital needed a community partner who had the trust of neighborhood residents. There had long been skepticism in East Harlem about institutions like hospitals, police, and governmental social service organizations; neighbors shared that if you called 911, the city's emergency number, sometimes the police came too. And sometimes hospital visits meant complicated, even frightening entanglements with social service authorities.

"They created a wonderful community health department and they invited us to partner with them," Sister Margaret remembered of Mount Sinai hospital in the early days, "a partnership that lasted for years and is still very engaged with LSA Family Health Service today."[82] In addition to Dr. Deuschle, the Little Sisters worked with other Mount Sinai physicians, including Dr. Charles Goodrich, and what Sister Margaret recalls as its "creative and innovative research department" led by Dr. Jane Moss and staffed by Renate Belville, who eventually worked closely with the Little Sisters. These early strong partnerships were all centered on community health.

But what was central in this partnership is that unlike the medical professionals, the Little Sisters (the nuns and the agency) had the *trust* of the community. They had been going into the homes of residents for years, and it gave them a much more on-the-ground, personal view of what was happening with families. Sister Ana's cultural knowledge was often the critical bridge between families and health resources in East Harlem. For example, Margaret remembers a meeting between Mount Sinai medical professionals and LSA staff to talk about shared families they were working with. Psychiatrists were assessing one particular family, diagnosing the Puerto Rican father as mentally unstable because he had cut his daughter's hair in an erratic, bizarre way. In their medical diagnosis, they even discussed the possibility of the children being taken away. Ana laughed and said he's a wonderful father; she was close with the whole family. He cut the kids' hair quickly because the girls had lice! The nuns had inroads to families that the professionals did not. The partnership was critical.

Sister Susanne recalled that initially, the work of the sisters was similar to the service that Father Pernet had envisioned in the nineteenth century. They would receive a referral or a request to go to a family's home where a parent was dealing with a medical crisis. "We would stay all day, do the cooking, the cleaning, the nursing, take care of the kids," Susanne recalled. "I can remember one house there were seven little boys, all different ages, and we had two sisters in there. Two of us would put four in the tub at one end, and three in the tub at the other end."[83]

Being inside these homes all day, for several days or even weeks at a time, the sisters came to understand the depths and complexities of the challenges these families faced. "You get to know them through what may be a medical issue," said another sister, "but realize there is so much there to the story." They learned that children often needed medical and nutritional assistance, that mothers were overwhelmed and required mental health assistance. Rats, dirty water, mold in the walls, and too little heat made it almost impossible to raise healthy children in these places, not to mention issues like domestic violence and unstable incomes.

"The level of poverty was overwhelming, overwhelming," said one of the early staff members at the agency, "and I had worked with poor families. I had worked in a shelter and I hadn't ever seen poverty like this poverty." Sister Margaret recalled of those early days, "We worked with very, very poor families, and they were living in terrible housing, housing that was decrepit and wasn't repaired or anything."[84]

They linked up with a sophisticated network of powerful doctors, community activists, and researchers, along with the neighborhood families themselves."We really couldn't be small," Sister Margaret said. "Whatever we did, we would have to do in partnership. Partnership was the key word."[85]

For example, the Little Sisters worked with Mount Sinai to create community health clinics in bodegas and church basements. "We also had a portable pediatric van that went around to all the projects in the poor buildings for pediatric care," Sister Susanne remembered, "because when we were getting calls from some of these families, it was a mess. They'd put a nutritionist on the bus, they'd put a pediatrician on the bus who had experience in Africa, and sometimes he said, 'I never saw this in Africa like I'm seeing it.' They had laboratory, they had just social work, they had counseling, and we were part of that. It was a wonderful experience."[86]

Over time, they began to make connections between poverty, substandard housing, and health issues like asthma. By the 1970s, the Little Sisters moved beyond nursing and began working on what we now would call the social determinants of health. As the sisters expanded their work to include community health with a focus on justice, Margaret's leadership was key. She was emerging as a strategic thinker and a coalition builder. She ensured that LSA's programs and initiatives were well-designed, were grounded in research, and drew from the networks of relationships they helped form across the neighborhood.

Sister Margaret remembers that their first major political action in East Harlem was Norm Eddy's idea. "Let's organize a movement with people," he once said. "Let's get them involved, particularly people who deal with housing and repair of housing." In 1968, Sister Margaret, Sister Ana, Peg and Norm Eddy, and other neighborhood leaders created an organization called East Harlem Interfaith, and their first project was called The 100 Worst Buildings Committee. Together, the Little Sisters and East Harlem Interfaith partnered with East Harlem Welfare, a tenants' rights organization. The first action of this interfaith coalition was to focus on five of the one hundred public housing buildings in East Harlem deemed to be in the worst shape.

In 1970, they interviewed 270 residents of those buildings to document trends in asthma, infections, flu, allergies, lack of hot water, cleanliness, and mold.

"Since 1968, when the Committee was organized, there has been a growing awareness and conviction that many of the health problems faced by East Harlem residents are in fact housing problems," their report concluded. On March 2, 1970, the report was presented to the Select Committee on Nutrition and Human Need of the United States Senate. It helped successfully make the case for greater governmental regulation and assistance on housing issues, identifying housing as a key pillar of health outcomes.[87]

This was a concrete example of the Little Sisters' new approach: the relationships they had built with families enabled them to go into people's homes, draw on what they knew about the correlation between health and poverty, and build the capacity of their agency through developing neighborhood partnerships and strategic coalitions. With these relationships, they conducted research on issues of neighborhood problems, published findings, and advocated for solutions.

Though that would be impressive enough, the changes in public policy were not the only goal. Out of the 100 Worst Buildings project, East Harlem Interfaith expanded to include not only Catholics like the Little Sisters but also Protestant churches and Jewish synagogues. In addition, they created a project called Adopt-a-Building that began in 1969 in East Harlem. With funds that East Harlem Interfaith helped secure, they worked to transfer the titles of these apartments in the run-down public housing buildings from reluctant city officials who were absentee landlords to East Harlem families who oversaw repairing their own new homes.

The Adopt-a-Building project was featured as a model project in the 1974 book on community and grassroots empowerment titled *Uplift: What People Themselves Can Do*. As the author wrote, "The title transfer making the tenants the owners of buildings was the work of a little-known project called Interfaith *Adopt-a-Building*. It was a remarkable feat for an organization that had started off only three years before in the slums of East Harlem under the guidance of a young ministerial student named Norm Eddy and a small group of nuns." It was strictly "a tenants' program," Eddy said; "All we do is provide some assistance, assurance and advice."[88] The emotional undercurrent was to affirm the assets of the neighborhood, strengthen relational ties, and develop capacity and leadership with the goal of the residents owning their own homes.

Sister Susanne remembers another early action the Little Sisters were part of. This effort was conducted in partnership with East Harlem Interfaith in response to hearing from families about the long, uncomfortable, and often painful waits in the lines at city welfare offices where there were not even chairs.

"Some of the women had small children, some were holding babies, some were pregnant, and they could stand seven hours and not be seen, and told to come back the next day," Sister Susanne recalled. One day the Little Sisters, dressed in full habit, "went to the welfare office at eight o'clock in the morning. We each had a chair. When they opened, . . . we went in with our chairs and because we were in habits, some of us, the guards didn't know what to do with us. They let us in. We sat down, each in our chairs. The first client that walked in, she got my chair, the next woman got the next chair, and so on. And do you know the next day, the place was covered with chairs."[89]

Yet another example of the Little Sisters' political advocacy was its response to East Harlem's frequent power blackouts in the early 1970s. During these evenings of darkness, the neighborhood felt under siege from the threat of looting and violence; some store owners stood guard in the windows of their shops with guns. It was even worse if police entered the neighborhood because police brutality was a well-known local danger. For several evenings during the blackouts, East Harlem Interfaith gathered clergy, including Sisters Susanne and Margaret, to be grouped in teams of three—the nuns wearing their habits, Protestant preachers wearing their collars—to patrol the dark streets and encourage peacefulness.

In a particularly dramatic event Sister Margaret was inside one of the member churches of East Harlem Interfaith when the Young Lords, the Puerto Rican activist group in East Harlem, took over the Parish in an eleven-day siege. Margaret helped defuse tensions; the nuns had treated Young Lords as patients. "It was an intense time," she recalled, but the sisters were "right there and knew the families so we felt we could help."[90]

In recalling these early days of activism in East Harlem, Sisters Susanne and Margaret remembered fondly what must have been a time of dizzying change for the community. Most of the sisters were trained strictly for nursing or social work alone. These experiments with community organizing, reading, and discussing theology and justice with neighborhood families and activists like the Eddys must have felt so new.

The Spirit and Program of Mutuality

The period between 1958 and 1980 was a time of both expansion and focus. Expansion in the sense that the Little Sisters' ministry was no longer limited to home nursing, but now included community health and political advocacy. And they now had a separate nonprofit agency with partnerships with hospitals and other community organizations. Their ministry took on a broader definition. But because they were no longer working all over the city, they were now more narrowly focused by working in East Harlem alone.

Amid all these changes, how were they to ensure a connection with the spiritual roots of LSA's founding? How could they have a mission that was capacious enough that it could consolidate these different projects under a shared set of values?

Under Margaret's leadership in the late 1960s, "mutuality" emerged as the ideal and guiding principle of the work, the singular term that defined the organization's self-understanding. Whether a sister was advocating at City Hall, helping a young mother with postnatal care, teaching a mother how to breast-feed, or urging her to volunteer to meet neighbors, mutuality was the animating force that consolidated the agency's work and made it distinctive.

Mutuality sounds like a soft, inoffensive word, but it signals mutual growth and empowerment rather than mere service. Mutuality is much more than an ideal. It is a practice that would make real changes in the lives of families in East Harlem. As Margaret conceived it, mutuality also had the radical potential to become a force for lasting structural social change.

The 1969 annual report of the Little Sisters in East Harlem, written primarily by Sister Margaret, is the first public document that employs this language. Three years later Margaret published an article, "Mutuality as a Catalytic Power for Growth." In the decades that followed, the agency had countless retreats, meetings, and reflection exercises on the term mutuality and how to "operationalize it," as they often put it. Even today, for people who have known the agency for a long time, mutuality is the key word they use to describe LSA's work in East Harlem.

Mutuality starts by recognizing that human relationships are central to every aspect of society. As the 1969 report states, "The power of growth is in relationships. It is essentially though the mutuality of relationship that growth potential—in persons, families, and communities, is stimulated and expands, and flowers out in dignity and goodness. Mutuality of relationship is bonded in the recognition of the need we have, one for the other."[91]

Mutuality was more than mere idealism. For the agency, it was practical. Each person who came to LSA was to be viewed in terms of their relationships. For a young, isolated mother seeking help, her own relationships had to be strengthened. In order for LSA to make an impact, real relationships of trust had to develop between families and the nurses, social workers, and advocates who worked with them. Sometimes trust took years to cultivate.

Crucially, when the staff entered relationships with East Harlem families, they always insisted both parties could grow and be transformed. "Those whose lives we have shared through home services remain our friends," wrote Sister Margaret. This mutual exchange recognized the gifts and strengths of all parties, and the nuns were always looking for ways to strengthen and draw on the assets of the families in the neighborhood. "They were in need of our direct home services at one time; now we are in need of them. We need their experience of life, their sharing of the human struggle, their understanding of what is really needed." Margaret added, "Mutuality is the belief that the power of growth is in relationships where we all become givers and receivers, the belief that diversity is a gift, and that ultimately we are all on a journey toward unity and communion."[92] LSA staff always aimed to include families in problem solving, evaluating programs, planning activities, even taking leadership (as we will see in coming chapters) to contribute to the agency.

Most importantly, the clients, mostly mothers, needed more supportive relationships to improve the well-being of their families and to improve their communities. Families in the neighborhood needed "mutual support and encouragement," they wrote, echoing the language of the Second Vatican Council, "in the joys, the hopes, and the anxieties of life in a complex world."[93] Discussion groups worked to build up the relational capacity of the neighborhood. These "group experiences" aimed to cultivate "a sense of self-confidence and self-determination" to "assist in acquiring feelings of self-worth, adequacy, and satisfaction in human interaction."[94]

THE POWER OF GROWTH IS IN RELATIONSHIP

EL PODER DEL CRECIMIENTO RADICA EN LA RELACION

The power of growth	El poder de crecimiento
is in relationship.	radica en la relación.
Even when life seems frail –	Aún cuando la vida parece frágil-
when there is	cuando nos rodea
darkness	la oscuridad
and pain,	y el dolor,
confusion	la confusion
and complexity –	y la complejidad-
the loving and caring	la capacidad de amar y cuidar
of a human person	de un ser humano
can be	puede ser
sunlight	el rayo de luz
and warmth	y el calor
to the growth power	para el crecimiento
of another human person:	de otro ser humano:
helping another	ayudar a otro
creates	crea
meaning and hope	sentido y esperanza
in both persons;	en ambos;
being sunlight and warmth	ser el rayo de luz y calor
to another's life	en la vida de otro ser
nurtures growth in both.	nutre el crecimiento en ambos.
To this growth we are pledged.	A este crecimiento estamos comprometidos

Sr. Maureen O'Keefe, LSA

Figure 5. "The Power of Growth Is in Relationship," 1969 poem written by Sr. Maureen O'Keefe. The agency had part of this poem painted on the door of the 119th Street building. It is copied in LSA's current mission handbook. (Photo courtesy of the Little Sisters of the Assumption archive)

In Margaret's early writing on mutuality, we see the impact of the developmental psychologist Erik Erikson, upon whose work she draws. Erikson's works emphasized the importance of seeing the individual in a societal matrix, and his insights suggested that political, economic, and social systems—all exterior forces—actually mold a person's interior emotional life. He was an important innovator in forging a union between psychoanalysis and the social sciences. These insights were ideal for an agency with religious roots and concerns that were both spiritual *and* political, inner *and* outer.

This personal component was key, but the LSA health agency was also thinking about systems and structures.

The emphasis on building relational capacity in the neighborhood was the first step for larger organizing campaigns in East Harlem that LSA was involved in throughout the 1960s and 1970s—projects like Adopt-a-Building, and eventually working collectively to demand that public housing units become safer and cleaner, for instance, and much more. But everything began with people connecting with one another at the grassroots level, sharing struggles and working together on solutions, demanding change.

The early leaders of LSA developed a set of practices, under what they described as a "three-phase model" to help turn these ideals into a program. The first goal was to provide immediate assistance to families and help them through their crises while developing trust; the second goal was to build relationships with families to develop their individual capacity and gifts; and the third goal was to support local leadership and community development.[95] In chapters 2 and 3 we will see how these three phases come to be felt in the lives of families.

Mutuality had symbolic force and resonated with the order's more explicitly Catholic ideals that were more present in their earlier devotional material. At the same time, "mutuality" placed religious language outside the organization's central purpose while still holding on to a spiritual, emotional resonance.

As Sister Margaret explained in an interview, "We've tried to define what we're doing out of deeper levels than religious tradition alone: love for one another, concerns for justice, relationships among people and the building of community. These are spiritual thrusts we can share with others of diverse traditions." Mutuality is this central spiritual value of the agency.

Sister Maureen O'Keefe, another member of the Little Sisters congregation, who like Sister Margaret earned a master's degree in social work, wrote a poem describing mutuality in 1969 that guided several of the organization's staff retreats. For many years, copies of the poem adorned the walls of the organization's East Harlem office (fig. 5):

The power of growth
is in relationship.
Even when life seems frail—
When there is
darkness
and pain

confusion
and complexity—
the loving and caring
of a human person
can be
sunlight
and warmth
to the growth power
of another human person:
helping another
creates
meaning and hope
in both persons;
being sunlight and warmth
to another's life
nurtures growth in both.
To this growth we are pledged.[96]

As the poem suggests, centering mutuality within the mission of the LSA health agency meant that even the most clinical medical work of the nurses, or the most politically strident actions from the advocacy department, evoked something more humanistic, even theological: hope, warmth, growth, meaning, power, alongside darkness, pain, confusion, the stuff of "inner" life too.

But this "softer," "slower" vision of change and collaboration was also no-nonsense and realistic. It was always meant to be a practice that met real families where they were.

One example from this time is illustrative. In 1970, a sixteen-year-old named Sonia was pregnant and living with her mother and siblings in New York City Housing Authority (NYCHA) housing in East Harlem. Her mother also had a baby at home. Doctors who had seen the mother learned that the daughter needed prenatal care. They connected the family with Sister Margaret who, along with other LSA nurses, helped Sonia navigate prenatal care and manage appointments. When she gave birth, the nurses and Sister Margaret helped Sonia develop parenting skills to gain confidence as a new mother. She was so young, but they had her come in to the agency, meet other mothers who were in a similar situation, and learn from older mothers. The staff at LSA aimed to develop Sonia's confidence, teaching young mothers that you can parent effectively with few resources—babies need to be stimulated with sound, touch, and sight, but no need for expensive rattles, "a bottle of pills will work just fine." But Sister Margaret encouraged Sonia to continue to imagine a future for herself too. Sonia said she was interested in studying nursing. The sisters helped Sonia enroll in a local pre-nursing program for high school students and do the difficult work of combining mothering with taking classes. "You will never understand what Sister Margaret did for me," Sonia said decades later. "She is like family."[97]

Mutuality seeks to develop the leadership of the people being served—helping them take control over their lives and develop their own capacity. Even when Sonia was an overwhelmed teenager, the Little Sisters worked to help her develop her own agency. For example, they knew that a neighbor a few floors up in Sonia's building needed nursing care to change her bandages weekly. They gave Sonia the task. Even though she was a busy young mother completing nursing coursework, they told Sonia they could tell she'd be a good nurse and could help the Little Sisters in this way as a skilled volunteer. Through the small act of helping a neighbor, Sonia gained confidence and the encouragement to continue with her nursing degree.

Sonia graduated and got a job as a nurse. But there were still many crises to come in her life. The father of Sonia's baby had served in the Marines. When he came home, he became physically abusive to Sonia. "We thought he was going to kill her," remembered Sister Margaret. Sonia recalled that the Little Sisters helped her start the process of securing a restraining order. This only enraged him. One night, as Sonia and a friend were leaving the subway, her boyfriend was waiting for her. In a rage, he beat her severely. She eventually got away and made it home with the help of her friend.

In the middle of the night, the police knocked on the door of her apartment. The boyfriend apparently had slit his wrists after beating her and called the police and said *she* slit his wrists in their argument. The police came to arrest her. Sonia couldn't believe her ears. She showed them her bruises and cuts. She was tiny, he was huge. How could she possibly cut him? But the police said they were obligated to arrest her. She called the nuns and was taken to jail in a state of shock.

Sister Margaret and a small group of Little Sisters went to the jail in the middle of the night to get her released, but they mostly had to wait outside the jail cell. Sonia remembers feeling the lowest of the low—beaten, now arrested. Then she heard the Sisters outside her jail cell singing hymns and saying prayers for her. "Hearing them sing got me through one of the worst nights of my life," she recalled. "It kept me sane. I thought I was going to go crazy."[98]

Sonia was released the next day, and the charges against her were dropped. Sister Margaret encouraged Sonia to find a new apartment, to move where the boyfriend couldn't find her. The nuns had a connection with someone at Mount Sinai Hospital, who had an extra room in their apartment and took her in for a short time. Eventually, Sonia was able to move out of East Harlem to Florida. She completed work for her RN degree and became a radiology nurse. In Florida, Sonia got married and raised three children. She eventually became head nurse of the Miami Dade radiology department.

"Everyone knows how I feel about the Little Sisters," Sonia said many years later. "I owe so much to them and try to teach everything I learned from Sister Margaret to my own children, and all of them went into nursing too, a helping profession."

Many years later, when an elderly member of Sister Margaret's family was facing a medical crisis in Florida, she called Sonia, who came and oversaw the person's care, like family. This time Sonia was the one who solved the crisis, something she has done many times as a successful RN and mother. With mutuality, the dynamics of power and care circulate back and forth within a relationship. Both Sonia and Sister Margaret have skills, gifts, and capacities that are forged in long-term commitments to people and that do not rely on quick fixes.

Mutuality is more than charity. It does not mean simply helping the poor navigate a system. Sometimes it means political action, like documenting unhygienic conditions in NYCHA housing and demanding change. Sometimes it's more face to face, like a ten-year commitment to a teenage mother until she's on her feet, stable, safe, working, thriving, and eventually able to lead, take charge, and serve.

"I think that it's a neighborhood agency," said Sister Susanne in describing the organization. "Whatever the neighborhood is, is where we're at, but the focus is always on the poor or those who are up against it the most. Hopefully, that we can do something. Also, there's room for people who can take some leadership or learn some leadership."

The practice of mutuality was not always easy for the Little Sisters, who were accustomed to taking charge. In an article published in July 1969 in the *American Journal of Nursing* titled "Assignment: East Harlem," a young white Little Sisters of the Assumption nun—a nursing student at Boston College named Sister Joyce Michael—described the summer she lived in East Harlem, spending her days in the home of a Black family with a mother and her eight children. She describes at first being overwhelmed by the litany of problems: toddlers in need of potty training, an unresponsive landlord who refused to address a rat infestation, an underweight infant, two preschool-aged girls in need of nursery school enrollment.

Some of Sister Joyce's early reflections exhibit a kind of paternalism, a subtle sense of a savior from the outside swooping in. She saw problems and deprivation in the family that she came to "fix." But after two summers with the Little Sisters of the Assumption, Joyce reflected again on learning that gradually, over time, she had understood something of the ideal of "mutuality." By the end of the second summer, she described innate *strengths* of the mother, how much she had done for her children once she knew where the resources were, and how much Sister Joyce, a young white nun, learned *from* the family.

For example, Sister Joyce saw how totally inadequate and broken the systems of help were for East Harlem families. For example, she described how a mother had to wait in the sweltering lobby of the city pediatrician for four hours for a minor appointment with no childcare for siblings. It was no wonder low-income families found it challenging to keep appointments, Sister Joyce mused. Families "who have gone through many crises" have "taught us that positive strengths may well lie dormant in young families even when they have multiple problems."[99] Words like strengths, hope, growth, and mutuality gradually appeared more and more central in the Little Sisters literature from the late 1960s onward.

In an archival video, the way one nun described her work was typical—it was not especially Catholic but certainly not secular. "It's a joy to help people discover the resources they have within themselves," the sister said, "to come in touch with their own preciousness, their uniqueness in God's eyes and to realize that they're wonderful men, women and children. And when I look into their eyes and know they are believing in themselves more than they had formerly believed in themselves, that gives me tremendous satisfaction."

Meeting and retreat notes from this period show that LSA leaders like Sisters Margaret, Ana, and Susanne knew "mutuality" required a real, embodied commitment from the staff. And it may not come naturally to everyone. In a 1972 retreat they asked staff to imagine "What happens if we think of the families who we work with as 'clients,' or 'welfare people'?

On the contrary, what happens if we think of them as families, individuals with names, with their own gifts and contributions to make to our own work and lives?" They encouraged families to volunteer, provided opportunities for them to host parties, to work at the agency, in an effort to exercise leadership.

Looking Backward, Looking Forward

It is remarkable to think how the agency in East Harlem began in 1865 with a small group of six nuns in Paris. Trained as nurses, they were young women who entered the homes of the poor to care for sick family members, prayed and begged for alms, and eventually crossed the Atlantic to New York. By the mid-1960s, long threads still tethered the East Harlem Little Sisters to their earliest forerunners in Paris and to Pernet and Fage's original vision: a commitment to attend to the health of the poorest and most vulnerable, to live in the neighborhood they served, to bring members of different classes together, to emphasize personal relationships, and to connect with the full family where *they* were. This work meant finding strengths and untapped assets within the local neighborhood.

So much had changed since the Little Sisters arrived in New York City in 1891. The sisters no longer focused exclusively on individual medical ailments but instead contemplated community health issues like safe and clean apartments, education, nutrition, and pre- and postnatal care. By 1958, when they were starting to establish themselves in East Harlem, the sisters also saw themselves less as an alternative to secular institutions, as in the past, than as a partner with other institutions and organizations in East Harlem—hospitals, schools, welfare agencies. Their work included direct care and service, but also marches, protest, and advocacy.

In East Harlem the Little Sisters sometimes made themselves "little" and in the background, as their name suggests. Instead of stepping in to solve problems, they offered structures and support to enable solutions to emerge at the grassroots level, like enlisting local grandmothers to assist young mothers who came to them for help. But the diminutive language of smallness can obscure the national, political impact these sisters had even early on: their achievements in East Harlem were evoked in congressional hearings in 1972, in a 1981 article in the *New Yorker*, and as a case study for federal policy in 1974. As we'll see, in later years this effectiveness at the level of city, state, and national policy would only grow.

The particular changes the Little Sisters experienced in East Harlem are best understood as changes that emerged from their relationships in the unique neighborhood culture of the 1950s, '60s, and '70s. Little Sisters grew and evolved differently in Dublin, Mozambique, Philadelphia, Morocco. But in East Harlem, residents of the deteriorated public housing buildings were skeptical of white saviors.

They were, however, desperate for help. They welcomed advocates who lived in the neighborhood and shared in their struggles. In East Harlem, the Little Sisters learned to emphasize grassroots power rather than external salvation or solutions, highlighting those solutions that drew on assets and strengths of families rather than deprivation and need. Mutuality meant that the Little Sisters listened and were *themselves* transformed in East Harlem.

As Sister Margaret wrote in a 1972 article, "Nowhere in this universe does life exist isolated and alienated. Within our own lives, and the lives of those with whom we interact, however, we too frequently see the forces of isolation and alienation. Alone and alienated, we can do so little. . . . Together we can do so much. Together we could be whole. The answers to today's questions lie in our mutual search and struggle. Only together can we all have greater life, create more hope, more peace, more goodness."[100] This vision is not limited to a critique of widespread American ideals like rugged individualism, or the deserving and undeserving poor. Rather, it enacts a living, breathing alternative.

What about the neighborhood residents who created this alternative network of care with the sisters and lay staff? We now turn to their stories.

Chapter 2

"LSA Is Like a Second Home"

The Story of Melina Gonzalez

ON A RAINY AFTERNOON in May 2022, Melina Gonzalez sat in front of several hundred attendees—academics, community leaders, politicians, students, and media representatives—on a panel about migration justice sponsored by Fordham's Center for Community Engaged Learning (fig. 6). We had come together to celebrate the work we do in and with the community, but also to talk about the unmet needs of immigrant communities and how to help them realize their full potential. The daylong summit, hosted by the Bronx Zoo, was a fancy affair. White tablecloths. Catered lunch. Formal attire. But Melina in her flowered blouse and black cardigan was calm, clear, and to the point as she spoke expertly, authoritatively, on behalf of the populations served by LSA.

Melina wears her hair pulled back in a tight bun and gives off a professional air. Even at the height of the pandemic, when most of us were frantically moving between housework, childcare, and professional meetings, Melina showed up for our Zoom interviews seated at a desk, wearing a blouse and makeup. She speaks in measured tones and thinks carefully about what she wants to say, and how she wants to say it.

As Melina took the microphone on a panel she shared with Carey, she made a point before doing anything else to thank their fellow panelist, David Shuffler, executive director of Youth Ministries for Peace and Justice, for acknowledging his staff. She knows that the heart of the work that nonprofit organizations do, that LSA does, depends on the staff's dedication and hard work. Now in her late forties, Melina has been working at

Figure 6. Fordham in Community Summit, sponsored by Fordham's Center for Community Engaged Learning, May 2022. *From left to right:* Zeinab Eyega (Sauti Yetu), David Shuffler (Youth Ministries for Peace and Justice), Ray López (LSA), Carey Kasten (author), Melina Gonzalez (LSA), Lucia Bravo (LSA). (Photo by Argenis Apolinario, courtesy of the Center for Community Engaged Learning)

LSA for more than twenty years. In her role as client advocate and immigrant outreach coordinator, she serves an essential role in connecting clients to the services they need. She is also a fierce advocate for migration justice and speaks passionately about how the United States should do better by its immigrant populations.

She should know. When she was just fourteen, she and her little sister crossed the border alone. Her journey from undocumented teenager to community leader and advocate is remarkable and owes much to the agency. She first came to LSA as a client in 1995. Her professional and personal successes since then are a testament to the transformative, personalized work LSA engages in and the profound impact it can have on entire families.

Melina traced the story of her life and her connection with LSA as she and Carey spoke two months before the summit panel on a springlike day in March 2022. We sat at a table on the third floor of LSA's light-filled building amid colorful signs and decorations hung as part of the after-school program celebrating Women's History Month. We shared a meal as we talked about her more than two decades at the agency. She took a bite of the enchiladas rojas prepared by a long-term client who cooks for the food pantry volunteers every Wednesday as a token of her appreciation.

"My sense of service was born here," Melina explained, describing how the nuns who ran LSA in the 1990s embodied the attentive, kindhearted spirit that drew her in. She explained how cared-for she felt one evening in the winter of 2008 when she was pregnant with her third child and working in the organization's development office. That day her doctor had sent her home to rest after determining that her pregnancy was high-risk. That same evening the agency's director, Sister Judy Garson, who led LSA for more than twenty-five years, visited Melina at home.

"She gave me her own personal saint's pin," Melina recalled, tearing up as she remembered how touched she was that Sister Judy had paid her such a personal visit. "She told me it would protect me."

Earlier the day of her meeting with Carey, Melina displayed a similar sense of concern in her role as client advocate and community outreach coordinator in the agency's advocacy department, where she has worked for more than five years. As she met with community members, she expertly handled a broad range of tasks: dealing with a request for a taxpayer identification number, helping an older woman address her completed income tax forms, organizing paperwork so a parent could apply for a child's green card, reviewing benefits such as SNAP (Supplemental Nutrition Assistance Program, commonly referred to as food stamps) and residency requirements for the city's public housing, helping complete a SIJS (Special Immigrant Juvenile Status) visa application, reviewing legal documents for a blind woman, and helping another woman apply for legal status under the federal Violence Against Women Act.

With each person, Melina asked after family members by name—a mother with long-term COVID symptoms, a younger sibling who had recently encountered bullying at school, a child who needed diapers. She gently urged clients to hold themselves accountable for tasks that needed to be done.

"Put that follow-up date in your calendar now," she'd advise. Or, "Remember to tell your lawyer about your exchanges with ACS," a reference to the city agency that intervenes when families are in crisis, especially in suspected cases of child abuse or neglect.

Melina also helped clients keep their goals and dreams alive, reminding one woman to sign up to take the GED test, the exam that provides high school equivalency, and helping another figure out how to establish a steady income stream in order to qualify for a lottery for low-income housing. Her vast knowledge and the care and attention with which she approached each person were impressive, an embodiment of LSA's mission in action.

Melina first came to LSA in 1995 when her two oldest children were one and two years old. Like the other members of the cohort considered in this study, she is originally from Mexico; she first came to LSA in the mid-1990s; and her family participated in LSA's Parenting and Child Development (PCD) program.

Having made the transition from client to full-time staff member, Melina is both exceptional and typical of the kind of powerful work LSA engages in. All of the agency's clients are transformed in numerous ways, both big and small, and many engage in volunteer or advocacy work at LSA or other organizations long after they first come into contact with the agency.

But Melina's story, more than that of any other of the mothers we interviewed, uniquely exemplifies the three-phase model of mutuality that LSA developed as a way to implement the philosophy. In this way, her story provides a bridge from the history of LSA's founding and mission presented in chapter 1 to the stories of the seventeen mothers we interviewed that appear in chapter 3. Melina's trajectory with and at LSA points to the radical possibilities of the three-phase model of mutuality, which empowers clients in all areas of their life, ranging from personal and family life to their role in their community.

The first phase focuses on clients' direct needs. Here LSA assists with nursing services, access to food, school transfers, landlord disputes, tutoring, housing and job searches, and more. The second phase focuses on building skills and relationships. For example, clients can take English classes or participate in parenting groups while learning to trust

Figure 7. Melina Gonzalez and her husband, Raymundo, with their children, Ricardo and Mila, late 1990s. (Photo courtesy of Melina Gonzalez)

themselves, their own abilities, and their community. In the third phase, which centers on advocacy and community building, clients take their newfound skills into the community to advocate for positive change for the community at large.

Melina's journey from English language student in the agency's PCD program to award-winning civic leader and LSA staff member embodies the results of LSA's mutuality in action. Her financial independence was directly connected to her community engagement as she became gainfully employed at LSA. Her journey with the organization reveals how the emphasis on mutuality empowers women to develop skills and self-confidence, first to address primary needs and then to apply these skills to the benefit of the community, all the while working toward personal fulfillment. In fact, Melina's work reveals the extreme possibilities of the three-phase model as she, in her various roles at LSA, now helps others undergo the same transformative process that the three-phase model brought about for her.

The concept of mutuality is embedded in how Melina describes her work. She says her job centers on listening and validating the stories and experiences of the people she works with. In this way, Melina has brought the three-phase model full circle, allowing others to begin the process of finding their own voices.

Unlike almost all the other interviews we conducted for this study, all of the interviews with Melina were entirely in English. Her fluency is both a testament to her success at integrating into her community in New York and an indication that she enjoys certain privileges (linguistic and otherwise) that remain unavailable to the other seventeen mothers whose stories are told in this book. In addition, while the names of all but one of the other clients have been changed for this book, we decided in consultation with Melina to use her real name since her identity would be impossible to conceal, as it is clearly revealed on the LSA website. The same is true for Yolanda Tovar, who was originally a client and who currently works at LSA as an early education specialist. Her story is included in chapter 3. We have, however, changed the names of both of their children.

Melina's Story

Melina and her four siblings grew up in Mexico City. In 1982, when she was seven, her father came to the United States, where he worked in restaurants and sent money home. This income, along with money that Melina's mother earned as a seamstress and by making and selling ice cream, afforded Melina's family a comfortable life. She and her siblings lived in a large house that the family had built with the remittances her father sent.

"Actually, to tell you the truth," Melina said in one of the four interviews we conducted over Zoom, "for me I was very frustrated to come to this country, extremely frustrated.

"We were in a good position where my mother did a lot of things with the money that my father sent," she added. "She built a huge house. She had her own business. I had my own room. I had my friends. I was going to high school. I didn't feel the need to come to this country."

Although Melina's family did not live in an affluent neighborhood, she led a comfortable life. She was fourteen years old, attending high school—something not all Mexican teenagers do—and was generally happy.

"We lived in a very poor neighborhood," she said, "but we were considered one of the upper-class in that neighborhood. My father was here. My mother had her own business. I always had a hot meal. I had enough money to travel from my neighborhood to the school without worrying about our financial situation." Her 1989 migration to the United States disrupted this comfortable life.

Unlike many Mexicans in New York at the time, Melina's father had traveled north to join relatives who were already living and working in the city. In 1986 he acquired a green card under the Immigration Reform and Control Act (IRCA), federal legislation that provided amnesty for more than two million undocumented immigrants who had been living in the United States. With his newly acquired status, Melina's father petitioned for his immediate family to join him. But family reunification petitions can take years, especially for Mexican nationals who have very high petition numbers. For example, in February 2022, the United States was processing petitions for children of legal permanent residents that were filed in September 2000, twenty-two years earlier.[1]

Faced with a potential twenty-year wait, Melina's parents decided that Melina, her mother, and her siblings would journey to the United States to join their father even though they would not yet have legal status. Their move coincided with a rise in Mexican migration to New York, due in part to the amnesty offered by the legislation.[2] In fact, the Mexican population in New York more than tripled from 1990 to 2000, according to census data, and that figure probably represents an undercount.

Melina and her family made three separate trips to the United States, all accompanied by coyotes who specialized in smuggling migrants across the border. First Melina's older sister came on her own, then Melina and her younger sister, and finally her mother and her younger brother and sister. This risky journey has become increasingly dangerous since Melina and her family crossed the border. Many migrants die every year as a result of increased militarization at the southern border, as well as rampant gang violence that controls migratory routes all the way from Central America up through the United States. When Melina arrived in 1989 at age fourteen, there was no way to know that migration would become one of the most fraught political issues of the late twentieth and early twenty-first centuries.

"This is one of the reasons I do a lot of volunteer work at the border," Melina said, pausing as her voice cracked. "Please forgive me if I get emotional, especially now with the youth that is coming across by themselves. I understood why my father made that decision and that it's not easy to be away from your children, but at the same time it could be very traumatizing for a child to do that trip. My sister and I crossed the border by ourselves. I was fourteen years old, my sister was twelve, and it was really scary."

First the two girls flew from Mexico City to Tijuana, where their uncle who lived in California met them. He initially tried to bring them through customs, but they were turned away because they lacked the proper paperwork. Instead he took them to the house of a so-called "crosser," who helped them jump the flimsy border fence that separated the two countries at the time. From there, they walked to a highway where they were met by a van that delivered them to a mall where they reunited with their uncle. Two weeks later, Melina and her sister boarded a plane to New York City.

Their father had prepared for their arrival by moving to an apartment he had rented on East 111th Street in the heart of East Harlem, where a small Mexican community was beginning to take root. To afford the apartment, he sublet the main bedroom to another couple.

Melina describes the jarring experience of surrendering her personal space as she adjusted to her new life in New York. "When I arrived to this country," she recalled, "my father was sharing an apartment with another couple. I had to live in the living room of the apartment. I didn't have privacy."

There were other issues. "I went to a high school where we were always bullied because we didn't speak the language because we were Mexican," she said. "It was extremely frustrating for me not to understand the language, not to be able to communicate, to be responsible for my youngest sister all the time. Not having my privacy, I had to share my own bed with my sister, which I had never done because I was able to have my own room. It was extremely frustrating. Extremely frustrating for me."

Shortly after her arrival, Melina began attending ninth grade at the Julia Richman School, a large public high school on East 67th Street that was notorious for chaos, violence, and failing academics. According to a *New York Times* article, by 1992, when Melina was a junior, the school had the worst graduation rate in all of Manhattan, just 37 percent.[3] The problems at Julia Richman were not new. The school had been on New York State's list of failing schools since 1979.[4] And it was commonly referred to as "Julia

Rikers," a reference to the prison complex just east of Manhattan known for violence and abuse.[5] The problems were so great that by 1993, right after Melina graduated, the school stopped accepting freshmen in preparation for its reconfiguration into six smaller schools to be housed within the Julia Richman school complex.[6]

The school environment that fourteen-year-old Melina stepped into in 1989 in no way provided a friendly, supportive safety net. Ann Cook, codirector of one of the schools that found a home in the sprawling high school complex, described tensions at the high school: "At one end of the larger room that housed the vice principal's office, a wire-mesh cage was used to separate adversaries or hold unruly students until police arrived. By 1993, in what can now be seen as a last-ditch effort to control safety within the building, metal detectors were installed. Still, safety remained a troubling issue. Neighborhood merchants continued to complain about an increase in the number of incidents, and local residents reportedly moved from the area, citing street danger and falling property values."[7] Understandably, Melina found the experience of attending her new school traumatic.

"Julia Richman was one of the—I don't want to use the word worst or terrifying experiences for me because I came from a different educational background in Mexico," Melina continued, "but it was very frustrating."

Today Melina speculates that she was sent to Julia Richman because of its bilingual program, which she characterizes as "a complete disaster." She remembers disengaged teachers and tensions between different social groups. "There was racism between African Americans, Puerto Ricans, and Mexicans, us," she recalled. "It was very severe. We were bullied constantly to the point that—I don't like to say this because I regret that—I had to physically defend myself from someone because of the bullying."

Melina eventually fell in with a handful of Mexican students who, like her, were recent immigrants.

"All of us knew that we were from Mexico," she said, "so we created this support group, whatever you want to call it, gang whatever, back then to support each other because we were always being bullied or made fun of. We didn't understand the language. We created like a group support, and we were always together through the four years. Some of us graduated, some of them didn't graduate, but whoever graduated, we would stick together for the four years."

Melina's husband, Raymundo, was one of the students in her friend group, although they did not start dating until after high school. Even in a school with a bilingual program and numerous undocumented students, Melina remembers that no one—neither teachers, nor staff, nor school social workers—reached out to inform her of available assistance or to connect her family to social services.

Given this situation, it is not surprising that Melina did not immediately thrive at Julia Richman. "For me, it was a constant frustration because I didn't know the language," she said. "I didn't understand what was going on. I was not engaged in the classrooms."

Then something changed. "In my second year of high school," she said, "I noticed, if I don't do something, I'm not going to graduate."

After hearing from a friend about the Navy Junior ROTC program at the school, Melina decided to get involved as a way to help her stay on track. "My friend said, 'They're very good. They take you on trips. You don't have to take all these classes because if you are in the program, you can skip many classes, and it's all good.' I always liked discipline. Once I was there, I really liked it. They actually took us on a trip to the Coast Guard and we stayed there for a week."

In addition to instruction on maritime history, the curriculum focused on ways to improve graduation rates, grades, and high school attendance.[8] While Melina initially joined the program in an effort to lighten her academic load and ensure that she would graduate, the program fostered a sense of belonging that helped keep her on course.

"It gave me a sense of community," she said, "because this program had that, a sense of community, the sense of belonging to something, so wearing the uniform, being on time.

"What I liked there is that they didn't care if I didn't speak the language," she added. "They were focusing more on building my personality and my persona to make us feel comfortable in the atmosphere that they created."

The Navy Junior ROTC program focuses on leadership development by emphasizing ideas of patriotism and citizenship. As anthropologist Gina Pérez explains in her book *Citizen, Student, Soldier: Latina/o Youth, JROTC, and the American Dream* on Hispanic participation in the program, the current curriculum for Navy Junior ROTC citizenship focuses on "both the rights and duties of citizens and highlights the imperative for citizens to be actively involved through, among other things, identifying problems (such as violence in urban and rural America) and promoting solutions to these problems on a local and broader level."[9]

The program allows noncitizen participation, as the group's website stipulates: "students in grades 9–12 who are otherwise ineligible for regular NJROTC enrollment may enroll as special NJROTC cadets. Special NJROTC cadets may participate in school approved NJROTC activities, be called naval cadets, wear the uniform, participate as cadet officers, and go on field trips and orientation visits to military installations."[10] Navy Junior ROTC defines citizenship not by legal status, which Melina still did not have access to, but by civic engagement. As Pérez explains, "JROTC cadets . . . are invited to think of themselves as catalysts for making the world a better place. But what seems to distinguish JROTC students from others is the way the program consistently binds up 'making a difference' with the duties and obligations of good citizenship. . . . Young people in JROTC are repeatedly encouraged to understand their conduct as enacting good citizenship."[11]

Despite not being a United States citizen, Melina benefited from these lessons on engaged citizenship, many of which are echoed and exemplified in LSA's mission. At the same time, because of her undocumented status, Melina knew that she could not avail herself of the most significant benefit the United States military had to offer: financial aid for college.

"I really liked it and I wanted to join the army or the navy, actually the navy, but because of my immigration status back then, I couldn't do it," she said. While the program fostered a sense of purpose, belonging, and engagement for Melina and bolstered her inner resolve to graduate high school, without legal status, Melina couldn't access the college scholarship benefits that ROTC offers.

After graduation, Melina enrolled at Borough of Manhattan Community College (BMCC) where she completed two semesters of remedial English coursework because, despite four years in the ESL program at Julia Richman, her English was not yet at the college level. At the time, Melina's migration status was still in limbo and she was told that she was ineligible for CUNY's in-state rates because she was considered an international student, even though in-state rates had been available to undocumented students at CUNY who could prove they had lived in New York for at least a year since 1989.[12]

It is widely acknowledged that misinformation and miscommunication regarding college access for undocumented students runs rampant in New York. As CUNY sociologist Robert Courtney Smith explains, "Based on my research, I have reported to the DOE numerous cases where undocumented students in New York City high schools not only were not told by their guidance counselors that they could get in-state tuition at public colleges—as New York State provides—but were also told they could not go to college at all because of their legal status, again, contrary to New York State law."[13]

Melina's tenacity in forging ahead with her studies despite misinformation and excessively high tuition rates is notable. As Carolina Bank Muñoz, sociology professor at CUNY's Brooklyn College, notes in an article on the challenges undocumented students at CUNY face, "Only the most persistent students who do their research, know their rights, and access the very limited support resources available end up making it into CUNY."[14]

Since Melina enrolled as an international student, her tuition was considerably higher than it should have been and the financial burden proved too much for her family. But her decision to abandon her studies was not taken lightly.

"I was working from five a.m. to one p.m. in a bakery, then going to college from three p.m. to ten or eleven p.m.," she recalled. "It was really expensive because back then if you could not present documents that you were a green card holder or a citizen, you were considered an international student, which is triple the tuition that you pay even in a community college, and most of my salary would go to pay my tuition.

"When I became pregnant, my husband helped me, but I told him that it was just too much, that it wasn't worth it for us to spend all this money. Even though he wanted me to continue, it didn't seem fair to me to continue paying, because it was going to take me three or four years to get an associate's from BMCC, and then transfer to another college for four years to get a bachelor's."

So Melina left college to start a family, all the while working in the bakery. Her first child, Ricardo, was born in 1993. Her oldest daughter, Mila, followed soon after in 1995. Continuing her education seemed a distant dream. "I always wanted to go back," she said, "but I couldn't."

Over the following years, Melina was able to adjust her immigration status, which dramatically improved her ability to access opportunities that shaped the course of her life.[15] The process was by no means quick or simple. Having waited for years on the petition that Melina's father filed for her in 1986, she aged out of her father's case seven years after arriving in the United States when she turned twenty-one because she was no longer a minor.

According to Melina, many green card holders who petitioned for family members were in a similar situation: "A lot of lawyers didn't tell their families that they had to rush, or they had to do another process, or they had to become a US citizen or otherwise, their children who were going to be twenty-one or older, they were going to lose their admission to the process."

As luck would have it, the family of Melina's husband was going through the same process, although unlike Melina, Raymundo was able to become a permanent resident, also known as a green card holder, because his mother had become a naturalized US citizen. Melina's father was still a green card holder, so he could no longer petition for his adult daughter.

At the time, Melina was pregnant with Mila, and she and Raymundo were not yet married. Since her own family's case came to a standstill when Melina turned twenty-one, she and Raymundo decided to marry so she could join his family's petition. Because of Section 245(i) of the 1952 Immigration and Nationality Act, which allowed undocumented spouses of citizens to adjust their status without leaving the country, Melina could complete the entire process from the United States despite the fact that she had not entered the country legally. This provision, however, has not been revised or extended since 2001, and it is nearly impossible for a person who enters the country without inspection to gain permanent residency through a means other than asylum, even if they are married to a US citizen.[16]

We have included the details of Melina's migration here to document the complex and confusing pathways that immigrants navigate, often unassisted and in foreign languages. Melina's journey to adjust her status is only the tip of the iceberg for migrants who travel through an unstable landscape of policies amid government websites that are often inaccessible and almost always unavailable in languages other than English. Even when these documents are translated, they contain convoluted language that is difficult even for native speakers to understand.

It is also important to point out that for Melina the process was, in many ways, straightforward and highlights the unique privileges that her family had access to, such as the 1986 amnesty, the likes of which have not happened again, or 245(i), which is accessible only to a negligible number of people whose petitions were submitted over twenty years ago. For all intents and purposes, this path to legalization has been essentially eliminated from our legal system. That Melina had a stable partner whose case she could join underscores yet another privilege, not to mention what this privilege means for her children's fortunes and her own career success. This bit of luck transformed her ability to navigate the education and employment systems and, due in no small part to her own intelligence, achieve that elusive "American dream" for herself and her family.

Melina at LSA: Motherhood

Melina first came to the agency in 1995 at age twenty as a newly minted green card holder. By then she was a full-time working mother of two young children living less than one block from LSA at 115th Street and

Pleasant Avenue. "I was a young parent living in the neighborhood of East Harlem," she said. "I knew about Little Sisters because one of my sisters received services from one of the nurses. She told me that Little Sisters had a parent guidance program for families, so I started attending the parent meetings and also, I took my two younger children to their program back then, where there was a daycare and a grandmother program where seniors, sixty-five and over, used to take care of the kids while you participated in some of the programs from Little Sisters."

Participating in the agency's programming altered the course of both Melina's career and her children's education. It provided her with essential linguistic and educational skills and reawakened in her the deep sense of service that she first experienced in high school with the ROTC program. In addition to helping Melina and Raymundo understand their children's unique strengths and weaknesses, the agency's Parenting and Child Development program empowered Melina to navigate the complex New York City school system to meet their needs. Melina's confidence in describing the convoluted high school application process for her third child—who was born in 2008 and never participated in the agency's programming precisely because Melina felt she already had the tools she needed—is remarkable. Melina has made it her life's work to share her knowledge with other families, helping them navigate New York City's complicated education, networks.

Without question, Melina's encounter with LSA proved life-changing. "LSA is a second home," she said. "I think most of the long, long-time staff members and volunteers would say the same thing, that this is their second home. I feel that for me. I know that the work that I do here has value for our community. And I have been able to grow so much. In a way, I feel that I'm paying back everything that was given to me."

During the first year in which Melina's family participated at the agency, social worker Marion Velez visited their home monthly to observe family interactions and assess needs. Melina described a typical interaction, "They would invite us to Christmas parties, to events outside the agency, see how they can assist the family, and then how to make sure that the family knew about daycares, schools for the kids if they needed to."

Initially both of Melina's children attended the agency's on-site Grandmother program. When the children turned three, the agency referred them to a nearby Head Start, a federal program established as part of the Johnson Administration's poverty elimination initiatives that makes free childcare available to three- and four-year-olds who qualify in terms of their families' incomes.

Participation in both the LSA and Head Start programs likely had lasting impacts for Melina's children. Studies have shown that center-based care programs such as these greatly improve educational outcomes for children. As New York University Professor of Education Hirokazu Yoshikawa reports in his book *Immigrants Raising Citizens: Undocumented Parents and Their Young Children*: "This form of care is associated with higher early cognition skills in children, especially for lower-income families."[17] While Mexican families have been shown to use out-of-home childcare much less often than other groups in New York, such as Dominican or African American families,[18] LSA's Grandmother program (described in detail in chapter 4) served as a bridge that helped people like Melina feel comfortable seeking out childcare programs beyond the walls of LSA.[19]

And while it's essential to acknowledge the linguistic and cognitive gains that Melina's children likely received at both LSA and Head Start, it's also important to remember that her children, unlike many families in this study, also benefited from undeniable privileges, such as two parents with high school degrees who had begun their assimilation to New York several years before they became parents. In addition, both Melina and Raymundo had extended family nearby, were able to adjust their migration status, and were moderately proficient in English.

According to Melina, the most important way that LSA contributed to her children's future success was through participation in an early childhood study that assessed cognitive, linguistic, social-emotional, and motor development. At the time Jacqueline Shannon was working in LSA's early childhood department while completing her doctoral studies in psychology at New York University. Through Jacqueline's research, Melina and her family participated in the Early Head Start Research and Evaluation Project, a multiyear, multisite study designed to evaluate the impacts of federal programs for low-income children from birth to age three. Through this participation, Melina and her husband not only gained a greater understanding of their children's strengths and weaknesses, but also recognized the importance of advocating on behalf of their children to ensure that their academic and social needs were met.

Five VCR recordings from the study that Melina shared reveal an engaged young family. We see Melina and Raymundo individually playing with Ricardo and Mila as off-camera voices give the parents instructions on carrying out free or directed activities. Melina is a patient and attentive mom. Her hair, which she now wears pulled back in a tight bun, falls loosely around her face. Both parents talk a lot with their children, switching between English and Spanish. They teach them colors, animals, and numbers, and the children eagerly repeat their words.

A particularly sweet moment captures Raymundo saying "Araña" as he points to a picture book about spiders. Ricardo tries to mimic him, saying "aña" over and over again. In another video, Mila looks at the same spider book and starts singing "The Itsy Bitsy Spider" to herself, indicating a familiarity not just with the concept of spiders, but also with popular children's songs. The children play with blocks, beads, Duplos, and dress-up clothes. Ricardo and Mila appear engaged, happy, and bright.

This window into the family's past lets us witness a watershed moment for Melina's understanding of her kids and their needs. According to her, the study identified Ricardo's remarkable academic abilities: "When they did the study with my son, which was almost two hours, the early childhood specialist told me that my son had either a photographic memory or a very high capacity to learn very quickly and she was impressed with how he was able to—because I think he was three at a time—to be able to stay with her almost the whole time. They told me, 'You have to take advantage and put him in a program that will develop his capacity,' so that's how I started looking for other schools that would be able to give him the knowledge that he needed, not just any school." From this moment on, Melina and Raymundo actively sought out schools that suited the individualized needs and strengths of their children, availing themselves of the myriad options available in New York City, including public, private, and parochial schools.

Melina and Raymundo were helped along in these steps by Norma Benítez Sánchez, author of the foreword to this book. As we will learn in chapter 4, Norma came to LSA as a client, just like Melina. Over time, she took on leadership roles within the organization, working as a development associate and coleading a women's group. As Melina explained, "Norma is the mother and the person from the community who has opened doors for many women like myself, and who has helped many community members. . . . She did a lot of things with community members. She was a social justice person who was protesting back then in the eighties and nineties. If I am where I am right now, it's because of her."

Melina met Norma in the late nineties when she began working at LSA. When it came time to find a kindergarten for Ricardo, Norma provided crucial assistance in navigating the system. "Norma is the essential key for me to learn about schools, the private, the Catholic, all the school system because she has kids older than mine," Melina explained. "When I met her and I started talking to her about my kids, she said, 'Oh, Melina, if your son is gifted, he needs to go to this program, this program, this program.' She knew about all these things, and she shared information with me. That's how I started with my son to enroll him. All these programs that he went through because of her."

When Ricardo entered kindergarten, Melina worked to find a school that would challenge him: "I knew that the public school that was located near my house was not the best," she said. "I knew that in order for him to get into a gifted and talented program, he needed to pass this test. I took him, he passed the test, he attended [the gifted and talented program at] BBMS [P.S. 182, the Bilingual Bicultural Mini School]."[20]

The inequitable nature of gifted and talented programs has been widely acknowledged. Schools in these programs have traditionally favored families with greater economic and educational resources. According to a 2018 report on school choice published by the New School's Center for New York City Affairs, "National research has documented that families with fewer advantages are less likely to exercise school choice, even when policies explicitly make it available to everyone."[21] The biases implicit in such programs, with low-income families of color exercising their rights to choice with less frequency, are compounded in a large, highly diverse city like New York.

Elizabeth H. Park makes this point in her 2021 dissertation, "Diversity in Gifted-and-Talented Programs: The Role of Family Engagement and Bureaucratic Rules": "In New York City, the disparity is even more dramatic with Whites comprising about 40 percent of students in gifted programs, Asians comprising another 40 percent, and Black and Hispanic children making up less than 20 percent of the city's gifted students."[22] With Norma's key assistance and the networks of care that LSA provided, Melina and Raymundo learned to become powerful advocates for their children, navigating a clearly biased and complex system to ensure their children's needs were met. Following in Ricardo's footsteps, Mila attended the same gifted and talented program as her brother. The personal support and knowledge that LSA provided Melina's family through Norma and others helped interrupt a cycle of isolation and lack of access to educational opportunities, thus contributing to the future success of Melina's children.

After elementary school, Ricardo attended De La Salle Academy, a need-blind independent school located on Manhattan's Upper West Side for academically gifted students from low-income backgrounds. He then attended Xavier High School in Manhattan, a prestigious Jesuit all-boys institution. He went on to graduate from New York University in less than four years with a degree in nursing.

Mila's education was similarly tailored to her needs, indicating how Melina learned to differentiate her children's needs. "She prefers a small atmosphere, small schools, more personal interaction," Melina said of her daughter. "From the beginning, when she saw all that was happening with her brother, she told me, 'I'm not my brother. I need more personal attention. I need smaller schools.'" She attended a public middle school in East Harlem near her home and a Catholic all-girls' high school. Mila graduated college with a degree in business administration from LeMoyne College, a small Jesuit school in upstate New York.

The mixture of public, private, and parochial schools that Ricardo and Mila attended signals how Melina and Raymundo individualized their children's education according to their needs as they learned to take an active role in identifying appropriate educational settings. Melina credits much of her children's academic success to LSA. "I have to say my own children are the result of this support," she said. "That support and the continued commitment to our families has made my children be able to be the first generation in my family to graduate from college."

Melina recognizes that the structural support coupled with personal connections allowed her to access resources that would otherwise seem off limits. "A lot of our families are very afraid or don't understand the private system," she explained, "because it's very common that we don't even try because we say, 'I'm not financially well off. I can't pay for those things.' We don't sometimes ask questions.

"Sometimes you need to get to know somebody inside or get somebody who has the resources to connect you with those programs," she said. "Thanks to Little Sisters, even though I was a staff member, they saw potential in my kids too. They referred my kids to programs. Coworkers of mine helped me make sure that my kids had the chance to get a private education, which back then was not very common."

The early childhood study helped Melina's family begin advocating for her children, navigating, information gathering, and seeking out appropriate educational settings to best address their needs. This empowerment in the face of NYC's education system stands in stark contrast to Melina's own experiences as a student at Julia Richman and at BMCC, experiences characterized by resignation, confusion, and misinformation. As Melina says about her experiences at Julia Richman: "I didn't know back then that there were other schools. I went to the school that my father put me in."

Beyond helping Melina navigate a complex school system, the knowledge and confidence she gained from LSA's PCD program, the early childhood study they participated in, and Norma's attentive guidance helped the family avoid potential pitfalls and unnecessary diagnoses, particularly regarding Ricardo.

"They would see him as a child who wasn't paying attention or who wasn't invested in things and he would get bored really quickly because he would learn things more quickly than others," she said. "He would start looking for things to do.

"I wouldn't be surprised if they diagnosed him with ADHD," she said with a chuckle, "because he was all over the place. So we had to look for something that actually would occupy his mind and his time."

Knowing that Ricardo needed to be actively engaged at a higher level, Melina sought outlets to help her son focus. At age six he began studying martial arts with a sensei, which greatly influenced him and became an integral part of his identity. Currently he works as a jiu jitsu trainer and competes nationally, although he stopped practicing martial arts in high school and college due to the demanding nature of his studies. Upon graduation from New York University, he asked for his parents' blessing to interrupt his nursing career and pursue martial arts, although Melina is clear about the fact that he did not need their permission to follow his passion. He lives independently and plans to start his nursing career once he is too old to compete.

Melina's daughter, who also lives on her own, works at a bank and hopes to open her own business.

That both of Melina's older children are following career paths and live independently in New York City is no small feat, particularly given the fact that these days far more Black and Hispanic offspring live with their parents than do white children, mostly owing to socioeconomic factors.[23] While there is no normative rule in which adult children's independent living signals some imaginary benchmark of success, Melina herself acknowledges how her family's success challenges the structure of the "typical" Hispanic family.

"As a Hispanic mom and a mama bear and a helicopter mom who wants to know everything, it was very difficult," she said, "but I also understood that they needed to be independent. We need to break that barrier because we Hispanics tend to live with our parents until we are forty, fifty and we have our own families living in their own parent's house. I didn't want that for them."

With the knowledge and support they received at LSA, Melina and her husband have carved out a different future for their children.

Melina at LSA: Career Opportunities

When Melina joined the PCD program, her main professional goal was to improve her English. As a cashier in a bakery, she felt limited by her language skills and also knew that she would be unable to secure a better job without better English. At the time, LSA offered parenting groups in both English and Spanish. With encouragement from LSA staff like Gail Gordon, Melina decided that by joining the English group, she could improve her linguistic skills and employment prospects while also gaining valuable parenting skills.

"I knew that if I participated in the Spanish-speaking program, I wasn't going to be able to do that," she said of the opportunity to practice her English. "At the same time, I was very afraid to participate in the English groups because I didn't want to feel intimidated, or that I didn't understand one hundred percent of what they were saying. Gail Gordon and the other nuns, they encouraged me to do it. They said, 'You are in a secure space. You are in a space of non-judgment. We're going to help you develop your English. We're going to correct you without judgment.'"

Having completed four years of high school ESL, plus a year of coursework at BMCC, LSA's ESL program was not challenging enough for Melina. But she was not fluent enough to secure a job in English. The crucial linguistic support that LSA provided allowed Melina to work on her English in a highly contextualized environment that she cared deeply about. Talking about her own parenting assured a high motivation to learn. Just like students in community-engaged learning classes, Melina was motivated by classroom topics and quickly learned skills that were of actual use to her. Furthermore, the supportive, trusting environment that LSA fostered became a secure space for Melina to practice her English as she developed her self-confidence.

"The other community members, most of them were African American and Puerto Ricans, were very nice to me," she said. "They would tell me, 'This is how you pronounce it; this is what it means.' Some of them translated if I didn't understand what they were saying. I got a lot of support from them." This increased confidence and self-sufficiency became a stepping stone to professional autonomy. For Melina, language acquisition was critical to the goals of mutuality. In developing her own strengths and capacities, she become more capable of exercising her voice to help others.

After Melina had spent a year participating in the PCD program, her social worker, Marion Velez, recommended that she continue her studies at Manhattan's Grace Institute, a free professional training and job placement program for low-income women. "One of the social workers who worked at the time," Melina explained, "she saw a potential in me that back then I didn't actually think I had." After learning that Melina was a green card holder and hearing how frustrated she was with her job at the bakery, Marion encouraged her to apply to Grace.

"She said to me, 'You can go back to school. You have so much potential. There is this program at Grace Institute where they give you the skills to become an administrative assistant. And you can work in a bank, you can work in an office. You don't have to do this.'"

Melina said that she learned about the program on the last day of enrollment, which added a sense of urgency to her decision. She briefly consulted with Raymundo, who fully supported her decision, and together they picked up a recommendation letter from LSA and drove to Grace's office in the East 60s to hand-deliver her application packet just before the enrollment deadline. Melina then began a year and a half of full-time coursework at Grace, an experience that launched her professional career and eventually brought her back to LSA. Had Melina not been a legal permanent resident, she would have been ineligible to attend Grace. And while her case is remarkable because of her intelligence, adaptability, work ethic, and dedication to the community, she also had the distinct and arbitrary advantage of having a green card, something that many other immigrants do not have.

As part of the Grace Institute programming, students complete a six-month internship to put acquired skills into action. Melina fulfilled her internship at LSA in a program that they created for her. Her time there was so productive that, after the internship ended, LSA made the decision to hire her to work full-time in the organization's development office, where she worked for fifteen years as a development associate and backup receptionist. "I'd make sure that the donors received the letters, making copies, helping with events, everything that an administrative assistant would do back then," she said, describing her job.

The bilingual skills that she had honed at LSA were particularly useful as a receptionist. But Melina notes that one of the things she liked most about LSA was the absence of an imposing hierarchical structure. "Back then they didn't have titles. That's one of the things that I love about Little Sisters. I knew who the boss was because that was the person who would make decisions, but they didn't use titles as much."

Over the fifteen years that she worked in the development office, Melina took on multiple roles, mainly because she is a fast learner and good at multitasking. In 2004, when the agency moved into its new building on 115th Street, Melina worked directly with the agency's director, in part because of the technical skills she acquired at Grace.

Around the same time, Melina also began working intermittently with the advocacy department, filling in when they were short-staffed. "They knew that I knew the community, they knew that I had the skills, so they asked me to come and help them as a backup person," she said. "They trained me, they showed me how to do public benefits applications, things like that."

In 2014, as part of an organizational restructuring, Melina was officially transferred to advocacy, where she worked as a client advocate and immigrant outreach coordinator. In her role, she connected clients to public benefits and identified pro bono support for people who wanted to adjust their immigration status.

For Melina, this reassignment marked a change for how she felt at the organization. With the former director Sister Judy retired and more and more of the nuns aging out of full-time work, the mission and spirit of LSA felt more diffuse. "It was a very difficult transition," she said, "because the person who came in [a new chief executive officer], even though we were very excited because she was a woman, she was the kind of person who believed that if you don't have a degree, you don't have what it takes to be part of the development or the administration department. I didn't have the degree that she was looking for, even though I had the experience.

"They couldn't fire me or they couldn't get rid of me," she continued. "What they did is they gave me the option to move to the first floor in a very nice way saying, 'We know that your skills would be better used in the advocacy department.'

"I knew the connotations, it was either you take this or you lose your job. I wasn't happy, I knew that this administration wasn't who I wanted to work for. I think I was also tired of working as a development associate. I said, 'I'm going to work with the community. I'm going to take this challenge.' Then, I moved to advocacy."

In this position, Melina actively involved herself in citywide and national networks that educate community leaders and advocate for migration justice. LSA has long been a member of New York Immigration Coalition (NYIC), an umbrella advocacy organization that works throughout New York State. Through this liaison, Melina attended trainings on immigration law. This led to her nomination to the WE Lead (Women Empowered to Lead) Community Navigator Training Program, which promotes women's leadership and professional development to take on legal work in migration similar to that of a paralegal.

Just as Melina finished her work with WE Lead, the Jones Day law firm was launching the Laredo Project, a pro bono endeavor to open a fully staffed law office in Laredo, Texas, to serve women fleeing gender-based violence. In 2018 and 2019 Melina made four visits to Laredo to work as an interpreter with the Laredo Project. Through LSA she also participates with CUNY Citizenship Now!, a pro se legal assistance program that deals with immigration issues. In 2019 she was nominated for an award from the New York State Youth Leadership Council that recognizes leaders who fight for justice at the intersection of migration and gender issues. And in 2022, LSA's long-term partner "Groove with Me," a nonprofit that offers free dance classes to promote young female leadership, nominated Melina as a DYCD (New York City's Department of Youth and Community Development) Community Mom for her support of families and communities. Clearly Melina's work is recognized by her own community.

While Melina was not initially thrilled about her transfer to the agency's advocacy department, this work is undeniably more public facing than her work in development and administration. Here her leadership inspires direct, positive change for other members of LSA's community.

Melina recognizes the increased responsibility and creativity she has taken on over the years at the agency.

"Professionally it has been a huge growth for me," she said of her evolution. "I started as a development associate, which was more administration work, doing reports, creating events, connecting with donors. Carrying the change to working directly with the community as a client advocate, it is a huge impact. I know my community, I grew up in East Harlem, so I know the needs of my clients. I think some of the clients can identify with me because a huge population of our clients is from Mexican descent, either for generations or just new arrivals. It's easy to identify when someone speaks your language, looks like you, and they can understand your needs."

Having gone through the process of adjusting her own migration status, Melina has a unique understanding of her clients' needs. Through her direct engagement with the community, her sphere of influence has widened and she has become a leader and a model for other mothers who through her see an encouraging future of possibilities: "I know that the work that I do here has value for our community. Even if it doesn't have value for the administration," she says, referencing the organizational changes and challenges LSA has faced as the staff becomes increasingly secular. "And I have been able to grow so much, so much. In a way I feel that I am paying back everything that was given to me."

In this way, Melina's work goes beyond the third phase where clients are encouraged to apply skills gained to tell their own story as a way to model leadership development and to advocate for positive change in their community. Melina now provides others with the same space to tell their stories. "We need to take a minute to hear people's stories," she said. "We need to start just not focusing on our job description, on what we are hired to do. We need to start communicating among each other so we can assist families and we can do the best to help them."

This constant reenactment of mutual learning in which staff and clients alike learn from each other to enrich the personal, professional, and civic lives of all involved is explained in a 1991 article cowritten by Gail Gordon and Sister Susanne Lachapelle together with several faculty members from Mount Sinai's medical school. The authors describe LSA as a nonhierarchical agency where staff and families work seamlessly together to lift up the community. "LSA is committed to empowering both clients and staff. Work organized along non-hierarchical lines in complementary [*sic*] without strict boundaries between disciplines. Where one worker leaves off, the other continues. There is strong peer support. Supervisors act as moderators and input from every staff level is encouraged."[24] This flexible structure highlights cooperation and shared mutuality that, according to the article's authors "extends beyond the usual restricted realm of professional responsibilities."[25] When Melina refers to LSA as a family, a second home, she is referencing this collaborative spirit that allows for a blurring between roles, and where a client, like Melina, can become a staff person and a powerful spokesperson for her community.

For Melina, LSA is a family affair, and her work would not have been possible without the support of her husband Raymundo: "His heart is also at LSA. He worked for LSA. He understood the mission and he still understands the mission and that's why I can do the work that I do. I think this is a family. I'm part of what LSA wants to do in the community, to make sure that families are integrated and they are bonded." Through the years, Melina's commitment to LSA remains unwavering.

And as structural relations have been under stress in recent years, it is a reminder of the importance of reinvigorating the founding mission: "People continue asking me why I'm still there, why don't I move forward with my career, why don't I work somewhere else when I can get a better paycheck and more money? I always said to them that when you do the work that I do, and when you find that you're making [a difference in] people's lives and children's lives and families, that's a better reward than a financial reward that you can always have. Of course, we would all love to make and earn a better living, but seeing the changes that we can create in families and children, I think it's better than the financial earnings that you can make in your lifetime."

In mid-May 2021, our group of Fordham students and faculty researchers arranged a meet-up at Thomas Jefferson Park in East Harlem. We had been working together on this project for nearly a year, but most of us had never met each other in person. The weather was finally nice enough for an outdoor gathering, and COVID hospitalizations were receding as vaccines became increasingly available. Things felt safer, but by no means had city life returned to normal, especially not in East Harlem. After sitting on park benches chatting about our grueling semesters, exciting summer plans, and what we had learned together through this unique collaborative research, we decided to head over to LSA for a look at the building from the outside. Most offices were still closed and almost all of the agency's staff was working remotely. When we got to the building on East 115th Street, however, we were greeted by Melina and her husband, Raymundo, who had stopped by to check on a few things at the agency.

At the time, we hadn't thought to include Melina's history at the agency. She'd been interviewed for the project solely as a staff member. But her warmth and her dedication to LSA were striking. Even though she was on her way out, Melina insisted on bringing us inside for a tour of the building. As we walked through offices and play spaces and saw the supplies piled up for the following week's food pantry, Melina became our knowledgeable docent. She rattled off statistics about clients served, programs offered. Her years of experience at the agency were apparent. And her dedication to her community was clear.

As Melina and Raymundo drove away, we all looked at each other, dumbfounded. How lucky we had been to run into Melina and to see the building through her eyes. "We should follow up with her," we remarked. "Her story is incredible."

Chapter 3

Voices from the Neighborhood

Immigrant Mothers at Little Sisters

TO UNDERSTAND THE WORK of LSA in East Harlem and the profound ways the agency has helped transform the lives of families—especially women—in the community, one could do no better than to listen to the story of Raquel.[1] Raquel is thirty-nine and lived with her grandparents in the countryside in the coastal state of Guerrero, Mexico, until she was six years old. In 1987, when her grandmother died, she moved to the small city of Tlapa to live with her mother, her stepfather, and his children. Her mother had married a widower with seven children, presumably to support herself. She hadn't taken Raquel in earlier because she had too much to deal with and didn't think she could add to her burdens.

"My grandparents said she couldn't take me with her because she had a lot of work with seven children," Raquel reported from her East Harlem kitchen over an hourlong Zoom conversation in January 2021 while the COVID-19 pandemic still raged through New York City. "When I got to the city at six years old, they put me in school, but it was hard because I spoke Mixteco [a Mesoamerican indigenous language spoken in Oaxaca and Guerrero] and they spoke Spanish. I knew I wasn't happy there. My grandfather couldn't take care of me, either, because then he couldn't work, and where was he going to leave me?

"It was a very sad and difficult experience," Raquel continued. "Almost from the time I was with my mother, at around ten years old, I started working, because I liked having shoes and my mother couldn't give me all that." As she told her story, Raquel's reserved, soft-spoken manner offered a smile.

By the time Raquel was fourteen, she was living independently, supporting herself as a street fruit vendor. But she was frustrated that she hadn't been able to finish her schooling. As a young child she had loved school, and she resolved to figure out how to continue.

"I'm going to finish primary school, at the very least, because I like studying," she told herself. "But if I study, who's going to help me?

"It was very complicated," she added. "I worked and at night I went to school." By attending night school, she managed to finish her elementary education up through sixth grade.

In 1998, at the age of eighteen, Raquel migrated to New York, and a cousin who already lived in the city with her own family brought Raquel with her on one of her visits to LSA. Two years later, when Raquel got pregnant, she began participating in LSA's home visiting program. They helped her get ready for the baby's arrival, securing a crib and showing her how to care for a newborn. Soon after, she and her daughter, Mayra, joined parenting classes. In fact, all four of Raquel's children, who at the time of our interview ranged in age from eleven to nineteen, were active at the agency, taking part in programs that ran the gamut from early intervention and speech therapy to preschool and home asthma intervention.

Because two of Raquel's children have special needs—Mayra has a developmental delay for which she receives in-school supports to supplement her learning, and Raquel's youngest, Hugo, was born with Goldenhar Syndrome, a rare craniofacial condition that causes irregular development of the face and head—their mother has dedicated herself to caring and advocating for them. Since Raquel has been unable to hold a steady job, the family relies on her partner's income as a day laborer, as well as occasional money from her partner's aunt, who collects recyclables.

Raquel's family still regularly receives food from LSA's weekly food pantry. But Raquel also works as a volunteer there, explaining: "At the pantry I'm happy helping out, because thanks to LSA I've been able to spend a lot of time with my children and I have LSA's support. I feel *en familia* there." Her eyes light up and she describes how volunteering makes her feel: "In my spare time, I go to LSA, I clear my head a bit, and I'm happy to give food to people and help the community."

Raquel's story is an example of LSA's philosophy of mutuality in action, whereby the strengths and capacities of all individuals are recognized and built upon. At LSA, Raquel can be in relationship with neighbors and fellow volunteers, helping inoculate her from the dangers of isolation as an immigrant mother in an apartment with special needs children. Helping others has cultivated self-confidence and a sense of connection with her community. Raquel's energy enabled her to continue her education despite numerous obstacles, not least of all having to support herself at such a young age. Her resilience, adaptability, and maturity are apparent not only in her move to New York, but also in how she advocated on her daughter's behalf when she noticed that the child was not hitting regular developmental milestones.

When Mayra's pediatrician ignored Raquel's questions, she sought support from LSA, where Inginia García, the former supervisor of the home visiting and socialization programs, helped the family secure a formal medical evaluation that Mayra still benefits from today at school. At the time of our interview, Mayra was a high school senior in an integrated classroom where students with and without documented disabilities learn together. She was preparing to apply for college.

Raquel's steadfast dedication to her children has clearly paid off. The staff at LSA, instead of ignoring these qualities, or treating Raquel like a charity case, recognized these strengths and built upon them. Most striking, perhaps, is that two decades after her first encounter with the agency, Raquel is both client and volunteer, serving her community just as the community serves her.

This reciprocity is part and parcel of the three-phase model LSA follows in carrying out its philosophy of mutuality. The first phase addresses clients' direct needs while establishing trust between clients and LSA staff. In the second phase, clients take on more responsibility, building personal strength and self-confidence as they participate more actively in the community. In the third phase, clients are encouraged to advocate for themselves and for their community, as they are empowered to become leaders and powerful agents of positive change. Clients like Raquel move in and out of different phases at different times, and sometimes even simultaneously inhabit two phases at once, volunteering and advocating for the community at large while also being served by it. This unique model of mutuality is more than a standard mission statement. It is the inspiration for all that the organization does, its organizing principle, its ethos.

It is no coincidence that Raquel describes the people at LSA as being like *familia*. Family relations are at the heart of the agency's mission, just as family is typically at the heart of one's identity. One of the Little Sisters wrote of the primacy of family to the agency, "The family is the privileged place where each one is loved and recognized for what he is, 'called by his own name' where his personality develops, his creativity is encouraged and where he learns to live his role in society."[2]

Healthy family interactions and relations help people understand themselves, their role in society, and how to contribute productively. Raquel's story, like so many of the stories shared by the eighteen mothers interviewed for this book, demonstrates how LSA builds upon families' strengths as part of a larger process of growth and transformation. Just as the Little Sisters are anything but diminutive "little" nuns, so the families they serve in East Harlem defy stereotypes commonly assigned to Hispanic immigrant mothers. Their stories of strength, success, and determination are in many ways the agency's true legacy.

Understanding the role of the nuns who founded LSA helps us understand one facet of the agency's work. The stories of the families who grew from their relationships with the agency reveal another facet. Here we focus on the stories of eighteen families who participated in parenting and socialization groups through the agency's Parenting and Child Development (PCD) program when their children were preschool age, from 1995 up to 2017. Their narratives of migration and resettlement in East Harlem—drawn from interviews carried out over Zoom and by telephone from November 2020 to January 2021—show how these families integrated the ideals and practical skills learned at LSA into their daily lives. Our team of three faculty members and eight undergraduate and graduate students who carried out the interviews in Spanish relied on an extensive questionnaire developed in consultation with LSA to direct our interviews. At the same time, we also encouraged interviewers to allow for a natural flow of conversation and follow the interviewees' lead.

As we trace the basic characteristics of each of the three overlapping phases of mutuality as demonstrated in our interviews, we highlight how LSA's philosophy of mutuality recognizes and celebrates the strength and resilience that the women interviewed bring to their experiences, even when experiencing crises or acute needs that force them to seek assistance from the community. The multiplicity of voices in the chapter serves as a testimonial to the common experiences these immigrant mothers faced in moving to East Harlem.

The women's stories are personal, yet at the same time they reveal broader common themes. All the mothers are from Mexico, mostly from small towns in the states of Guerrero and Puebla. On average, each mother has three children, who, when the interviews were conducted, ranged in age from six to twenty-eight.[3] Many of these women maintain active relationships with the agency. Some continue to receive services; others volunteer; some, like Raquel, do both; and still others have adult children and grandchildren who now participate in the agency's programs. These long-term, multigenerational relationships help us understand the slow, steady, and lasting outcomes of mutuality.

In addition to taking part in the parenting and socialization groups where mothers discussed everything from approaches to parenting to nutrition and self-care, all the women interviewed participated in additional programs at LSA, ranging from the food pantry to programs in maternal infant health or environmental health, to name just a few. Their children received services and also participated in programs, such as early intervention with speech and physical therapy, or gardening. This wide-ranging engagement speaks to the agency's holistic approach to community health, addressing short- and long-term needs to effect durable qualitative change.

By telling LSA's story from the perspective of the clients, we see firsthand how the three-phase model of mutuality leads to transformative change. Clients who come to the agency with an acute need for food or medical care, for example, are not simply treated and sent on their way. Rather, their need becomes an opportunity to deepen clients' relationships to their communities, their families, their work, and themselves. In this sense, our focus on the Parenting and Child Development program is, in some ways, arbitrary. Other clients at the agency experience the bulk of their interactions through programs such as Environmental Health or Nursing. But because of the PCD program's unique focus on family relations, it was a natural place for our team to identify study participants, as well as for us to discuss how the agency's practices of mutuality can transform entire families, shaping child rearing, careers, and educational opportunities and in general grounding a family in practices of understanding and empathy.

For the eighteen mothers interviewed, the PCD program is the heart of the agency. Their stories communicate the unique, personalized, asset-based approach that LSA employs. With staff and clients alike engaging in respectful, reciprocal relationships, all parties start to realize their potential and their true selves more fully. When Raquel says that volunteering at the agency makes her feel *en familia*, she is referring to the way LSA helped her come into her true self: "I'm thankful they taught me about my rights as a person, as a mother. I'm grateful they've always been there for us."

Raíces: Roots of the Parenting and Child Development Program

The PCD program has its roots in the agency's Grandmother program, described in detail in chapter 4, in which neighborhood grandmothers worked with LSA families to support and encourage parenting skills. As the grandmothers' work with high-risk families shifted to focus not just on helping mothers cope but on preventing families from entering the foster care system, the program incorporated ideas of child development. To assist them in their work, the grandmothers even received training in skills such as first aid, early childhood development, and behavioral diagnostic skills.[4]

By the late 1980s, the agency began tracking the development of the children in these families using standardized assessment tools in order to provide extra support and necessary referrals for children with developmental delays. By the early 1990s, the grandmothers were mostly working on-site with children in LSA's early childhood center while their parents attended classes or groups at the agency. Home visits took place under a separate program designed to teach parenting skills and identify developmental delays early on. With the establishment of New York State's Early Intervention Program in the early 1990s, the agency began offering in-home services to children, such as speech and occupational therapy. These three programs—the grandmothers, early intervention, and home visiting—became the center of the PCD program.[5]

Of the eighteen mothers we interviewed, seventeen of the interviews—including our conversations with Melina—were recorded and transcribed, and researchers maintained extensive notes for the unrecorded interview. All but one of the interviews were conducted in Spanish. Melina spoke in English, mainly because her first interview focused on her role as a staff person at LSA. After reviewing that interview, we decided to feature Melina's experiences as a client, not only because of her exceptional story, but also because her profile fits in with the broader cohort of our study. She is Mexican, and her family participated in the agency's PCD program between 1995 and 2017. Her information has been included in all statistics cited in this chapter, but her direct experiences are featured in chapter 2.[6]

Comunidad: Where We Come from and Why We Come

To put these mothers' interactions with LSA in context, we must first understand where these women come from and the kinds of experiences they had growing up compared to the experiences of their children. While there had been a modest Mexican population in New York City for years, it increased sixfold between 1990 and 2010,[7] precisely the decades in which the women interviewed arrived.[8] The sociologist Robert Courtney Smith, who has written extensively on Mexican New York, cites Mexicans as the fastest-growing ethnic group in New York City; in 2000, Mexicans accounted for between 275,000 and 300,000 of New Yorkers.[9] Furthermore, this group is notable for having a high foreign-born population; in 2000, nearly 97 percent of all Mexican women who gave birth in New York City were born outside the United States.[10]

The community that LSA serves is naturally determined by population trends in East Harlem. The rapid growth from the late 1990s to today of "Manhatitlán"—the word is a mash-up of Tenochitlán and Manhattan used to describe New York's burgeoning Mexican population—necessarily meant adjustments at the agency. Whereas the Black and Puerto Rican families traditionally served were often proficient in English, this Mexican influx made ESL classes and immigration legal assistance essential. Similarly, these newly arrived families tended to share already cramped apartments that accommodated multiple family units. Providing tools and support to manage the stress and complex dynamics involved with cohabiting amid crying babies, energetic toddlers, and overworked parents of multiple families also became part of LSA's focus.

Despite the obstacles, the promise of migration offered a powerful incentive to these families. People don't migrate on a whim. They don't uproot their entire lives for nothing. They seek to flee impossible circumstances: meager wages, barriers to education, anemic economies, violence, and discrimination. In coming to this country, these women made incredible sacrifices, forfeiting their legal status and abandoning their homes, so that they and then their children could have a chance at a future denied them in Mexico. In keeping with the Little Sisters' ministry focused on those who live at the margins of society, many of these women live or lived in the shadows. The agency's emphasis on mutuality worked to empower them to acknowledge and harness their own strength and power, despite the often grim realities of their circumstances.

Every mother who was asked if her children have better educational opportunities than she did replied yes. These women come from humble, mostly rural, backgrounds. Many were forced to work or care for younger siblings when they were still children themselves. Most of them did not study beyond middle school in Mexico, not only because of family demands, but also because of ingrained notions of gender that give little priority to women's education.[11]

In their journeys, these women have made great strides. While their proficiency in English varies greatly, all of them have learned to live and often to work in a second language. And in all cases, they have become staunch advocates for themselves and their children in ways both great and small. Whether their children are studying at renowned American colleges or receiving treatment for rare medical conditions like Raquel's son, Hugo, these women have witnessed their children's growth and advancement far beyond what could have been imagined for them in Mexico.

These are their stories.

Superarse: Immigration as Aspiration

Paloma, who was thirty-six at the time of our interview, has two children, ages eleven and sixteen. She is on the cusp of completing her GED, a process she began thirteen years ago when she enrolled in adult education classes at LSA after being referred to the agency because of her son's asthma. Paloma is from a small town in Guerrero, Mexico, where she completed half of her primary school education. When she came to the United States at fifteen, she could barely read and write. She and her sister scraped by as migrant farm workers on the West Coast.

After a year of itinerant work, she moved to Mississippi to take a job at a poultry plant, where she met her husband. He had family in New York City, and, lured by higher wages, he persuaded Paloma to move. They journeyed north by bus and, because they spoke no English and struggled to read the road signs, carefully followed along with a paper map so they could make necessary connections in North Carolina, Virginia, and other states along the way. When asked about her own schooling in Mexico, Paloma laughed, tucked her long black hair behind one ear, and then recounted the following.

"I'll tell you about my childhood experience. I come from *un lugar pequeñito, pequeñito, como dicen* [a tiny place, tiny, as they say]. Maybe it didn't even exist on a map then. It's in Guerrero, the state of Guerrero, but you know that there are a lot of *lugarcitos pequeños* [tiny places] here. It's the same there, there were small towns and my town is Jicayán, that's where I'm from. At that time there was a school, it's not like here where you have fancy schools. That's what I always say to my children, 'You have so many opportunities for schools, teachers, all the supplies you need, you have it here and still *no le echan ganas* [you all don't try hard].'

"It's not like where we came from, that if we had money we could study, if not, not. At that time people said that women didn't have to study because their work was being home, making food, cleaning, and men had to study, but men also had to work. That was what my parents had in mind: 'You studied a little, now stop and let's get to work.' There were a lot of us in my family, we are ten kids. Eight girls and two boys, so we always needed money.

"My father farmed, he planted everything. Perhaps we weren't so poor food-wise; we always had food to eat. But as far as money or clothes or shoes, *eso sí* [yes indeed]. If we had a pair of shoes, it lasted us for years or until they broke. My schooling wasn't very continuous. Here children start school in September and finish in June. There teachers showed up when they felt like it, if they came for a week or two weeks, you got to take classes regularly. We didn't know why we were going."

When we spoke, Paloma's two children were in sixth and eleventh grades, respectively. "I am so grateful to Little Sisters because they helped me *superarme*," Paloma said. "The dream I had when I was little to graduate, finish elementary school, middle school and get my degree, I couldn't do it then, but as an adult I was able to. They helped me a lot because on the other hand my son grew so much. He got that caring help." The anthropologist Alyshia Gálvez explains how the word "superarse" is key to stories of female Mexican migrants. In her 2011 book *Patient Citizens, Immigrant Mothers: Mexican Women, Public Prenatal Care, and the Birth-Weight Paradox*, which focuses on Mexican mothers in New York City, Gálvez describes how "superación" refers to the process of bettering one's life circumstances: "To migrate is a dramatic rupture that is also often seen as a means to proactively alter one's path," Gálvez explains. "*Superarse*—literally, to surpass oneself, or better oneself—is the answer frequently given to the question '¿Por qué te viniste?' [Why did you come?]: 'Para superarme.'"[12]

This desire to better oneself and the life of one's future family was a motivating factor for many of the women we interviewed, women who grew up amid adversity. As Gálvez reminds us, "Striking out for a new country is, by definition, an aspirational act."[13] The anthropologist Jessica P. Cerdeña employs the term "imperative resilience" in her book *Pressing Onward: The Imperative Resilience of Latina Migrant Mothers* to describe the necessary strength and focus migrant women demonstrate in the face of the systemic injustices and oppression they confront: "Imperative resilience enables migrant women to press onward against these forces [violent social and political systems] and to enact political resistance by imagining the future of themselves, their children, and their community."[14] That future-focused aspiration drives the women in our study as well, as their stories demonstrate determination to pursue their studies and create circumstances through which their children have more opportunities than they did, while also demonstrating resistance to inequities they experience.

Estefanía, forty-nine, was twelve when her mother died. When her father remarried and moved to the United States, Estefanía moved in with an aunt and took care of her four younger siblings.

"I became like a mom to my four siblings," she said. "There are five of us, but I always liked studying, learning, and even though I had to work, I kept studying and I graduated from university by working and studying at the same time."

Before emigrating, Estefanía had completed her undergraduate studies in foreign languages. In the United States she pursued a master's degree in bilingual education. All the same, she earns a living today cleaning houses because she was undocumented and didn't have working papers when she completed her master's. Although she is now an American citizen, she has never worked as a teacher. Her two children, however, are on a different path. When we spoke in December 2020, Estefanía's daughter was completing a master's degree in cybersecurity at SUNY-Albany while her son attended tenth grade at Xavier High School, one of the city's most prestigious Catholic schools.

Evelyn, who was forty-seven when she was interviewed, lost her mother when she was just nine years old. After being abandoned by their father, Evelyn's younger siblings went to live with other families and Evelyn was forced to start working.

"*Trabajo duro* [hard work]. I finished elementary school working and studying. I finished middle school working and studying. I wanted to go to high school, but it was an expense I couldn't afford. I decided to come to the United States, *supuestamente* [supposedly] to work and save money to go back. Years passed, *no he regresado* [I haven't gone back]." Of Evelyn's four children, her twenty-eight-year-old daughter recently completed a master's degree in education, her twenty-four-year-old daughter graduated from college with a degree in education, her seventeen-year-old son is about to enter college, and her youngest son is starting high school. The opportunities her children have availed themselves of far surpass the ones Evelyn had access to.

Sometimes it was illness or simply poverty that interrupted schooling and forced these women as children to take on huge responsibilities. Andrea grew up cleaning houses in Puebla to help support her sick mother. After graduating from middle school, she started studying accounting in a pre-vocational high school, but had to abandon her studies after less than a year.

"I couldn't do it," she explained, "because I worked cleaning homes to provide for my mother and I spoke with the teacher, and even with the principal of the school, agreeing that I could cook for her in order to pay for school, but she paid me very little, and I couldn't pay for the semester. I had to quit. I didn't keep going because of my mother's illness and the economic situation. It's not like the same help that they give you here."

Similarly, Clara, mother of five, was able to attend school only up to third grade. "My parents were poor so I had to start working very young in order to help them with the expenses at home," she explained. "In addition, in my culture, school is not seen as important and much less for a woman who is expected to just get married and be a caregiver."

Leonila, forty-five, came to New York from Puebla when she was just fifteen. And while she was raised with certain limiting beliefs, New York offered the promise of a different life for her three children. "Where my parents live it's a very small place," she said. "For example, there wasn't much hope of going to university there because it seemed very far away.

"Coming here, for example, in my case, I arrive here, in my mind almost immediately I begin to change that," she added. "If it was very difficult or it was practically impossible there, not here."

As for how she describes her past to her children, "I have always talked about it with them," she said. "I used to tell them my story, where I came from. It still makes me a little melancholy, but it was a story that helped a lot too, that they understood why I stayed in this country, or why I came and why I decided to stay. I decided to stay for them, yes, *por ellos* [because of them]. Because in them I felt that, even though I didn't speak the language, even though I came very young, and I did not have legal status, I was undocumented, they could do things. After living with their father, he was also a hard-working man. Limitless. He believed that it could be done despite where we came from. That was what we were putting in their heads, yes. So far it has worked out with a lot of work; it hasn't been easy at all."

However, she added, "I decided to stay here because I had great hope that here they maybe could break that chain of limitations, of shortcomings that we have. And that the new generations, their children, their grandchildren, will have another life, different from ours."

These women shared certain experiences—child labor, deceased parents, truncated schooling, extreme poverty, and gender discrimination—as a result of which they were typically vulnerable and underprivileged. In moving to East Harlem, they faced unique challenges—discrimination, language barriers, and the struggle to find housing and work despite their undocumented status. But these challenges also forced them to assert their strength, their independence, and their great capabilities. For people so accustomed to fending for themselves, their encounters with LSA provided a surprising yet welcome change.

Many of the women interviewed commented on the warm welcome they received upon arriving at the agency and the ways the organization and its staff offered help. As women and mothers, they had been brought up to serve. To suddenly have the tables turned and to be served, not least of all by mostly older white nuns, was a novel experience. In supporting these women in their goals of *superación*, LSA's work contrasted with dominant ideals of rugged individualism. Mutuality insists that self-improvement does not happen by pulling oneself up by one's bootstraps, but by entering into relationships that cultivate connection and self-confidence. In this way, families exercise agency by forming connections with others, volunteering, broadening their experiences and neighborhood connections. Mutuality means supporting women through the sometimes years-long process of finding resources for children, healing from the traumas of migration, discovering opportunities for additional schooling, and more. Mutuality insists that this is not an individual process, but a deeply relational interaction. With time, as these mothers' work with the agency continued, the nuns and staff addressed their needs. But they also began to celebrate their gifts.

Primeros Encuentros: Arriving at the Agency and Building Trust (Phase One)

Most of the mothers arrived at LSA with an acute need. Oftentimes, they came with the recommendation of a family member or a friend. Rosario, forty-two, came because an acquaintance told her that the agency could help her get formula for her newborn. When she arrived, staff members told her that they'd notify her as soon as they could help her. "I headed back home," Rosario said, "but when I got about halfway, someone caught up with me and told me to come back and that they were going to help me."

Others were referred by doctors for LSA's medical services, a tip of the hat to the community partnerships that first the nuns and later the agency had worked hard to cultivate. When Yolanda experienced high blood pressure with her second pregnancy, a clinic referred her to LSA so she could take part in its home-nursing program, which monitors women throughout their pregnancy.

"So they sent me off with an envelope to look for Little Sisters when they were still on 119th Street, and I went there," Yolanda recalled. "I didn't know there was an agency called Little Sisters here in East Harlem, I didn't know anything. And I remember that when I arrived they said, 'Do you want food?' And I thought, food? Maybe they will give me food to eat here. I said, 'No, thank you.' Again they asked me again, 'Do you want food?' and I said 'No, thank you.' But I didn't know anything about the services they offered and what they were telling me was that they were going to give me access to the food pantry, right? That is how I met them."

As was the case with Yolanda, it was not uncommon for mothers who arrived for one reason to receive other services in addition to the one that sparked their first visit. Paloma, the mother of two who traveled to New York by bus from Mississippi, also arrived via a medical referral; her pediatrician connected her to a nurse at the agency to help treat her son's asthma.

"I met the nurse named Sister Suzanne Deliee," Paloma said "She was a good person. She visited the place where I lived with my son because he has this very serious asthma, and she started visiting us. Then she explained the programs at Little Sisters, she asked me what I was doing, if I had any activities, anything, anywhere. At the time I did not know anyone, I wasn't familiar with places. She said, 'Would you like to participate in a mothers' group? Little Sisters is a place that offers help to families, there are classes for adults, for people who haven't finished primary or secondary school or a GED or if they want to study English, it has that service.'

"In my country I didn't even finish elementary school. I got about halfway. I told her, 'If there are classes for adults, I would like to do that. If possible I will finish my education.'"

In Paloma's story, we see the very beginning of the three-phase model where, beyond a standard assessment of needs, trust is established, and a relationship is built particularly as clients see their strengths recognized by others. Acknowledging that these mothers might have desires to continue their own education while also seeing their children thrive is part of the idea of "superación" or bettering oneself. Through this process, Paloma was able to study English, complete her primary school education, and continue her high school studies while also caring for her two children.

Mónica, forty-five, initially came to LSA to take advantage of the food pantry. But after showing up several times to collect her food items, she learned about other agency services, such as nutrition and English classes. A few months later, her eight-month-old son was attending preschool at LSA while Mónica studied English.

Estrella, forty-two, came to LSA with her pregnant cousin in 2000 when her oldest son was a baby. "I had my little boy, I think he was just three months old," she said, smiling as she remembered. "I went with a cousin of mine, who was pregnant. In the hospital they gave her a piece of paper, because at the agency they were going to help her with parenting classes and she took me with her. When we got there, because we arrived with a sheet of paper that she got at the hospital, I thought the services were only going to be for her, but they told me that if I was interested in signing up, that they could help me too, and that's how we both started going to classes together."

Andrea, who was forced to abandon her pre-vocational high school studies in Mexico, came to LSA before becoming a mother. In 1999, a year before her daughter was born, a local hospital recommended that she seek services from LSA to help pay for her own medications.

"When I was leaving the hospital, a lady told me, 'That medicine is very expensive. Go see *las monjitas* [the little nuns].' I said, '*¿Qué monjitas?* [What nuns?]' 'The ones on 119th Street and First Avenue.' '*¿Las monjitas?*,' I said, 'do they help?' 'They're called Little Sisters,' she said. I left, and later I went there and they treated me and gave me medicine. Then I took my husband there, and they frequently asked, 'Do you have food at home?' 'No.' 'Come on Tuesday and we'll give you a bag of food.' And that's how it started. When they moved, I went to ask for more help with my daughter."

Over the years, Andrea participated in all kinds of programming at the agency, including English and computer classes. She recognized how essential it was that the agency provided childcare so she could study, a logistical detail that many programs overlook. This support helped Andrea feel less alone, more capable as a woman, as a mother. Most importantly, the agency helped Andrea assess her daughter's developmental delays at nine months old and secure the appropriate treatments. At the time of our interview, Andrea's daughter had completed high school and was looking at university programs. The long-standing support she felt from LSA helped Andrea seek out assistance when perhaps she might not have otherwise.

Like Andrea, Leonila came to the agency before having children and was then able to transition to the parenting programs. She was first brought to LSA by her aunt.

"At the time my aunt got food from them," Leonila said. "One day I went with her and got to know the agency, which was very small at the time, very small." From then on, Leonila received food from the pantry. She also signed up for English classes: "Before I had [my first child,] Ryan, I attended English classes that *las hermanitas* gave," she said. "From there I got to know them more. At the time, the nuns worked there, *las hermanitas hermanitas*." She smiles warmly as she remembers, "They were *un amor de hermanitas* [lovely nuns]."

These firsthand accounts reveal how these mothers arrived at LSA in a variety of ways. But whether they came with a friend or family member or were referred by a trusted neighborhood partner, like a local hospital, the first order of business upon arrival was to treat concrete, urgent needs, like hunger or medical emergencies. When needs exceeded LSA's capacity, the agency provided viable referrals to established partners. For the agency, this important step is a key element of the first phase of the three-phase model of mutuality, as LSA staff establish trust by listening and responding to clients. Through such an encounter a relationship begins to form as clients and staff get to know one another and begin learning from one another. This is the first step to addressing longer-term needs and growth.

Convivencia: Capacity Building in Community (Phase 2)

As clients move toward phase two of the three-phase model, the emphasis shifts from one-on-one relationships to relationships in and with the community. After the urgent needs that first brought clients to LSA have begun to be addressed, in this second phase clients begin nourishing themselves in a deeper way, as they develop their self-confidence, recognize their own abilities and strengths, and learn to trust themselves and their community through relationships. For all the mothers interviewed, this sense of community was fostered in the Parenting and Child Development program, which became the focal point of their experiences with the agency. Through this program, mothers participated in socialization and parenting groups where they discussed everything from approaches to parenting, nutrition, and stress management, while their young children often took part in enrichment activities and developmental play. Some children also received early intervention services, such as speech and physical therapy.

The impact of the parenting groups was profound. These young first-time mothers found themselves alone in New York and were expected to navigate the city on their own, without access to resources or community. Mercedes, a thirty-nine-year-old mother of four, described how the unique, life-changing solace the agency provided helped her escape her intense isolation. "Because being young, being a mother, it wasn't easy," she said. "You arrive here, you don't know the city and everything is . . . it wasn't easy to go just anywhere. LSA was the only place I would go with my children."

Other mothers, like Estefanía who had earned her bachelor's degree in Mexico, explained how the challenges posed by language barriers did not exist at LSA: "One arrives in this country, especially the language problem, for many people it's a problem. Fortunately there are always people there who speak Spanish. That makes someone more comfortable to come back or go and ask for help, because sometimes language has been a barrier in the community. Not there, there was never that problem, the classes or workshops we had, they were always in Spanish, or some people spoke to us in English, they also spoke English, but we always felt trust, *como en casa*, because of the language, above all."

Leonila, a forty-five-year-old mother of three, describes how LSA became a refuge for what she calls "people like us." Leonila came to New York at fifteen and started attending English classes at LSA three years later, before having children. When asked to explain what she meant by "people like us," Leonila teared up. "People who came without documents, people who didn't speak the language, people who were alone, who did not have, for example, family," she replied. "They supported us, that's how I felt at the time. It doesn't make me sad, but I remember and I am very grateful to them because I found very good people there. Even though it's been a long time, it's been thirty years, but that still gives me—I don't know what it gives me, but it brings up emotions."

For Leonila, the memories of those lonely, difficult years just after arriving in the United States still proved overwhelming three decades later. But she also recalled how her relationship with LSA helped create community. "When I arrived here I didn't know anything; nothing was familiar, but like I told you at that time I began to study English with them [the nuns], there was always communication with them about what else there was, how else they could help us. That helped the time to pass and the difficult times to pass and got a little better."

By joining the LSA community, these women experienced feelings of relief and gratitude. There they were seen and heard. As their loneliness abated in their newfound community, the mothers gained confidence in both themselves and their parenting skills as they built trust in their community of mothers and in LSA. Estefanía came to LSA in 2006 exhausted and worried. Her eighteen-month-old son was colicky, a phase most babies outgrow by four months. And she was concerned that he wasn't talking yet. "Inviting me to the group and seeing other moms and sharing stories with moms and their little ones," she said, "it was a relief, understanding that I am not the only mother who has a situation like the one I was living with my son, that there were other moms who experienced maybe the same or worse situations."

Similarly, Paloma, who described traveling to New York by bus, explained how, through contact with the group, she learned to be a better mother, partner, and friend. Most importantly, she learned how very capable she was.

"You felt this fear that I'm the only one who doesn't know anything or who didn't finish my schooling," she said. "I am the only one who has that problem. In reality, there are a lot of us, there are people who are worse off than you. It opened your mind and made you feel like you matter and that anything is possible if you set your mind to it."

Lina, a mother of four, echoed this sentiment: "They make you see what you don't see in yourself. Sometimes you think you can't do many things and I think we can do everything." The solidarity these women experienced in getting to know each other bolstered their confidence, making them feel capable. As Estrella said: "I believe that all families that Little Sisters has touched, it's been to influence them that they were going to be someone in life."

Much of the work to make these mothers recognize their own competence involved acquiring practical child-rearing skills. In parenting classes, topics ranged from information for first-timers, like how to change a diaper, to lessons on age-appropriate discipline strategies and homework help. Cecilia, who participated in programming from the time she was pregnant with her first child, recalled that doctors from the community were invited to present on child development. Other mothers remembered cooking lessons, art classes, professional massages, as well as the inclusion of topics the mothers themselves suggested. There were activities to educate, but also to acknowledge and honor the hard work these mothers were already doing.

Still, the most important knowledge gained came through the relationships that were formed. As Leonila explained when recalling the group of more than thirty women in her mothers' group: "They taught us how to *convivir*, moms with kids and kids with moms."

Leonila's use of the word *convivir* is important. The term evokes medieval Spain, when Christians, Jews, and Muslims all lived together in relative peace.[15] While this unproblematic depiction has long since been debunked, *convivir*, which roughly translates as cohabitation or coexistence, does invoke a sense of being with others—living together not in spite of, but because of. *Convivir* is a manifestation of LSA's mantra—the power of growth is in relationships—in practice. And the bonds formed in the PCD program—between parents and children, between families, between the agency's staff and the families it serves—are what motivate this growth.

For the mothers, learning to *convivir* with their kids meant reading with

Figure 8. LSA gardening program, 1999. Cecilia, one of the mothers interviewed, is fourth from left, holding her baby. Her son is in the front row eating an apple. The young girl smiling in the front row now works at LSA's Sharing Place. The boy standing on the far right works in LSA's environmental health program. (Photo courtesy of the Little Sisters of the Assumption archive)

their children, interacting in age-appropriate ways, helping with homework, or as Rosario said, "simply to talk with them." In some ways this was a change in perspective that the women, who mostly came from traditional backgrounds, had to adapt to.

As Lina explained: "They taught me to be patient, to see things differently. I no longer came with the Mexican mentality, how they raise us there, that men are in charge, women obey. All of that was different. They teach you to grow, to listen. At least for me, I learned to be more patient, which I wasn't. I was very impatient, I wanted my children, from a young age, I wanted them to be more mature and to help me more or at least not be messy. You may think that it's silly, but it keeps kids from growing up like they should, like a kid.

"They helped me to develop as a mom a lot," she added, "to understand children and myself a lot." This is part of *convivencia.*

For the kids, convivencia was equally important. Like their mothers, these children were often isolated and unaccustomed to interacting with other children at daycare, parks, or playgroups. As Paloma said of her sixteen-year-old son, George: "He really learned a lot. He learned to convivir with other children, communication, he learned to speak at an early age. I think they helped him a lot.

"He didn't know other children, other adults other than where we lived," she added. "Once I started there he had friends."

Rosario recalled how her son and daughter grew at the agency. Her memories are particularly poignant given that her daughter, Genoveva, was born with a renal disorder. She faced many developmental challenges and died when she was just eight years old after a failed kidney transplant. Through LSA's nursing program, Sister Suzanne Deliee was assigned as the family's nurse. In addition to weekly home visits to check on Genoveva, she helped the family manage their medication regime, translating instructions to Spanish and ensuring that they understood and followed doctor's orders. As Rosario explained, "Every time Genoveva was discharged from the hospital, Sister Suzanne was the one who received all the documentation about changes or surgeries or treatments they'd given her in the hospital."

Rosario remembered the key role that Sister Suzanne took on in her family, "She would explain everything to me so that I understood all of the procedures that had been done or that would need to be done in the future. Sister Suzanne Deliee was Genoveva's nurse practically from the day she was born until the day she passed away."

Despite Genoveva's illness, Rosario fondly recalled how the LSA community helped her children grow. "My son learned to socialize, *a convivir*. Genoveva too. Genoveva learned to walk there, she learned to manipulate toys with her little hands, she learned to speak. Out of that came all the learning, everything they needed for school later on."

When Genoveva died, the community came together to support Rosario and her family. Genoveva was in a coma for a month before she passed. Rosario recalled countless visits from LSA community members who sat with her daughter, singing and talking to her as they accompanied the family. After Genoveva's passing, the agency found a therapist for Rosario, who had understandably entered a deep depression. They also referred the entire family to a counseling program for families who had lost a loved one. Today Rosario works full-time at the Arcoiris Cooperative, a thrift store in East Harlem that operates with the support of the Little Sisters congregation. Because of her long-standing connection to the community and all the support she received, Rosario continues giving back. This too is convivencia.

Beyond simply coming together, *convivencia* means creating community, sharing space, and together overcoming obstacles. The profound solidarity the groups afforded these mothers, together with their common languages and cultures, allowed them to discuss shared challenges, which ameliorated feelings of loneliness. At LSA, these women felt seen and heard.

They described the relationships formed at the agency as intimate; the clients and staff became family and LSA a second home.

This intimacy opened a space for mothers to work through their complicated emotions around child rearing. For example, Lina, whose daughter was born premature, talked about the psychological support she found at LSA. "Because it's true," she said, "you blame yourself for things that happen. I used to say, 'Is it my fault that my daughter was born like this?' I felt bad. Sure, you do get depressed. They helped me move on, understand that no, things are not like that, it just happened. With her, they helped so that, for example, physically she could walk fast, that she was not behind in her growth, in her learning. Emotionally they have helped me a lot, I have had a lot of support because of them."

As forty-five-year-old Yolanda explained, "Families, when they get to the second floor, which is the PCD program, can feel the positive energy there. They arrive and feel at home."

Yolanda continued, "they make you feel like part of the family. It's not like a cold relationship, like at other agencies where you arrive and you just do your job and that's it."

Figure 9. One of LSA's parenting groups celebrating *convivencia*, late 1990s. Sister Susanne is toward the back left in a white button-down shirt; Gail Gordon is on the right standing on a bench; Elsie Sanchez is seated on the right in a button-down dress. (Photo courtesy of Gail Gordon)

Part of creating this supportive environment involved people coming together to mark special occasions. Festivities and celebrating achievements gave the agency the opportunity to acknowledge the cultural traditions of these families. Leonila describes the celebrations as both extraordinary and mundane. Big holidays and graduations were observed, but every day provided an opportunity to gather. "There was a lot of convivencia," she said. "They celebrated everything *tan bonito* [so beautifully]. Christmas. They celebrated everything. You celebrated in class. There was a wonderful, beautiful harmony back then. So lovely."

Leonila remembered how the nuns would give out small gifts to the families. "They were always concerned if we ate enough. Back then they had this big pot for hot water to make coffee or tea. And during our break time—it was convivencia—we'd get tea and we'd eat a little piece of bread. Whatever they had. It was really lovely." By bringing these women together to mark occasions great and small, the agency validated these women's culture and their humanity.

La esperanza del barrio: Yolanda, a Case Study (Third Phase)

Yolanda Tovar came to New York at nineteen from Santa Ana Necoxtla, a town with fewer than thirteen hundred residents in the state of Puebla. She left school after sixth grade because money was tight, and she recalled that books were rare in her town, especially for children. By twenty, Yolanda had her first child, a daughter. Three years later her son, David, was born. As we learned earlier, Yolanda came to the agency because of high blood pressure during her second pregnancy. Before then, her experience of New York was solitary, without friends, family, or even basic knowledge of how to navigate urban life. The farthest afield she traveled was to the park right in front of her apartment.

"I was unfamiliar with cities, even Mexico City," she said. "I'd only lived in that small town. And to arrive here, a super big city, I didn't even know how to cross the street with traffic lights. So you get here. You leave your parents in Mexico, your whole family. You don't know the language. You feel alone. There's no older person like an uncle or aunt to take care of you. You only have your husband's support. Meeting the nuns, Sister Susanne Lachapelle or Sister Suzanne Deliee, for me they became, all of them, like my mother, right? Like I'd found the support of a mom who cared about you. That helped me so much. I was able to find affection, respect, maternal love, spirituality.

"It was a base, I would say, a super-strong base to be able to be who I am now," she added.

Since then, Yolanda completed her bachelor's degree in early childhood education. She has worked since 2010 as an early education teacher in the agency's PCD program, the same program that nurtured and supported her years ago. For Yolanda, the convivencia she experienced at the agency not only helped her become a better mother, but also awakened a passion to work with families and young children. And it helped spark her return to school so that she could pursue her passion to work with children professionally. Yolanda's long-standing relationship with the agency, from young mother to long-term volunteer and, now, staff worker, shows the power of LSA's three-phase model of mutuality. Her story also helps us understand the third phase of mutuality and its focus on leadership and community building.

Yolanda found her voice as a young mother in the parenting and socialization groups. "I began to discover that there was another world. I started participating," she said. They encouraged me, telling me, 'Oh you can start English classes.' They taught me how I could be a better mother. How to take care of my children. They began supporting me, motivating me, and then there was this one time when they told me that they believed in me. That I had enough potential and charisma to be able to continue my education if I wanted to."

The acknowledgment and practical skills she acquired through her interactions with the agency promoted confidence and independence, which led to a sense of empowerment. "It was a group that helped empower women," she said. "To have a better quality of life as women, as mothers, as families. Because the families we come from, I think in all our countries there's always machismo. And that women can't go to school or can't study English. That they have to stay at home. That they always have to say yes. They can't say no. All of us, the participants, we learned to change our way of thinking." For Yolanda, learning how to be a better mother went hand in hand with learning to trust herself and recognize her own potential. As she developed trust in the community, her belief in herself grew.

This confidence and newfound knowledge made Yolanda a better parent, she said, more attuned to her children's needs. And, in fact, this connectedness is a key element of the PCD program, which promotes healthy family relationships to lay the foundation for children's development into adolescence and beyond. Yolanda explained that mothers must learn to engage children, even babies, from an early age to help them learn to self-regulate: "Because we think that's the base for children to have better

Figure 10. Poster on the wall showing typical activities in a parenting workshop at LSA aimed at cultivating inner strengths of mothers with young children, date unknown. (Photo courtesy of the Little Sisters of the Assumption archive)

adolescence, to have better relationships and to have a better future. Because children will have high emotional intelligence, and they will be able to be good human beings, people with empathy."

Yolanda's own experiences putting the knowledge gained in the PCD program into practice serve as an example. When her son David was five, he went through a rough patch at school. Yolanda repeatedly received phone calls reporting misbehavior. Managing his emotions, particularly in dealing with other children, presented significant challenges to David. Initially, Yolanda felt frustrated and helpless. "I was going through an extremely difficult time," she explained. "I had no experience at the time. But since I was already participating in a [parenting] program at the agency, they supported me."

Yolanda recalls fondly the support she received from Inginia García and Susanne Lachapelle. "They guided me, telling me what I could do with my son. And I realized that first I had to change so my son would change his attitude. So I spoke with my husband and we formed a team. We worked together to help my son manage his emotions. I learned that the parents first had to change to help him. Thank God my son was able to have a more relaxed childhood."

The family was successful in coming together to help David manage his emotions. So much so that when David's school referred them to a therapist at Mount Sinai to address the situation, after only a week the therapist congratulated them, telling them they'd already done their work as a family to help David.

"I told her that my husband, me, and my daughter worked as a family helping David to understand and strengthen his emotions," Yolanda said. "We learned to understand him. I mean, instead of when he threw his tantrum, saying 'stop it' or whatever, like hitting the table or things like that, well I changed all that. I changed to be more patient and help him to recognize his emotions and he changed. But it was also thanks to the support of Little Sisters." As Yolanda became more confident and knowledgeable as a parent, her family grew more adept at communicating and working together.

Today Yolanda speaks like the true child development expert that she is. Not only did she learn to build trusting relationships with the community and gain confidence and skills to become a more capable parent with her own family, she developed her leadership skills and took on a key role in helping foster community at the agency. Her journey from client to volunteer to staff member shows the effectiveness of LSA's philosophy of mutuality; thanks to the help Yolanda received in learning to see her own strengths as a parent, a student, and a community member, she could grow in a supported and encouraging environment in all aspects of her life.

Early on in her time at the agency, Yolanda began studying English in LSA's adult education program. There her teacher, Sister Bea Baker, told the class about Section 245(i) of the Immigration and Nationality Act, the same legislation that had helped Melina adjust her status from within the United States. Sister Bea gently yet consistently encouraged her students to think about submitting a petition. Through her husband's job at a Korean fruit market, Yolanda thought they might be able to put together an employment-based immigration petition. She encouraged her husband to speak to his employers on their behalf. In the end, this petition resulted in a deportation order.

However, thanks to Yolanda's work in the community with LSA as well as local churches, she was able to win her deportation case. To defend herself in immigration court, Yolanda solicited character references from LSA staff and other community members she volunteered with. "They gave me letters, recommendation letters, saying that it was worth it for me and my husband to stay in this country," Yolanda explained. "When the judge decided to tell us, 'you all are going to stay,' he told us we should thank the people that had given us the letters." Yolanda's investment in her community proved a key support in helping her family win its migration case.

At the same time that Yolanda was studying English at LSA, she started volunteering in the early childhood center. Through this she discovered her true passion: working with children and families. In order to continue this work in a professional capacity, Yolanda knew she would have to finish her secondary schooling, but she was nervous. As she recalls with a laugh, "I felt a little insecure because I didn't even remember if I started multiplying to the right or to the left." Lupita Martínez, one of the agency's teachers, encouraged her to face her anxieties and continue her middle school education through a program at the Mexican consulate.

"I told her, 'Lupita, I'm scared, and I feel insecure about going to middle school,'" Yolanda said. "'The other students will know more than me. I don't know.' And she told me, 'Don't worry, I'm going to teach you to multiply if you want so that when you arrive you don't feel so insecure.' They encouraged me to go finish middle school.

"Of course, it wasn't that easy, because it was on Saturday mornings. And I had to go with my young children. Well, they weren't so young. They could walk. And I would take them very early, we would stop to buy breakfast and we would arrive at school. So my children would come with me to school. And that's how I started. And I didn't give up. I finished middle school. From there at LSA they told me to go for the GED. And again I was, like, 'Oh no, it's the GED. They say it's so hard. I don't know.' And they're like 'No, no, you can do it, you can.'

"So, motivated by las hermanitas, I decided to do the GED and the same, and then I decided to do an associate's in child development called CDA. So that I could start working with them [the agency]. And then I decided to enroll in college to do early education." Yolanda's work, first volunteering and then working directly with LSA's early childhood team, brought her goal of finishing her education into focus. The agency did all they could to help her all along the way. Flor de María Eilets, the agency's former director of community adult education, tutored her in algebra. Flor also helped Yolanda's family understand culturally what college meant. She

Figure 11. Yolanda Tovar in 2009, celebrating her secondary school diploma, with Sisters Suzanne Deliee (*left*) and Sister Susanne Lachapelle (*right*). (Photo courtesy of Yolanda Tovar)

invited Yolanda and her husband to her home to help with the registration process.

But she did not simply help Yolanda fill out paperwork. She explained the importance of a college education to Yolanda and her husband and emphasized how the whole family would need to support her studies.

"They made me see that I had to think of this as my priority and that I had to leave other activities as a second priority," Yolanda said. "She said to my husband, look, this is something new for us. Maybe for second-generation families here or young people like you [the Fordham undergraduate interviewer], they know everything about education, but I don't. For me, it was like a child with a new activity. So all those gestures, all those details helped me a lot."

In her leadership position, Yolanda has moved squarely into the third phase of mutuality as her "sphere of influence" has grown beyond her own family to the larger agency community that she helps foster. Backed by her educational credentials, Yolanda is now a public-facing leader at the agency, a staff member of the PCD program who ushers families through the same journey of self-discovery that she has been through.

"Thanks to the nuns who empowered me, helped me to grow as a person, I no longer have the need for services," she said. "And that's the goal we have in that program. Not only helping parents with their kids, but aiding the personal growth of moms, women, dads, parents. Their personal growth so they can be independent."

Yolanda's commitment to her community is so steadfast that during the early stages of the pandemic when most New Yorkers were isolated at home, she began sharing motivational videos with families from the PCD program.

"I was thinking about the children stuck at home," she recalled. "How families here in the community live in very small apartments, some with three, four children. Maybe they don't have their own rooms. Sometimes they share apartments with other families. I imagined the parents' stress, with kids all home. And if the father or the mother is in a bad mood, what's the kid gonna do? I worried about the families."

The videos included meditation exercises, nuggets about child development, and ideas for fun family bonding activities, like cooking together. In effect, Yolanda designed her own curriculum to reach out, make contact, and continue the work of inspiring and building up others.

For Yolanda, the most important part of her job at LSA is helping families think about children's growth from a human perspective. "I have the opportunity not to help families, but to accompany families in learning about the development of their children, in learning to be more empathetic as parents." She feels strongly that academic outcomes should not be parents' primary focus, and she encourages families to think about their children as full human beings. "Working with the community fills me with joy and happiness," she says.

Yolanda has not only helped advance work with families at LSA. She has also embraced the mission of the Little Sisters so fully that in 2017 she was chosen to travel to France along with other laypeople from across the world who support the work of the Little Sisters congregation. In Paris, they learned about the history of the order, the trials and tribulations of Father Étienne Pernet, Marie Antoinette Fage, and other early participants. The group made pilgrimages to sites of importance to the order. More importantly, the group spent time discussing how to center the Little Sisters' mission in moving the order and its numerous organizations into the future. Yolanda describes this experience as formative: "For me being part of Little Sisters, it completely changed my life. It was where I met people I had the same vision, the same life's mission, our life's work."

When Yolanda came back from France, she felt even more grounded in her work at LSA, self-assured, and, as she says, brave. Being able to enact the mission of the Little Sisters brings her joy. "It's beautiful," she explains,

Figure 12. Yolanda in 2003, when she began volunteering with the PCD program. (Photo courtesy of Yolanda Tovar)

"because we, since we work from within the agency, we can inspire and transmit that empathy, that love for service to the community."

Yolanda calls the agency the *esperanza del barrio*—the hope of the neighborhood. "Many families feel lonely when they get to this country," she said. "But when they get to know the agency, they find a big family. Then they don't feel alone anymore. They feel they have someone supporting them, giving information, information that helps them grow as people. They stop having a poor mindset and have a more open mind, with more energy, more heart, and more enthusiasm wanting to move forward, to go to school. Or to learn English. They start to change their way of thinking."

Calidad Humana: Helping Children Succeed

So far, this chapter has focused on how the agency's mutuality practices help parents establish trust in themselves and their community while empowering them to find their own voice and build on their strengths. Yet the picture would be incomplete without a consideration of the children who were directly affected by LSA's programming. They received early intervention services, played in the agency's early childhood center, were helped along in school placements, and joined gardening and art classes. Today some are still studying in high school, college, and graduate school. Others are working and pursuing their dreams. Some are parents themselves. Naturally they have encountered hardships. But, like their parents, growing up at and with the agency helped them acknowledge and develop their unique gifts. The support these children received from the agency, together with the educational advantages they gained access to in the United States, has altered their paths. From early childhood through their lives as young professionals, these children have struggled and thrived not in spite of but because of where they come from.

Estefanía's two children, Elsa and Gabriel, are twenty-three and fifteen. We mentioned earlier that at the time of our interview, Elsa was finishing her MA in cybersecurity and Gabriel was studying at Xavier High School. But things did not always look up for them. Gabriel's challenges went beyond the colic discussed above. He suffered speech and psychomotor delays so severe that, by age two, he would frequently bang his head and bite out of frustration at not being able to express himself.

One time at a party, he bit a little girl's face. The girl's father was infuriated and started beating the wall. Estefanía was beside herself feeling frustrated and helpless. Afraid of similar recurrences, she was reluctant to take Gabriel out into the world. Agency staff, however, helped get Gabriel evaluated, and he began receiving speech and occupational therapies as part of the early intervention program at LSA.

Over time, the therapies helped Gabriel manage his frustrations and develop his speech and motor skills. One particularly effective strategy came when staff at LSA introduced Legos with his occupational therapy. As Estefanía explains, "Since he didn't speak, he cried a lot, he got exasperated. He couldn't concentrate much on things. The Lego was incredible. For him it was something that taught him to calm down, to concentrate, to move his hands. At first it was a bit complicated because he got frustrated, he couldn't do it. But with help little by little he started learning. And that helped a lot for his concentration." For years, Legos were the family's go-to to calm Gabriel down when he was upset.

Gabriel received speech and occupational therapy from age two through eighth grade, at LSA as well as through in-school services. When he was admitted to Xavier for high school, Gabriel resolved to enter high school without these extra supports. The years of therapies and hard work had prepared him, empowering him to feel able to manage on his own.

Estefania's older daughter Elsa also benefited from the agency's support. When she was in fifth grade, she became depressed and experienced school avoidance. She said her teacher ignored her and she felt isolated, discriminated against, even. Most of Elsa's classmates were white, and there were very few Hispanic children at the school. Estefanía reached out to the school but had a hard time getting a meeting with the teacher.

On one occasion the school counselor advised her to stop speaking Spanish at home. As someone who had studied foreign languages in college, Estefanía was confused. "I told my husband, 'I don't believe that. I know people who speak two, three, four languages. That can't be the problem.' Clearly, I think that since the school was completely monolingual, and most of the kids were white. I don't know, I wasn't happy.

"But at the time I wasn't familiar with the education system," Estefanía explained. "I didn't have friends or people to help me."

So the family turned to LSA. Martha Andrade, the now retired director of education and youth services at the agency, helped Elsa transition to a local Catholic school. There she received extra reading support—she had fallen behind at her other school. Within a year, Elsa's reading was back on track.

When it came time to apply to high schools, Martha helped the family identify and apply for a scholarship through Student Sponsor Partnerships, an organization that pairs eligible students with sponsors to provide financial assistance and mentorship to attend a New York City private school. Over time, Elsa found her footing, gained confidence in herself, and graduated with honors.

The agency gave Estefanía's family the necessary tools to navigate New York City's complicated education system. "When my children began to have emotional problems, learning problems, all that, Little Sisters for me was that door that I needed to open to everything that I didn't know or didn't have within my reach," she said.

"Meeting the people who were there at the time, that I talked to, and who made me feel that everything was going to be okay. That I only had to do this, that, and the other thing. A lot of times as a mom you need to listen, because sometimes you get caught up in the emotional problems you're going through and you get desperate and don't know what to do. Talking to someone who said, 'Well, this is happening because of this reason, but now we are going to be able to do this for your kid,' it was like it changed my life, the perspective."

When asked what she values most about the agency, Estefanía mentions the "*calidad humana*" (human quality) that staff bring to the table, treating their work as if it were a calling. "Because I've had to seek help in other places where, from the time you arrive, you feel rejection, coldness, like there is no interest in what you are asking for. It's very different." The incident with Elsa's schooling helped bring into focus Estefanía's desire to pursue her master's degree in bilingual education as a way to put into practice the values she learned at and with LSA.

The impact of specialized therapies and individualized attention were mentioned time and time again by the families we interviewed. These interventions, which occurred mostly during early childhood, affected long-term outcomes for these children. Without them, their success today would be less robust as the families' energies would have been redirected to childhood delays and illness.

Forty-one-year-old Josefina explained how her daughter Begoña received physical therapy until age three to correct a spinal misalignment that affected her feet. The weekly therapies at LSA and at home helped correct Begoña's spine. But Josefina explained how the therapists engaged Begoña not just physically, but as a whole child. "They came to the house twice a week. They took her out walking," Josefina recalled.

"The lady who gave her therapy had a car. She took her out. She said, 'Well, let's take her out, I want to see her run, I want to see how she plays.' I liked how they treated her. She got better." At the time of our interview, Begoña was a senior in high school with plans to go to college and study law or finance. In treating her, LSA staff saw Begoña not just as a patient with a physical misalignment, but as a kid who deserved to play freely like any other child.

Beyond providing essential therapies, the agency also helps families by introducing them to schools and programs they would otherwise not know about, just as they did with Estefanía and her family. New York City is home to the largest public school system in the United States. When you factor in the more than three thousand charter, parochial, and private schools, all with different missions, focuses, and target audiences, the navigation of such a behemoth is overwhelming for anyone, much less someone who does not speak English and is new to the American education system.

A reasonable reaction amid such immense choice is to hold one's children close, putting them in the nearest school instead of exploring options and seeking out enrichment opportunities. However, it is often in traveling further afield that children gain ground, as families take advantage of personalized programs for individual children. LSA helped families exercise their right to choose, showing them that finding good schools was not only something available to them, but an option these families deserved.

Teaching families to value the choices available to them in New York City often began when their children were just preschoolers.

As the education expert Hirokazu Yoshikawa states, parents act as "powerful gatekeepers" to resources for their children.[16] Young children who participate in center-based care experience undeniable cognitive advantages that last well beyond early childhood. Through LSA's on-site early childhood center, families were introduced to the benefits of learning and socializing in a group setting while remaining in a trusted environment. In this way, LSA helped families understand the importance of parental engagement in schooling. As the Harvard education professor Gabrielle Oliveira explains in her book *Motherhood across Borders: Immigrants and Their Children in Mexico and New York*, "mothers' school involvement and children's academic performance are heavily correlated."[17] Despite the lack of formal education for many of the women we interviewed, with LSA they learned to take on an active role in their children's schooling.

Leonila, a mother of three, fondly remembers when her middle daughter Ana attended the early childhood program at LSA, where she sang and played with puzzles and other manipulatives. At the same time, she received speech and physical therapy to address delays that were quickly remedied with individualized attention. But Leonila says the most important lesson her family learned when her children were little was to give them more independence.

"With LSA I learned that I had to let go and look at what was good for him," she said of her oldest son, Ryan. As a young boy, Ryan was smart, but he was restless and in need of constant stimulation. With the help of LSA's education director, Flor de María, Leonila enrolled Ryan in numerous programs. Flor helped Leonila find classes and even fill out forms. "She was always there, helping. She always made space to welcome us, anything we needed," Leonila recalled.

These experiences of using a trusted partner to engage her child helped Leonila feel more confident when Ryan ventured further afield for high school. "I didn't want Ryan to go to a school that was far away, because it scared me," she said. "But with LSA I learned that you have to let go and look at what's good for your kid." Ryan attended the High School for Environmental Studies, a well-regarded public school in Midtown Manhattan. He went on to graduate from Hunter College with a bachelor's degree in biochemistry. At the time of our interview, Ryan had started a master's program at City College. Although his studies had been interrupted due to the pandemic, Leonila spoke confidently about his plans to return. In the meantime, he was working as a research technician and laboratory assistant at Weill Cornell and as an adjunct lecturer for Hunter's chemistry department. His laboratory work had even led to a publication in a scientific journal on the presence of COVID-19 antibodies in saliva. Ryan's sister Ana was studying computer engineering at City College while working at the Hospital for Special Surgery.

By participating in the PCD program, families became increasingly comfortable with their children's independence which, in turn, prepared the whole family for later experiences in school settings. Lina describes the PCD program as a rehearsal for sending kids off to school. "It was like pretraining for Head Start. Like the uncoupling of mother and child," she explained. "Sometimes moms suffer more than children when they leave them. It's a process. 'Let's start getting used to the fact that the child is going to be in school and, in the meantime, we'll have talks, we can chat about whatever you want.' Meanwhile the children were elsewhere training to start school whenever they were due to go to Head Start."

While the possibility of earning a college degree seemed far off on the horizon for these preschoolers and their families, the correlation between early engagement and long-term outcomes is long established. A report by the Brookings Institute on the impacts of Head Start programs, for example, shows that Head Start attendance in the Hispanic population increases the likelihood that a child will complete a postsecondary degree by 15 percent.[18] In engaging preschoolers, LSA had long-term goals of improving college access for families. As Estrella said: "They helped me, guided me to lead my children toward an education, toward college. Now for me it's very gratifying to see that everything we have been through has been worth it." When we spoke, Estrella's two sons were studying at Rochester Institute of Technology and Stony Brook University, and her daughter, age twelve, was attending a local charter school.

For Rosario, whose daughter Genoveva passed away from kidney failure, the support that her son Andrew received at LSA with speech therapy and socialization programs helped him overcome his extreme shyness and learn to relate to others. Today he is studying for a master's in public policy at Northeastern University, having completed his undergraduate degree at Boston College. Like many college students, Andrew studied abroad and completed prestigious internships. According to Rosario, the social exposure he got at LSA has been key to his success. "He likes school, that's the most important thing," she said. "We always encourage Andrew to continue studying, that he has a great future in this country and that, without studies, it is a little more difficult. So he has to fight for his dream, he has to have goals and try to achieve them. Up until now he has done it, he has studied where he wanted."

Mónica was a single mom working to support her three children. When her oldest daughter started playing hooky from high school, she sought support from the agency. "I didn't know what to do," Mónica recalled. "The police called me and told me that they have her. That was when Martha [Andrade] was working. She helped students at Little Sisters and she told me, 'Don't worry. I'll go with you. Let's go get her.'"

Martha not only accompanied Mónica to the police station but helped Mónica devise a system to get attendance sheets signed by teachers to confirm that her daughter had been to class. This way Mónica didn't lose precious work hours in making sure her daughter made it into the school building. "I just wanted my daughter to stay in school, to not go down a bad path. Thank God my daughter finished high school. Now it makes her laugh because she says when you're young, you don't really think. But she says, 'Thanks to you, Mami, because you were always there and didn't abandon us, I finished school.'" With the help of the agency, Mónica was able to support herself and her daughter through an extremely challenging time.

Without a doubt, the most important element of the LSA's mutuality model is a deep and continued sense of community. Through this, mutuality is able to replicate itself, bringing more women and families into the fold to be nurtured and trained in mutuality practices. They can then, in turn, give back to their own communities, teaching others to do the same: to see your neighbors and community members as partners in lifting each other up and making the community stronger.

Lina, mother of four, recently returned to the agency after many years. She was picking her baby granddaughter up from the early childhood center. Lina's own twenty-six-year-old daughter had joined a parenting group and sought out psychological support from the agency after her partner left soon after their daughter was born. Picking her granddaughter up at LSA rekindled in Lina a sense of community and a desire to give back. "I think one day I'll go back. I've always thought about it. I say to my kids, 'When

I'm old and I've stopped working, I'll go back, even if it's only to read a book to the little kids."

The agency provided an example of service that transformed the lives of these families, helping them settle and succeed in their new East Harlem homes. At its best, that example offers an invitation to continue serving the community and inspiring others. As Yolanda explained, "I had an example. The nuns' actions helped me and taught me to enjoy and feel satisfied serving my community. Service shouldn't start from the outside, but from inside myself. They have taught me that everything starts from my nuclear family and then you expand that love and that service, that compassion and that empathy outside, with others."

Chapter 4

Mutuality for a New Era

IN A PHOTOGRAPH from 2017, six young indigenous Mexican and Guatemalan mothers are gathered in LSA's kitchen (fig. 13). They are looking over the stove at Irwin Sánchez, the renowned Nahuatl-speaking chef and educator from Puebla, Mexico, who is cooking an indigenous recipe. Most of the women have their backs to the camera. We see their long black hair pulled back in ponytails. LSA staff member Inginia García looks on, her curly hair a head taller than the mothers. Her hand rests gently on the back of one woman. The women smile as they watch Sánchez at the stove. Another photo from the day shows Sánchez pulling out needles from a bowl of *nopales* (the Nahuatl word for prickly pear cactus) in a workshop on how to prepare a salad from the nutritious cactus leaves.

Inginia and her LSA colleague Wendy Miron had been experimenting with new programming to meet the needs of indigenous families who had been arriving in East Harlem since the 1990s. In the 1990s, two-thirds of all Mexican migrants to New York came from the Mixteca region of Mexico. Many of them had indigenous ancestry, belonging to the Mixtec, Nahuatl, Amuzgo, and Tlapanec communities. New York City is now home to the largest population of indigenous peoples living in any urban center in the United States.[1]

Inginia grew up in the Dominican Republic, and Wendy was born and raised in Guatemala. Both are native Spanish speakers who are fluent in English. LSA had no on-staff speakers of indigenous languages, and like the Little Sisters before them, Inginia and Wendy knew they could only

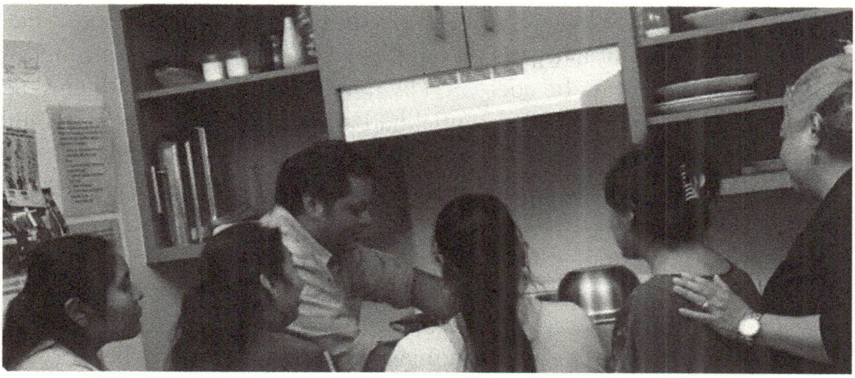

Figure 13. Indigenous Mexican and Guatemalan mothers gathered in LSA's kitchen with Irwin Sánchez, the renowned Nahuatl-speaking chef and educator from Puebla, Mexico. Inginia García (*far right*) and Wendy Miron ran the program, called the Xilonen Project, in partnership with the Endangered Language Alliance from November 2017 through January 2018. (Photo courtesy of Little Sisters of the Assumption Family Health Service)

meet the changing needs of East Harlem by forming partnerships and building coalitions. They connected with an organization called the Endangered Language Alliance and in 2014, the two organizations started a small group of Mixteco-speaking neighborhood parents who met weekly at the agency to form community, preserve the indigenous language and culture, and build Spanish and English fluency.

Following the success of the literacy programs, and after talking with the indigenous parents about their needs, Inginia and Wendy then set up a seven-week cooking, literacy, and nutrition program at LSA. The program—called the Xilonen Project for the Náhua goddess of corn—focused on indigenous food, language, and community. The group consisted of fifteen young mothers who met weekly to promote ties to healthy traditional indigenous cuisine and learn how to find ingredients locally on a budget. They explored the benefits of maintaining natural diets from their home regions, and learned of the dangers of processed foods and sugary drinks that are so widespread in low-income parts of the city. As one mother explained the need for the program, "In my home country, I rarely ate meat; I mainly ate vegetables in my country of origin. My diet has worsened since I arrived in New York. I cannot eat chipiles, failes, cacayas because I cannot find them."[2]

Almost sixty years after the Little Sisters of the Assumption first came into the neighborhood, experimental programs like the Xilonen Project reveal the continuity of the nuns' original vision. LSA had always focused on health, with the knowledge that health is inextricably linked to social factors. The spirit of mutuality meant tapping local knowledge and strengths. Solutions should always be cocreated by families and staff. Health and the development of people's full potential had physical, social, emotional, and even spiritual components. Community and connection were the starting places for making change in the lives of those who are so often isolated and in the shadows. "Inner" work was just as important as assistance in finding resources for medicine, schooling, legal aid. In addition to the indigenous programming, Inginia added a mental health component to LSA's work, creating the Building Bridges of Hope Program in her first year to help isolated young mothers process traumas endured crossing the border.

While much of the original vision and ministry of mutuality has persisted over the decades, lay staff members like Inginia, Wendy, Trish, Gail, Norma, Yolanda, Melina, and many others have transformed the agency. How could they not? The Little Sisters who came before them were trained as nuns and, for the most part, as nurses. Their lives were structured around a disciplined rhythm of prayer, communal life, and the work of service. They each earned an annual stipend of $4,000, which was returned to the religious order and distributed to projects run by Little Sisters around the world. The Sisters were trained—in heart, body, mind, and soul—to internalize Christian ideals such as sacrifice and service and to express these ideals into the world.

The laypeople hired by the agency beginning in 1970 were also committed to service and care, but they came from all faiths and from no faith. Perhaps most critically, they had to earn a living wage in New York City—already an expensive place to live—so they could pay rent, mortgage, and taxes, care for family members, and pay school fees and babysitters. Hiring laypeople required the agency to have a different relationship with money, a different relationship with the secular world. To put it simply, hiring and, more importantly, paying laypeople required finding ways to increase the amount of money coming into the agency and developing closer relationships with a wider range of funding sources such as large grants from government, foundations, and corporations that had their own priorities.

While the language of mutuality provided the agency with a long-term vision, reliance on external funding made some of its less concrete deliverables trickier to maintain. How has the agency been able to combine this mutuality idiom with the quicker outcomes and result-oriented work that meet funding requirements? Even apart from funding, how do the mission and worldview of the Little Sisters get passed along, taken up, and, at least in part, transformed by laypeople?

The story of how LSA navigated this transition to secular staff speaks to an issue that communities are dealing with around the world. Who takes up the mantle to run the massive organizations—schools, shelters, hospitals, home nursing programs, orphanages, neighborhood agencies like LSA—that religious orders created on a global scale in the nineteenth and twentieth centuries? How can lay staff be tethered to the founding spirit of the religious community when they come from such a different, typically secular, culture?

In today's culture, nuns are often viewed as distant from ordinary people; even their dedication to extreme morality marks them as so different from most laypeople. But this belief overlooks how much nuns have inspired and been in deep relationships with communities all over the world. Perhaps it is best to envision their organization in East Harlem as moving along together in webbed relationships, networks—not so much the nuns proceeding first, and then the laypeople taking it up. The bonds between the Little Sisters and lay staff like Inginia, Gail, and Melina, along with the neighborhood families, are the sorts of bonds that have long been central to LSA's work, even in the early days in East Harlem in 1958. Gradually, the leadership of LSA moved from the nuns to the laity, but partnership has been central to their work for decades. They have long been aware that the bonds between the sisters and the lay communities flourish and strengthen through concrete practices like retreats and deliberate community reflections on the topic of mutuality and so much else. The bonds have also been energized by genuine friendships and shared commitments to projects to improve the lives of families in East Harlem at the personal and the structural levels.

The stories in this chapter focus on the staff and LSA's programing from 1970 onward, when the nuns began hiring laypeople. The purpose here is to amplify the organizational context that makes stories like Melina's and those of the remarkable women in chapter 3 possible. The stories of those women transcend individual tales of overcoming obstacles. They emerge from a structural, communal ground where new experiments of sociality and care were intentionally created.

First Lay Staff: Neighborhood *Abuelas*

Over fifty years ago, in 1971, Sister Margaret Leonard published an article in the *American Journal of Nursing* about a novel experiment she had initiated in East Harlem that led to the hiring of the agency's first lay staff from the neighborhood.[3] In 1970, LSA received a grant from the National

Council on Aging to tap into an underused neighborhood resource—local Puerto Rican grandmothers who could serve as part-time "community health workers" to help overwhelmed young mothers who lived nearby. At this time, most of the mothers the agency served were newly arrived immigrants from Puerto Rico who were isolated, were dealing with poverty and language barriers, and had little family support.

As Sister Margaret wrote, "Culture shock is experienced by this family in various forms: strange languages, congested populations, high-rise deteriorated buildings, climatic differences, role differentiation, strange consumer patterns, blocks filled with drugged people, and impersonal, complex health and welfare systems."[4]

Unsurprisingly, the culture shock generates fear and confusion. In response, many women and children in East Harlem, particularly immigrants, become insular and, as Margaret put it, "make cocoons of their apartments." The isolation of many new mothers had an important impact on the family's health and general well-being. It prevented them from having access to parks, fresh air, and other neighborhood resources that could help their children, especially when the children enter school—an institution, as Margaret put it, that neither "they nor their parents understand."

Searching for ways to "strengthen this vulnerable family," LSA aimed to "recreate" extended family patterns from Puerto Rico. As Sister Margaret wrote, "Our belief in the family challenges us to look for those elements in an apparently threatening environment which can be transformed and created into growth potential for the struggling families in transition."[5] The result of these efforts was what the agency called the Grandmother program. Neighborhood *abuelas* were each assigned one family to help with cooking and infant care, to give them encouragement for their parenting, and to connect them with pediatricians and community health resources, including other programming at LSA.

The agency initially hired and trained three grandmothers paid by the grant to work four hours per day, twenty hours per week. In 1977, LSA expanded the program with a grant from the Ford Foundation to have eight grandmothers. When families were facing crises, the grandmothers were known to stay all day and even spend the night. An undated report submitted to the Ford Foundation underscored how the abuelas helped mothers gain skills and independence: "The Grandmother 'does *with*' the mother that which the mother can learn to do."[6]

Abuela Carmen, for example, was matched with the Rivera family, and their needs were many. Neither parent could read Spanish or English. In Puerto Rico they had not gone beyond first grade. They couldn't understand written medical instruction. They made mistakes with their children's medication, and when one family member had a doctor's appointment at 1 p.m., the whole family, including all four children, showed up at 9 a.m. Carmen became trusted babysitter, interpreter, household manager, and someone with a larger view of available resources.

With Carmen's assistance, the mother made a family calendar to help everyone keep track of various appointments and commitments. The abuela had many neighborhood connections, and helped the mother enroll in English classes.

The Rivera family had biological extended family in the Bronx who could be a valuable source of support for the family, but after once getting lost they were afraid to take the subway there. Carmen showed them how to make the trip, accompanied them on the journey, and helped them rebuild relationships and gain confidence in moving around the city. Like a grandmother, she celebrated baptisms and birthdays and brought treats and gifts to the children, among them crackers and balloons. One report comments on how the older siblings yelled out "Abuela here!" when she arrived at the house and reached out to hold the baby.[7]

Sister Margaret described another Puerto Rican mother with four children who seemed "completely overwhelmed and lost" in the city and lived in a "heatless deteriorated" apartment. The family was referred to LSA because an emergency room doctor was worried about the children's mental and physical health. The grandmother assigned to the family, Iris, a fifty-eight-year-old Puerto Rican woman, initially focused her efforts on helping the mother, twenty-nine, who desperately needed assistance. Iris helped her learn to cook, get organized enough to confidently take her children to the park, and generally gain self-assurance as a parent. The emphasis in the training was "doing with" instead of "doing for."

"Companionship helped reduce the anxiety [of the young mother]," Sister Margaret wrote. "The mother needed constant encouragement. Together, they even searched for a new apartment, decorated it, and planned furniture placement. The environmental changes stimulated creativity for both Mrs. Fuentes and Iris." Iris had a "real love of the family," Margaret continued, something that was clear to everyone at the agency when she stopped by with them.[8]

The Grandmother program was an ideal project for LSA because it was an exemplary, creative embodiment of mutuality. It helped address issues of isolation, giving meaning and purpose to the lives of elderly neighborhood residents, who now had a paid job that drew from their own skills and experiences. In fact, the initial government grant the agency secured to support the program came from the city's Department of Aging, a program intended for the abuelas themselves rather than for the young families. Health, as Sister Margaret explained, is "a shared process." Under the auspices of mutuality, "relationship established on a person-to-person level between the Puerto Rican senior citizen and the young family has brought mutual growth and meaning into the lives of both."[9] As one sixty-two-year-old grandmother put it in 1985 when the program was profiled in the *New York Times*, "It keeps us active after the children are gone," she said. "It's better for us than staying home and rotting in our rockers."[10]

The Grandmother program also embodied mutuality by drawing from internal, grassroots assets, rather than relying on experts swooping in from outside the community. In doing so, it creatively addressed one of the main obstacles preventing East Harlem residents from getting access to better health care. Within the Spanish-speaking community, mistrust of health care providers was a key barrier. Fear of deportation, an inability to speak English, the overwhelming medical system of New York City were all factors that prevented East Harlem residents from connecting with health care resources. The work of LSA was increasingly seen as a model because the agency incorporated trusted, bilingual neighborhood liaisons like the abuelas, provided programming in Spanish, and incorporated cultural competency into their programming.[11]

The abuela program was a huge success. The November 16, 1981, issue of the *New Yorker* described it as representing a creative and successful response to poverty in the city. "The surrogates," the writer Ken Auletta said of LSA's abuelas, "were grandmothers from the neighborhood who were invited by young women to come into their homes and help them learn to mother, help make appointments with the hospitals and state agencies, garner the confidence to take the baby places in the neighborhood."[12]

The *New Yorker* article went on to say that in 1974, the Ford Foundation, along with a group of federal agencies, "scrutinized LSA's grandmother program" when they developed federal policy recommendation plans for teenage mothers. LSA's Grandmother program served as a model for similar programs in the Bronx neighborhood of Mott Haven with the Dominican Sisters Family Health Service; and in Worcester, Massachusetts, with the Pernet Family Health Service. In 1985 Marybeth Shinn and Margaret Rosario, two community psychologists who worked with the program as it expanded, wrote about the prescient approach of LSA's Grandmother program in the *Community Psychologist*, a newsletter for the community psychology division of the American Psychological Association. As they explained, "In over a century of service to poor families and

Figure 14. The abuelas, together with Lorraine Tierney, director of the Grandmother program, and children, early 1990s. (Photo courtesy of the Little Sisters of the Assumption archive)

communities, these orders of Catholic sisters have developed an ideology of empowerment and an ecological approach strikingly similar to what community psychologists have advocated more recently."[13]

In 1987, Dr. Shinn published an article in the *American Journal of Community Psychology* emphasizing the life-changing effects of the Grandmother program: "Together, the Grandmother and the agency provide a coordinated, ecological approach to intervention, bolstering families and helping alter the circumstances of their lives."[14] In May 1990, *National Geographic* ran a cover story under the headline "Growing Up in East Harlem," which documented the work of the agency and highlighted the Grandmother program as a model of support for young immigrant families dealing with poverty and isolation.[15]

The growth of the Grandmother program coincided with a period of significant expansion for the agency. Programs grew in both size and number. LSA rented more and more space in East Harlem, mostly around East 119th Street. By 1983 the agency occupied "a patchwork of two brownstones, two storefronts, and borrowed school classrooms," as one document in the LSA archive described it.[16] By 1990, the agency had been in the neighborhood for more than thirty years and now had twenty-four staff members, half of whom were nuns and half of whom were laypeople.[17] In addition to the Grandmother program and home nursing, programs included home management assistance, a food bank, a play group, parenting skills classes, counseling for housing and welfare, physical therapy, emergency assistance, a mothers' group, English and high school equivalency classes, arts and crafts groups, prayer meetings, summer programs for children, tutoring, pastoral ministry, a group for middle school girls, and sewing classes.[18] But the fact that the first lay staff were these local abuelas, assets from the neighborhood itself, shows how mutuality informed the agency's earliest decisions of whom to hire and why. LSA insisted that relationships and connection were the first steps to improving the neighborhood's well-being. In this case, both the senior citizens and the isolated mothers forged new connections, and this meant more health and well-being for the whole neighborhood.

To oversee some of these programs, LSA hired the gifted social worker Gail Gordon, the first of several lay social workers, nurses, advocates, community health workers, grant writers, and volunteer coordinators who came into the agency and helped deepen its mission.

Gail Gordon: "There Is a Mutuality Which Takes Place When You Enter Another Person's Home"

Gail Gordon is in her eighties, physically fit, with short gray hair. She retired from LSA in 2007. When you first meet Gail, she comes across as spirited, practical, and smart. Much like the Little Sisters, when she reflected on more than twenty years of working with East Harlem's parents and children, she radiated a tender, profound emotional intelligence.

Gail lives on the West Side of Manhattan, where she raised her family just a few miles from East Harlem. She earned her graduate degree in childhood early intervention, specializing in high-risk families. Gail was initially hired in 1982 as a social worker focused on preventative health, and early on served as the coordinator of the Grandmother program, a role she held until 1997. In her final position at the agency, Gail worked as coordinator of the Early Childhood programs until 2007, overseeing the home-based visiting programs for young parents and their babies. Although technically retired, she still is a beloved figure at LSA, now volunteering on a research project assessing the adult children of parents who received long-term services at the Little Sisters.

Archival video footage of LSA's activities dating back to 1989 shows Gail as a committed young woman riding her bike across East Harlem to families' homes to check on mothers and children.[19] In these old clips we see Gail in the apartments of Black and Puerto Rican mothers in the neighborhood whose children have been identified as being at high risk. She was so gentle with these mothers, coaxing them to feel confident with their babies. But she was highly skilled too, showing the mother how to keep track of the baby's milestones without missing anything: how to assess a baby's grip, their crawling and walking, the signs to look for that indicate that a child might need help. As an intervention specialist, Gail taught mothers to track a child's progress and be confident, active parents.

Gail wrote articles in the social work journal *Early Childhood Development and Care* describing some cases that were so difficult it took years to see changes. It sometimes took more than a year to earn the trust of a mother. Gail and her colleagues often focused on a family for many years, extending even over more than one generation, seeking to connect with the family from many different angles. In difficult cases, they first aimed to connect with the mother, who was sometimes suffering from depression, had few parenting skills, and maybe had been abused or neglected as a child herself.[20] In a 1985 interview, Gail explained, "Over a period of time, the women are able to establish relationships. The first thing is to parent the mothers. Many say 'It's very hard for me to hug my child. I need to be hugged too.'"[21]

In describing her work, Gail said something we heard time and time again: going directly into the homes of families enabled LSA social workers and nurses to see the reality of their lives, the complexity of the challenges, and the assets too. "There is a mutuality which takes place when you enter another person's home," Gail explained in a 1985 article. "You are their guest, rather than they your client. In this way, we accept the families

Figure 15. Sister Marilyn Gremas (*right*) and Gail Gordon (*center*) during a home visit. Marilyn worked as a social worker, while Gail did child development assessments. (Photo courtesy of Gail Gordon)

where they are, making assessments in their own environment and building our treatment plans from their *strengths* as well as their weaknesses."[22]

Gail instinctively connected with this method. It kept her at the agency for over twenty years, giving her room to be creative as a social worker and go beyond conventional models of service. "I'm not even Catholic," she reflected. "I'm Jewish." But what she described as the "charism of the Little Sisters" drew her in. "It's always the emphasis on going out and meeting people where they're at," she said. "And the fact that we *both* grow through this mutual relationship we develop. It's not just a one-way process. We learn from the family; the family learns from us. That is what attracted me to the Little Sisters."[23]

She added, "They were one of the few agencies I knew who actually does what they say they do. The people who did not buy into the culture, they didn't stay."[24]

Mutuality meant warmth, development of strengths, and a willingness to be transformed. But it also simply aimed to make life better for East Harlem residents in a real, concrete way.

Gail, like the nuns, also had a no-nonsense commitment to results. Gail and Sister Susanne partnered with the research department at Mount Sinai School of Medicine to engage in qualitative and quantitative studies of best practices for the low-income families in East Harlem. The agency tweaked its programming based on findings.

One of the many impactful decisions Gail made was hiring Inginia García in 1999. Inginia was deeply involved in the lives of the women featured in chapters 2 and 3. Born in the Dominican Republic, Inginia had been living in New York City for twenty-two years when she was hired at LSA. As a young mother, she volunteered in her children's preschool, where the director noticed Inginia's leadership skills and encouraged her to go back to school to work professionally with families, as she had been doing as a volunteer. With support and encouragement, Inginia finished her GED and began a college program for which she was placed in an internship at a local hospital, working in early childhood development. There she met someone who urged her to apply for a job at LSA, where her language skills, cultural competency, and commitment to families could be put to use.

Inginia interviewed and got a position with LSA's early childhood program. It was an ideal match. Inginia was bilingual, and she also had an intuitive combination of compassion, down-to-earth commitment to families, and sharp intellect focused on results—all hallmarks of LSA staff.

Before Inginia joined the staff, the family support at LSA had primarily been a mix of English-language programming for Black and Puerto Rican mothers, and Spanish-language groups of newly arrived mothers from Mexico and Puerto Rico. But when Inginia started in 1999, the neighborhood demographics were changing, and the neediest families who came in contact with the agency were largely indigenous Mexican women. The living conditions of these vulnerable women were arguably even more precarious than those of earlier years. Many had experienced domestic abuse, were severed from family support, had young children in crowded, unsafe apartments, and suffered from extreme poverty. Inginia began as a home-based care worker, visiting young mothers and their children. She worked hard to avoid making families feel bad or ashamed about their living conditions or what was happening in their lives. "You know, it's part of life, it's part of life," she would assure the mothers. "It's okay, it's okay."[25] From the get-go, developing trust with families was key before they began making changes together. In our conversation, Inginia talked about her bonds of love with the families she worked with, sometimes the same mothers and children for several years. "It was like a family, I'm telling you."[26]

The home-based program enabled Inginia to know families deeply. She saw what they needed, helped them get out of crisis mode, and began the longer-term work of empowerment, self-development, and building relationships. Through her home visiting work, Inginia referred 370 children for early intervention services. All but two qualified (an astoundingly high number of children to have successfully connected with resources).

By the end of her first year at LSA, Inginia realized she could help more families in groups if they came into the agency. This would also support the mothers who were otherwise isolated. She kept working to earn their trust. Inginia often repeated that the most essential element to her work was respecting the mothers, listening to them, believing in them. "You have to trust them, listen to them about what they need, hear what they think." But even that was a skill the mothers needed support to cultivate within themselves. She told the mothers to "trust yourself, take care of themselves, be good to yourself, love yourself."

To support the work of confidence building, in 2000 Inginia began the Building Bridges of Hope program, which still exists today. In its first year, forty-one mothers enrolled. They met at the agency on Thursday mornings for a four-hour weekly program to engage in parenting classes and workshops about child development. They cooked lunch together and forged connections with one another. Eventually the mothers requested additional programming in wellness and mind-body practices. One nun, Sister Fran, came to practice massage. Inginia was trained in reiki, which she offered to mothers along with healthy cooking classes. In 2015, they did a "Yoga de Risa" (laughing yoga) workshop. The mothers were involved in planning the activities every step of the way. "The group liked the idea of a laughter workshop because they felt it would relieve stress and bring some warmth to the cold winter day," a report explained.[27] Most women stayed in the program for about two years, and then new mothers cycled in.

Inginia won grants for her programs. The Dominican Sisters, another religious congregation, provided $50,000 for programming, which the agency used for seven mothers to enroll in a program to earn associate's degrees in child development. This professional degree to become an assistant teacher dovetailed with many of the parenting skills the mothers were learning at LSA. Some of the mothers went on to college after this

Figure 16. Inginia García at her May 3, 2019, retirement party at LSA, where she was a key leader in the early childhood development programs for over twenty years. (Photo courtesy of Little Sisters of the Assumption Family Health Service)

training. Yolanda from chapter 3 was one of these mothers. She earned her bachelor's degree in early childhood education and now is a teacher in LSA's PCD program.

According to Inginia, the fact that Gail, Sister Judy, Sister Susanne, and Sister Margaret trusted *her* with the families empowered her work even further. She, in turn, loved the families and trusted and empowered *them*. "The goal is to *empower* these women, even empower these kids. Some people say it's about giving things—'Here, let me give you a bag of groceries.' No. It's not about that, not about giving, receiving things. It's about empowering. It's being patient with them, being there with them, building a long relationship." This subtle, inner work of confidence building took years and involved bonds of trust. By rejecting quick fixes, Inginia's creative programming flourished.

Inginia's approach was different from standard social work practices that East Harlem residents had experienced in the preceding decades. Alfredo Lopez's 1973 book, *The Puerto Rican Papers*, provides a scathing indictment of what he calls the "poverty professionals" in Puerto Rican communities of East Harlem and Washington Heights. He writes, "Social workers . . . use their positions of authority to induce shame. . . They impose the most brutally racist and reactionary notions on the people in an attempt to solve problems, which they have not even begun to understand." Social workers "want things better but *they* want to determine what is better. . . . It is so sad it might bring one to tears to see what talent and good will has been wasted."[28]

Staff like Inginia work from a completely different perspective. Rather than shame and blame, they lift up self-care, trust, and empowerment, inviting families to take ownership of programming and decisions.

Norma Benítez Sánchez: "We Found a Home When We Found the Little Sisters"

When Gail and the neighborhood abuelas were hired, some local mothers who had been volunteering came on board as staff, just as Melina would eventually do, as we saw in chapter 2. But the transition from volunteer to staff has not always been seamless.

Norma was born in Veracruz, Mexico, in a small town called Omealca. She comes from a big family that loved baseball and parties. She studied industrial chemistry, but never found work. In search of employment, she and her husband left for the United States in 1990. After a terrifying border crossing, they made it to a hotel room packed with strangers in the same situation.

By the time she and her husband arrived in New York, she was pregnant. She remembers feeling isolated and lonely: "We didn't have a TV, we didn't have a radio, nothing, just looking at the walls. I didn't speak the language, I didn't know the neighborhood."[29] Compared to life in Mexico, her new life was small, silent, lonely—and they had few resources. Her husband worked at a garment factory run by an immigrant family from China, and although Norma worked there for a brief time, the work became harder as her pregnancy progressed.

At one of her prenatal appointments at a health clinic in East Harlem, she heard women in the lobby speaking in Spanish about a mommy and baby class they were going to on East 119th Street with the "Hermanitas" or Little Sisters. Norma, who lived nearby, asked them for details. They told her it was a great program where they met and chatted with other newly arrived moms, got help, and attended workshops. They said she should come. One of the women picked up Norma on her way out and they walked there together. Norma was immediately hooked. She finally found herself embedded in relationships as she had been in Mexico. After so much loneliness, there were people in her life.

"I was so excited," she said. "It was a mothers' group. A mothers' group!

When I got there, and I see all these women, oh, my God, I was so happy. At that time, it was a big group, but it was bilingual."[30]

Leaders of the group helped her with practical things, how to breastfeed, how to parent a baby, and offered tips that were much appreciated since Norma's own mother, grandmother, and aunts were in Mexico. The group gave her a purpose and a community. Members did crafts and cooking. After a couple of years, Norma and her husband moved to Queens, but Norma missed the agency. East Harlem was her home, a place where she had finally built relationships. Every day she took her baby in a stroller and rode the train to East Harlem to attend LSA's workshops. "I was coming every day in the subway with a big stroller with my baby," she said. "It was crazy."

Eventually the family moved back to East Harlem to be closer to LSA. "It was home," Norma said. "I always think of the word home because I think for all the immigrants, we found a home when we found the Little Sisters. I registered in all the classes, nutrition classes, the arts and crafts, everything. I started volunteering. I came with my baby and didn't leave. I met them and I never left."

"It was beautiful," she continued. "The sisters were knowing people,

Figure 17. LSA workshop (likely summer leadership training), 1998. Sister Beatrice Brennan of the Society of the Sacred Heart is on the left. Norma Benítez Sánchez is at far right with her youngest son. (Photo courtesy of the Little Sisters of the Assumption archive)

just to know that somebody is calling you by your name because they knew everybody. 'Oh, you are here and the baby, how is my baby doing?' It was so nice. I got very close with one of the grandmothers. Then she became like my family."[31] The abuelas, in addition to working with families, also often worked at the agency, and cared for babies and toddlers while the mothers did workshops. They were trusted. This was in the mid-1990s, right when Melina started coming to LSA. Norma, Melina told us, taught her everything she knows.[32]

Norma began to take on more significant leadership roles at the agency, By the late 1990s, she co-led the mothers' group with Sister Susanne. She worked closely with another Spanish-speaking woman on staff who lived in the neighborhood, Elsie Sanchez, who ran the agency's thrift shop. According to Norma, the staff pushed her to improve her English, to gain confidence with people. Norma remembers, "One day my friend Amy, who was a social worker, she comes and says, 'Norma, I need to talk to you.' I say, 'Okay. What happened?' She said, 'You know, I notice that everybody on this floor answers the phone. Everybody answers the phone except you. Who are you? Are you the queen?' I said, 'Amy, it's so hard to answer the phone.' 'No, no, no, you are going to answer the phone.' I know she was looking out for me. She wanted me to speak the language. She was pushing me always. I know she loved me. It was like that." Mutuality meant Norma would always be so much more than a "client"; she was a gifted leader with talents and potential that had to be cultivated. The agency eventually hired her in a paid position.

But Norma was still undocumented, and this posed a problem, especially now that the agency was no longer run entirely by nuns and their wealthy patrons who supported them without a lot of red tape. This is how Norma's story diverges from Melina's. Melina had papers. As the agency grew and hired laypeople, it increasingly depended on government funding and foundations to pay staff.

If government agencies found out that LSA employed undocumented people, they could cut off funding. In the 1980s, under the leadership of Sister Judy Garson, a Sacred Heart sister who served as the agency's executive director for twenty-five years, LSA experimented with solutions that could protect all employees, regardless of citizenship status. But eventually, a new executive director felt any lack of clarity around employees' citizenship status was too risky for the agency. In 2012, Norma was honored with an achievement award at LSA's annual gala. In 2013, she was let go, along with all undocumented staff. It was a shock to many, and a dark spot in the

Figure 18. Mothers en route to protest for better schools at City Hall as part of a collaboration with East Harlem Partnership for Change, late 1990s. Norma Benítez Sánchez, smiling, is in second row. (Photo courtesy of the Little Sisters of the Assumption archive)

agency's history. Some moved on, some people eventually found work with the Sisters in other capacities—working not with the health agency but with the order of nuns, their international congregation.

Norma's voice is still shaky when she talks about it. "The nuns can take risks," she said. "The difference, I guess, between nuns and people that are not nuns is that nuns take risks for you, for people, and other people have to follow the rules. I understand the reasons why they let me go. I completely understand, but it hurt so much." Clearly, the transition from Little Sisters to a majority lay staff has had its difficulties.

Part of the explanation for crises like these stems from the fact that during LSA's early years in East Harlem, from 1958 through roughly the 1980s, the Roman Catholic Church enjoyed significant cultural and civic authority in the city. Although the sisters lived and ministered at some remove from the bishops and the archdiocese, their work was aided by the immensely powerful institution of the Archdiocese of New York. Catholics held many of the city's important government posts. The sisters often tapped into this power and channeled it toward the families they served.

One example in the archive is illustrative. In 1974, Sister Ann Hayes, a social worker and Little Sisters staff member, was helping a family living in a public housing unit that had no heat or running water and was infested with rats. The mother had eight children, including a fourteen-year-old who had a month-old baby herself. Sister Ann picked up the phone and called Father James Gilhooley, director of family services at the Archdiocesan Catholic Charities and an expert when it came to tenant problems. He, in turn, contacted City Councilman Carter Burden. By week's end the family had found new housing.[33]

This was not the only model of power the Little Sisters relied on, but it helped. Those days are, for the most part, over. The Roman Catholic Church has been diminished as a site of political and financial power in New York, and LSA's faith foundation is more integrated into the ethos of programming and mission, rather than seen as a power lever to pull. Today the agency moves through other channels of money and power that require compliance with federal regulations. There have been many positives from this transition, but it has also made some of the more creative, long-term problem solving for families and staff—hallmarks of LSA's approach—trickier to maintain. Norma described this tension when she explained, "I feel like when they turned into a formal program, they needed a different way to report. They have the social workers, they have . . . all the people that get involved. You miss something, right? Because that was like home. . . . They didn't have a title so they were like your mom, like your grandmother. It was totally different."[34]

Admittedly, the warmer, personal approach didn't go away, but it became vulnerable in this new funding landscape. There were still (and are still to this day) families of means who trust and support LSA's work, in a personal way, with little red tape for oversight, with parties at home that serve as fundraisers, and much more. The efforts of Dolorita Wallace and her family stand out in their support of the Little Sisters in the 1950s and '60s with fundraisers and dinners sponsored by family and friends. Many donors like this persisted through the years, such as New York City philanthropists and civic leaders George and Christine Stonbely. Christine for many years held lively Kentucky Derby parties at their New York home to raise funds for LSA. Many other generous donors and supporters through the years, like Paula and Thomas McInerney and so many more, have enabled LSA to keep its personal touch and familial atmsophere, and remain somewhat distinct from the larger agencies fully funded by government grants alone. Those sorts of relationships were (and are) critical to keeping the more personal, familial, programs alive.

Martha Andrade and Trish Gough, Early Live-in Volunteers: "I Had a Very Strong Feeling of Belonging."

Despite these changes in staffing and funding, the Little Sisters have always been creative in discerning how to adapt their mission to the changing cultural landscape. Though power brokers and wealthy Catholics no longer bequeath Upper East Side apartments to the LSA, over the years the agency developed other ways to bring people into their alternative project of mutuality.

In the 1990s the Little Sisters developed a live-in volunteer program through which people applied to reside in an apartment near the agency's office, live in community with one another and work as volunteers at the agency. Trish Gough, one of the first live-in volunteers, stumbled across a description of the Little Sisters Volunteer Program in a catalogue when she was thirty. She had moved home to Northern Virginia following a stint in New York City after college, and was wondering what to do with her life.

"I thought, wouldn't that be interesting to go back to New York City, but go as a volunteer and live in a different part of the city and do a service project," she said.[35] She moved to East Harlem in 1995 to the Little Sisters residence on 120th Street. She would walk the block south when the agency was at 119th Street and work as an advocate for the families who came into the agency.

Today, almost three decades after she began as a volunteer, Trish oversees all volunteer programming at LSA. She creates a welcoming presence for what is arguably one of the most diverse groups of volunteers in the city.

Mutuality's emphasis on relationships was central even to this volunteer program. "When I was a volunteer," Trish remembered, "we'd have community nights. There was a prayer, but it could be any prayer. People could bring all these different traditions; there was always a sense of being curious. The sisters were curious, and they really honored where everybody was coming from, even someone who said, 'I don't have a faith.' They honored that. What they cared about was just the sense of, 'We are a community. We are a family. This is a family that we support each other.' They accepted people where they were."

Trish recalled that many of the live-in volunteers bonded with the sisters, with one another, and with the agency. "I'm still in touch with quite a number of them," she said, "because they felt the Little Sisters community was very important to them, the sisters, the other volunteers they got to know. There's one marriage that came out of it. Two full-time volunteers

Figure 19. Trish Gough (*back row, second from right*) at the LSA Volunteer program's spring retreat in 2001. (Photo courtesy of Trish Gough)

who got married, they met in East Harlem, and I'm friends with both of them. They have an eleven-year-old son now."[36]

Even some of LSA's Spanish-speaking staff came into LSA from the live-in volunteer program. Martha Andrade is from Ecuador. She is highly educated and speaks Spanish, English, and French. She had moved to California as a young adult and raised her family there, working as a language teacher. After her children were grown, she was looking for a meaningful volunteer experience. She heard of LSA and visited them in East Harlem in 2004. "I had a very strong feeling of belonging. It was something that happened that I knew this was the place for me. I went home, back to California, sold my house, and I left to come to New York on the 15th of August, 2004. It didn't connect at the time, it was not until later on that [I realized] I had come back to New York on the Feast of Our Lady of the Assumption."[37] Martha dove right in. A year later, LSA hired her to direct the Education and Youth Services program she began as a volunteer. She worked with Trish, Inginia, and Norma to start a middle school mentoring program for Hispanic girls. She also did advocacy for kids in their schools to get them connected to services and became very involved in the lives of many young families who came through the doors of the agency.

The live-in volunteer program was shuttered a few years later when funding sources dried up and fewer volunteers came forward. The program made national headlines in 1993 as an example of a grassroots volunteer program that was vulnerable when the Clinton administration began the (otherwise admirable) National Service Program, which encouraged young people to enroll in Teach for America and AmeriCorps, offering health care, student loan forgiveness, and a $7,500 stipend to volunteers. As a small volunteer program, LSA offered a mere $100 monthly stipend, housing, and no loan forgiveness. National news stories circulated as LSA's live-in volunteer program was among those that would have a tougher time competing with these larger, federally funded programs.[38]

The Mission of Mutuality for a New Era

Given how many different people were coming into the agency for long-term commitments beginning in the 1980s—nuns from other religious orders, social workers, neighborhood mothers, young volunteers—LSA leadership experimented with ways to connect with the new staff around the vision of mutuality. The nuns had devotion, prayer, and reflection built into the structure of each day. But what about these new participants (almost all women): mothers in the neighborhood with families, Jewish social workers, young people just out of college, nuns from different religious orders, nurses of all sorts?

In these years of growth and change, the agency's leadership made a serious effort to explicitly instill the mission into the new staff and families that came in. They recognized that mutuality had to be taught, discussed, and set before people as a topic of reflection. It had to be made real, to be connected to people's lives and experiences, to be internalized. In 1990 the agency's leaders created what they called a Mission Team and Norma and Trish served as two of the leaders.

"When the mission becomes muddied or not really shared directly or intentionally," Trish reflected, "then I think people come in who don't get it. They just go, 'This is a social service agency.' Or, 'I'm here as a nurse,' and no sense of anything more than, 'Oh, it's a nonprofit, it helps the people.' I think people always say LSA is special but why is it special? Because there is a spirit of the people working, they really go beyond. Those are the people who have that connection to the mission, I think."[39]

Sister Judy Garson, for instance, was repeatedly mentioned during conversations as someone whose leadership style communicated the mission.

"She was such a perfect role model," Gail remembered. "She just treated everybody with the utmost respect." Whether it was a man off the street who "rang the doorbell and was inebriated, or the head of the board who was maybe a millionaire," she continued, "there was no contrast in terms of her demeanor and how she approached each person as a human being. Although she wasn't a Little Sister, she embraced the whole philosophy of the agency."

Sister Judy was more than just a good leader. Her moral and spiritual charisma was contagious. It spread from staff to the families they served. Ralph Siciliano, a lawyer who served as the chair of LSA's board for many years, began as a volunteer in 1986. He remembers these early years: "I have to mention Sister Judy Garson, such a driving force. A nun who taught at one of the schools in New Jersey, but then was recruited by Sister Margaret to the agency. I was working with her for many years as chair right up front, so I had the real privilege of understanding her extraordinary leadership and humanity. That was so gratifying. Now, of course, everyone just thought she was so wonderful. It was she who drew many donors. The privilege I had was working so closely with her during the challenges and euphoric times."[40]

"Sister Judy was a model that then got replicated with the people who came to work there, and the way we each worked," Gail explained. "Those of us who had programs really wanted to create that kind of modeling with the staff that then would be modeled when they go out and work with the family. It goes from the top down and from the bottom up. True respect, that we're all in this together." Trish Gough said that Sister Judy "empowers people," adding, "I think that spirit continues here."[41] After all, it was Sister Judy who demonstrated her care for Melina by gifting her a saint's pin, an act of care that Melina was able to carry into her own work at LSA.

Even board members at the time seemed to understand what mutuality was about. Ralph Siciliano describes mutuality as a "concept that I came to appreciate as a board member. I think what it was designed to do is make sure that board members and donors did not have a paternalistic attitude, which I think is a natural approach to charitable giving. 'Somebody is in need, so I give my time and money to help them.' What this concept of mutuality brings to that is, we're working together. Both Margaret and Judy Garson, who had been executive directors of the agency for over twenty years, really tried to instill that concept."[42]

The presence of women of deep faith who modeled mutuality, like Sister Judy, gave the agency a structure in the early days that emphasized nontangible activities: retreats, reflections, introspection, celebration. "There were times, this goes back many, many years," Gail recalled, "when staff were invited to go up to Walden, New York, where Little Sisters had one of their convents for retreats, reflection, and reconnection. There was always food, even at meetings; there was recognition of special days."[43] This approach trickled down into unique programming that made a lasting impact on both the staff and families. Trish also remembers visiting the Little Sisters' retreat house in Walden. "They always had just one of the programs where all these older sisters were there," she said, "and they interacted and the meals with the volunteers. You could see how it just affected the volunteers because they were all so nice. They were just so kind. You just felt this lovely group of nuns who were just so welcoming."[44] This is what the mothers in chapter 3 called *convivencia.*

The goal of one 2010 retreat, for example, was for staff to develop "deeper understanding together of mutuality, as a way to implement our core belief: 'the power of growth is in relationship.'"

At the retreat, participants listened to presentations about mutuality

Figure 20. A PCD program retreat at Little Sisters' retreat house in Walden, New York, late 1990s. Norma Benítez Sánchez is seated in back right, next to her son. (Photo courtesy of the Little Sisters of the Assumption archive)

and reflected on such questions as "How do I express mutuality in my relationship with coworkers and with families? What are some successes I would like to share? What might be some of the barriers to living out mutuality in our relationships?" At other staff retreats, participants explored such questions as "Have you ever felt you are a giver as well as a receiver in your work?" One meeting closed with a ritual naming the "gifts" that each staff member has and the gifts they recognize in families. "How can we have any mutual relationships if we do not name and appreciate gifts?"[45]

In browsing through the LSA archive, we glimpse other rituals and activities that draw from a religious imagination and are steeped in a longer sense of history, a sacred understanding of time. Though they are not explicitly Catholic or Christian, they couldn't be described as exactly secular. They were practices and deliberate experiences to help the staff feel, internalize, and make real the ideals and values they espoused.

For example, at one retreat, staff were invited to take part in an exercise of imagination. One of the (unnamed) staff members said:

> Now look at your hands . . . consider how, through the centuries, the creative and healing power of Mystery has been passed on through the gestures of the human hand and fingers. Give thanks for the many ways you give a hand to co-workers and to the families with whom we have the privilege to share life. Take a moment while you notice your hands to think about your power and gentleness, and of the incredible works you have done. . . . and let us bless these hands.
>
> Blessed are these hands as they use their power to join the struggle of those who are hungry and thirsty for good and jobs and shelter and health care and education and strong families and a safe, vibrant community. Blessed are these hands as they embrace with love, respect, and dignity. Blessed are these hands as they stop violence and seek social change. Blessed are these hands as they nurture mutual relationships. Amen! And so let us begin![46]

Through such exercises, lay staff members were asked to imagine the work they do as something much more than a job. It wasn't the contemplative and devotional structure of the sisters' lives in community. But staff were invited to see their work as connected to centuries of work of healing and social change. Lay nurses, social workers, advocates, and community health workers were asked to see their professions as not just generally sacred or powerful, but as *personally* powerful—look at *your* hands, imagine *your* work, think of all that *you* have done.

Instead of "saving" the "poor," participants see their hands as blessed when they "join the struggle" *with* those who seek better lives, to see their hands as anointed when they "nurture mutual relationships." Mutuality itself becomes a conduit for the power of mystery. The work done by staff is expressed almost as a spiritual experience itself.

LSA's retreats were not exclusively for staff and volunteers, but often included the families engaging in services. Gail remembered an experience from 1992 when she and her colleague, a religious sister on staff, took a group of East Harlem mothers and children in a van from the city to Rhinebeck in upstate New York for a retreat. The retreat house was a convent run by the Ursuline Sisters, and the long, low brick structure is perched atop a bright green hill overlooking the Hudson River and nestled amid rocks, fire pits, and oak, cherry, and maple trees.

At the retreat, Gail remembers doing trust exercises with the families. "We did an activity where people talked about something that they would like to remedy in their life," she said. "Everyone wrote down what they would like to change on a piece of paper and placed it into a fire. Next to the fire, members of the staff had placed flowers, and the mothers each got flowers to hold and take with them."

"Some of those more creative experiences really stuck with me," Gail remembered, "and I think created a bond with a lot of these women with the agency. It wasn't just with me, or with Sister Marilyn, or with Sister Judy, or with Sister Susanne. It really was with the Little Sisters, with the family health service."[47]

Gail's description of these experiences evokes the role of ritual, the lighting of candles, incense, and fires to radiate into people's thoughts and feelings. While not explicitly religious, these actions borrow from religion's emphasis on practices that attend to the inner life. Experiences like these retreats also helped East Harlem mothers reclaim time for reflection when so much else in their lives was stressful. These were central to making mutuality real, to helping processes of healing for each person, to cocreate experiences where the bonds of trust are strengthened.

These more personal experiences impacted families. A mother shown in an archival video from 1989 explained that she had "tried to get on my feet" but found that other programs were "harsh, demanding, with a lot of pressure, and I just couldn't take it."[48]

"But they accepted me the first day I was here," she went on to say. "I was shocked. It was so different, the loving, the caring." And she added, "It's the family, the closeness I've never had. I feel like this is my home, even though I know it isn't. I come here and don't want to leave. They make me feel like I'm more important than anybody else."[49]

Mutuality implies that both parties recognize the gifts and strengths of each other and are open to being transformed, vulnerable. Cultivating the strength of mothers who have experienced profound trauma—poverty, abuse, isolation—can proceed only once trust and connection have been established. Mutuality requires practices that are softer, slower, intangible. It insists that both the staff and the families served will be transformed. By 1985, there was a sign painted on the door of the brownstone on 119th Street that read: "Bringing sunlight and warmth to another's life nurtures growth in both. To this we are pledged."

In the 1980s through the early 2000s, there was a sense among staff that, as Gail put it, "if you had an idea and you wanted to do it, you would try it out." She added: "We weren't so data-driven, and we were not as confined to measuring everything, entering everything on computers. If I wanted, I ran a parent crew. We eventually got the mothers to begin to do the cooking for the parent group, and we got the money. We could give them the money, they could go out and shop, and then we would replicate going out for lunch for these mothers who never got that opportunity to do it. Things like that. There was a lot of opportunity to be as creative as you wanted to be, provided it was within the bounds of the kind of work that you were supposed to be doing."[50] By 2013, as we see with Norma's story, there were more concerns with legality, transparency, and structure.

This atmosphere of creativity and closeness enabled many staff members to go above and beyond for LSA's families, driven by a commitment that exceeded the bounds of standard professional social work. For example, Child Protective Services was threatening to take the children away from one family Gail had gotten to know in the 1980s because the mother wasn't sending them to school. She had a lot of children, suffered from health issues, and couldn't get organized to get everyone out the door in the morning. But after working with the family, Gail assessed this woman as a good, if overwhelmed mother, and knew taking her children away was not the answer. Gail began riding her bike across the city to wake the family up in the morning. The mother would dress a couple of the children, and Gail would help the others and get everyone out the door. "Then, when I felt I was doing that long enough, I gave her an alarm clock," Gail said.[51] The mother eventually got into a routine and the kids resumed schooling.

With Gail, as with Martha, Norma, Trish, Inginia, Melina, and so many others, one senses the same can-do spirit attuned to the potential of families that Sisters Susanne and Margaret demonstrate, combined with a realism that acknowledged the tragic undertow of the lives of so many families. Like Margaret and Susanne, Gail recognized that not all families could end up as models of success. Gail sometimes spoke about things that were startling to hear, challenges that are so profound and intractable they are difficult to process. Gail remembered a mother named Maria, "whose husband had just committed suicide. He had AIDS, and she had just tested positive." Gail was tasked with helping Maria navigate both her own illness and the care of her two children. As Gail explained,

> I grew very, very, very close to her. I did some things that were not really professional. I'm not recommending these as a social worker, but because I was at Little Sisters, my husband and I took her up to our house up in the country with her two kids. She knew she had AIDS and she knew that she was going to probably die. She was trying to decide what should happen with her children. She had a cousin in Massachusetts, we had the cousin come and they talked about the possibility of custody. The cousin eventually changed her mind after she got home, which was unfortunate.
>
> She just taught us a lot. When she would go into distress in the hospital, she would actually be calming everybody else down. She eventually died. A neighbor who she knew eventually took custody of kids. It didn't work out that well in the long run, but she didn't live to see that. She had a terrific impact upon me. She had terrific impact on a couple of the other people who got involved with her. That was just a really profound experience.[52]

One hears similar words often about the families at LSA: even when the women were in the most vulnerable circumstances, agency workers tell us that "*she* taught *us* a lot" and "She had a terrific impact on me." In 1991, the federal agency of Health and Human Services published a report on the Little Sisters and commented on the mother Gail described above. The document describes the two and a half years of services LSA helped Maria and her children with. "When one listens to people describe Maria with words like courageous, incredible, determined, and loving," it read in part, "one senses that not only have they lost a client, but also a friend."[53]

The report continued, "The support given to Maria might sound extraordinary, but at LSA it is the norm. The staff at LSA who became her family are not only special but also hard to find. . . . There is a real sense of community and family among the staff, and the clients acknowledge and appreciate the environment." This report was written when the Office of Inspector General in the U.S. Department of Health and Human Services selected thirteen agencies in the United States that were effective in their work integrating multiple services for families living in poverty. As a way to highlight best practices around the country, the authors described creative and effective organizations from places as distant as San Antonio and Baltimore, Iowa City and East Harlem. They said of LSA:

> Walking down East 119th Street in Spanish Harlem, one has to concentrate to find the Little Sisters of the Assumption Family Health Service. Without noticing the constant flow of neighborhood families in and out of the basement efficiency entrance, one would ignore the common brownstone in the middle of the block. From the outside to the inside, the building is very ordinary and unpretentious. Meeting the staff, one realizes that they are all equally unassuming and down to earth. While the need for more space, computers, and staff are common complaints, talk of "their families" dominates the discussion.[54]

Clearly, by the 1980s and 1990s, the reputation of the Little Sisters had extended well beyond New York City. The report added that success at LSA is "not measured in statistical terms, but from a different perspective."[55]

This different perspective came from the unusual combination of people the agency held together. The skilled neighborhood mothers, nuns, trained staff, and *abuelas* came together to focus on improving the lives of families in *one* neighborhood in an otherwise vast, complex city. The retreats, celebrations, and spiritual charisma of leaders like Sister Judy and the generosity and commitment of staff and young families were the intangibles that held them together.

"I don't know of another place quite like Little Sisters in the sense of the commitment that people have to the work that they do," Gail said. "You really get very close to the people that you're working with."[56]

Although Gail seemed more comfortable than most people talking about the sadder, tougher stories, that was never the last word. Her relationship with the mother who died of HIV was partly what motivated her to coauthor a 1993 article published in the academic journal *Social Work* based on her team's work with parents in East Harlem infected with HIV titled "A Community-Based Approach to HIV Case Management: Systematizing the Unmanageable." Gail also wrote articles describing the needs of grandparents who gained custody of grandchildren when a parent dies of AIDS or struggles with drug addiction, and she began teaching as an adjunct lecturer at Hunter College School of Social Work. Her work represented a combination of tenderness, commitment, realism, and intelligence at the service of vulnerable families. The staff was tender, but they were also researchers. They were committed to making a real difference, to engaging in best practices.

Of course, mutuality included more than these serious, somber encounters. LSA's archive from these years reveals parties and festivities that exuded joy. Elsie Sanchez ran the thrift shop called the Sharing Place and created a party to celebrate its one-year anniversary in 1999. One hundred fifty people from the neighborhood came. A newspaper described the scene:

> Clusters of bright yellow balloons bobbed in the breeze at the shop's entrance. Inside, the neatly arranged shelves and racks displayed gently used clothing, household items, baby clothes and children's books at very low prices. On the sidewalk, tables had been set up for trays of appetizing Mexican taquitos, vegetables, cheeses, wedges of juicy watermelon and cold sodas.
>
> Elsie Sanchez, staff store manager who lives in the neighborhood, conducted a free raffle. Winners received gift certificates to the store, children's books and other items. She read the winning numbers in English and Spanish. "One-eight-one, uno-ocho-uno. . . ."
>
> The culmination was a fashion show, featuring apparel from the Sharing Place modeled by a dozen customers and volunteers. Tots to senior citizens promenaded down the runway, as spectators called "Bravo! Bravo!"
>
> Commentator was Trish Gough, assistant manager. With appropriate flair, she described each outfit and its price. Her spiel for beachwear worn by a male model: "Hat with visor 25 cents, T-shirt 50 cents, shirt $1."
>
> Sister Judy Garson, R.S.C.J., executive director of the Little Sisters of the Assumption Family Health Service on East 119th Street, took a break to walk down to the celebration. She told CNY that besides giving community residents a chance to shop with dignity—and very little money—the Sharing Place serves many other purposes.
>
> "The purpose of the shop isn't to make money," she said. "It needs to cover its expenses, and it's doing that. The idea is to have people meet each other, discover how you get along, understand each other," she said. "It also becomes a place where people can learn by volunteering and develop their job skills and their confidence."[57]

In talking about developing confidence and providing opportunities for people to build relationships in East Harlem, Sister Judy, Elsie Sanchez,

CATHOLIC new york

July 15, 1999 Volume XVIII, No. 42 50 Cents

Good Business

The Little Sisters Sharing Place in Spanish Harlem is in business for a good cause. It offers bargains to people of limited means, but beyond that, the storefront is a gathering place where community is built and it's a place where people get information on the Family Health Service operated by the Little Sisters of the Assumption. The shop's second anniversary was celebrated with taquitos and watermelon, balloons and a fashion show.

—Centerfold

Figure 21. *Catholic New York* cover story of a 1999 neighborhood party celebrating the second anniversary of LSA's Sharing Place thrift shop. (Courtesy of *Catholic New York*)

and Trish Gough knew that even the parties, with their balloons and silliness, were part of the program of mutuality.

As the agency had to rely more heavily on external funders like governmental departments and foundations rather than on individual wealthy Catholics, it was harder to be creative, to commit to open-ended projects that helped residents with the intangibles gained in activities like retreats and reflections, cooking and eating together at the agency. These activities resisted narratives of measurable outcomes.

Many people think that larger social work agencies are more effective at solving problems. And in fact, larger institutions that approach poverty on a broader scale are often more likely to receive funding. But according to Gail, "Larger agencies are not the answer. Small community-based agencies where people really get to know families within a twenty-block area" offer something effective and unique. "The idea of having a neighborhood like East Harlem and having Little Sisters, who have been there for sixty years, and really having been in and out of almost every building in that community, and really knowing the families"—that, she said, is a model to hold up, study, and replicate.[58]

The agency had expanded from its humble origins. But the focus remained on the neighborhood. By May 2004 the organization had raised enough money to build a five-story building on East 115th Street in which they could consolidate their many undertakings. As Sister Judy explained in a 2002 interview about the new building published in *America* magazine, "The goal was not to get bigger, but to have everything functioning more effectively under one roof while staying small enough as an organization to know people—the key to creating supportive relationships."[59] It was a thrilling time for staff, to have raised two million dollars to build a new building right on 115th Street. The goal was a home, a new building with bright colors, outdoor space, windows, natural light, everything under one roof, and that is still the beautiful space that houses LSA today.

Not long after the move, Sister Judy was called to a new ministry, and the agency began hiring secular leadership. In this time of growth and change, it felt more difficult to maintain the connection to the softer intangibles of the mission. In 2008, a team of trusted staff like Inginia, Pura Cruz (a longtime committed staff member originally from New York with Dominican heritage), Melina, Lucia Russert (a wonderful client advocate who had been working at LSA since 1998), and Sister Susanne gathered to brainstorm ways to ensure families are included in decision-making about programming and have a chance to give feedback. Retreats about mutuality had to continue for staff to understand the mission, but it wasn't easy.[60] As one memo stated, "Many of us sensed losing community and losing sight of the mission. All staff need to be in touch with the mission and the reality of life for our families. How do we 'operationalize' the mission?" On June 23, 2010, an all-staff retreat called "Living Mutuality: The Power of Growth Is in Relationship" took place at the Mariandale retreat center in Ossining, New York. Staff such as Norma, Elsie, Lucia, Pura, and Sister

Susanne helped plan it and led the small groups. Sister Margaret came down from Boston to serve as the keynote speaker.

If retreats helped staff members internalize the idea of mutuality and see it as sacred, and if women like Gail, Norma, and Inginia extended the Little Sisters' extraordinary commitment to families, other staff members deepened the activist work the sisters initiated early on. Given mutuality's attention to the personal, relational, and emotional dimensions of the work, an issue becomes: How to move beyond a personal, individual empowerment model? How has the agency maintained a commitment to Sister Margaret's desires to create structural changes in the neighborhood, to cultivate power and change systems? How did staff take up that part of the vision of the organization?

The next section takes us beyond the scope of the parenting groups with which the women featured in chapters 2 and 3 were engaged. The story moves forward in time, and we broaden our lens for a wider view of the practices and impacts of the agency in East Harlem.

Ray López and Environmental Justice

On October 1, 2006, a headline in the *New York Times* read, "Ray Lopez vs. the Critters of the Night," next to a photograph of Ray, then a twenty-six-year-old staff member at LSA. One of the few men who worked at the agency, he wore a protective mask and was standing in an apartment in East Harlem.[61] On the wall behind him hung familiar images of Latin American piety: a poster of the Virgin of Guadalupe, a flier depicting the serene-looking Sacred Heart of Jesus.

Although the photograph of Ray evoked calm, the accompanying article described a devastating scene: Ray was helping East Harlem families who were terrified of a bedbug infestation then plaguing the city. "'It's horror stuff,'" said Ruth Reyes, the forty-five-year-old East Harlem resident who was quoted in the article and who, according to the reporter, "frantically scratched the constellation of red welts the nocturnal parasites had left on her body." "'I can't sleep,'" she continued. "'I dream of bedbugs bothering me all the time. I don't know what to do.'"[62]

"But if bedbugs sometimes seem like tiny bloodthirsty vampires to those cursed with them," the reporter went on to say, "Ray Lopez may be the closest thing East Harlem has to a full-time vampire slayer."

Ray ran LSA's environmental health program, where he first worked on issues like mold and cockroaches. But at the time the article was published, it was all bedbugs all the time. Ray showed East Harlem families how to seal their mattresses, scrub their furniture, trap, kill, and dispose of the bugs, and, most importantly, keep them out in the first place. For Ray, bedbugs were a basic health issue, but as he spoke with families in their apartments, he quickly realized that the bedbug infestation also represented a mental health emergency. One woman had been hospitalized for shingles due to the stress caused by bedbugs.

Although the vampire slayer image was a bit tongue in cheek, the article picked up on two things often said of Ray: he had remarkable success working with families dealing with formidable challenges, and he had an ability to get things done despite his soft-spoken manner. As one woman was quoted as saying, "As far as I'm concerned, he's a savior."[63]

Stories like this about Ray, who has worked at the agency for more than twenty years, abound. But he recoils from so-called savior language and its way of dividing the world into two categories, the ones doing the saving and the ones who need to be saved. The heartbeat of his work has been his deep relationships with East Harlem families, his interest in developing local leadership, and his commitment to addressing the larger, structural problems that lie at the root of the challenges faced by so many of the neighborhood's low-income families. Unsurprisingly, like the families who come to LSA, Ray lives in the neighborhood.

Ray was hired by the agency in 2001, not long after graduating from Amherst College. He wasn't the first lay person to work at the Little Sisters Family Health Service, but he was among a group of people who almost instinctively understood and embodied the mission of the Little Sisters early on and took it in new directions. Today, Ray serves as chief program officer at LSA, and is now one of East Harlem's most widely respected community leaders and neighborhood residents.

Ray was born in the Bronx to a Spanish-speaking family and as a child had been chosen by his elementary school teacher to enroll in a nonprofit program called Prep for Prep that strives to enroll promising students in some of the city's best private schools. Ray was accepted by the prestigious middle school at Dalton, located on the Upper East Side. Inhabiting these two worlds—home in the Bronx and Manhattan schools infused with tremendous wealth—Ray was attuned to issues of inequality early on. He also volunteered in high school, and the simple concept of what he described as "doing something good for someone else" made an impact on him. He was civic minded by the time he left for Amherst College in Massachusetts in 1997, where he majored in economics, focusing on issues of economic inequality in health care and education.

After graduation, a friend of Ray's from Amherst who was a medical student at Mount Sinai had an internship with Sister Susanne in the nursing program and a mother who lived in East Harlem. When the friend learned that LSA was seeking a director for its new asthma prevention program, he said to Ray, "You'd be perfect. You're bilingual. From the city. You had asthma as a child." Ray decided to give it a try and moved to East Harlem, to an apartment not far from the agency.

As with Gail, the home visits made a huge impact on Ray, and shifted his thinking about the families in East Harlem. "Just seeing what people were facing, the complexities of their challenges in their day-to-day lives, was eye opening, but it wasn't only that," he said. "You could also see the strength of these families too, what they were able to accomplish given the incredibly difficult circumstances of their lives."[64]

Ray initially worked on environmental issues in East Harlem's public housing apartments, helping families deal with asthma triggers like mold, cockroaches, and leaks. But seeing family after family struggle with the same issues, he realized that he had to address these issues systemically. "I won't be able to stay doing this kind of work if all I'm doing is helping one family at a time, and ignoring the systematic problems I see," Ray remembers telling his supervisor at LSA. That was over twenty years ago, and the atmosphere was loose, open. "Do as you see fit," Sister Judy told him. "This is *your* project now."[65]

Ray learned that children in East Harlem were almost thirteen times more likely to have an asthma-related emergency room visit compared to children living in the nearby wealthier neighborhood of the Upper East Side.[66] As Ray explains in one published interview, "We have made great strides in improving living conditions for NYCHA [New York City Housing Authority] tenants, but certainly many of these problems arose in the first place due to systemic racism."[67]

Public housing in America was first built in the 1930s to serve a white middle-class population. But by the late 1960s, tenants of color began to outnumber whites, and the buildings started to fall into disrepair as NYCHA suffered financial divestment from all levels of government. Today, NYCHA tenants are predominantly people of color and are at higher risk for health problems such as asthma that are caused by mold and water damage in their apartments. In fact, in recent years the troubles besetting the city's public housing apartments have grown, and the buildings have become increasingly plagued by problems ranging from crime and fire hazards to nonfunctioning elevators and power blackouts.

Sister Susanne had already been working on these issues when Ray came, and Ray took it to another level. One year after Ray began working

Figure 22. Sister Judy Garson and Ray López at Sister Judy's retirement party, August 14, 2017. (Photo courtesy of Little Sisters of the Assumption Family Health Service)

at LSA, in 2002, a national newspaper reported, "In New York City's Spanish Harlem, a group of nuns has taken on the mold fight. The Little Sisters of the Assumption Family Health Service works with landlords—or, if necessary, testifies against them in court—to clean up moldy tenements where asthma rates are double the norm, according to epidemiological reports provided by one of the nuns, Susanne Lachapelle."[68] The agency had some successes with individual landlords, but now the "landlord" was the NYC Housing Authority, which ran some of the largest buildings in East Harlem.

When Ray started trying to address the root problems of families living in hazardous housing conditions, to get city officials to make these buildings as safe as they were when occupied by white tenants, "I couldn't get anyone in power to listen."[69] Ray needed training in political organizing. Some of the Sisters at LSA encouraged Ray to connect with a grassroots citizens organization called Manhattan Together, a coalition of faith-based organizations in the city, and a member organization of the Industrial Areas Foundation (IAF)—the same organization that had trained Sisters Margaret and Susanne years ago with East Harlem Interfaith. Much of IAF's organizing philosophy overlaps with what Margaret has written about mutuality: the importance of developing leadership in the community and the belief that interpersonal relationships are the foundation to building power at the grassroots level.

Ray met Manhattan Together leaders and participated in training sessions. The executive director of the IAF led the trainings for Manhattan Together leaders, including Ray. At the time, IAF was led by a former Catholic priest named Ed Chambers. When Chambers stepped in as the head of the foundation, he put what he called relational meetings ("one-to-ones") at the core of the organization. Chambers offers advice for community organizers in his 2016 book, *The Power of Relational Action*, which he wrote shortly before his death. "If you want one skill," he wrote, "you have to be disciplined to build relationships in public life, to be vulnerable, know what makes you tick, listen to what makes others tick, and there is initially a very low rate of return but you build up trust, connection, community that becomes the foundation of grassroots power."[70] This segues seamlessly into Sister Margaret's description of mutuality.

A campaign to build relationships can transform a neighborhood from isolated, fearful individuals into a community with collective power. When people know and trust each other, they can discover common problems and goals and as a group focus on a concrete goal for their neighborhood to improve lives or change local, state, or even national policies. As a collective, and with training, neighbors can become less afraid to confront people in charge. They can become leaders who wield their leadership and power strategically.

Today, Ray still lives in East Harlem and works at LSA. He is an extraordinary leader in East Harlem and says that the major lesson he learned in Manhattan Together training sessions was "how power works, how to build it, and how to wield it."

"Then the fact that it's a never-ending thing," he added. "It's a process, iterative process that has to be done intentionally. I think that has sustained me. Let's choose an issue that's winnable and let's put some effort towards winning it. It's really all you can do.." Ray has also learned, as he put it, how to "identify and empower community leaders," adding, "I've learned how to advocate with public officials, and bring decision-makers to the table."[71] Relationships, as with everything at LSA, were key. It was only because of LSA's relationship with so many tenants, and their partnerships with other community-based organizations working on tenant issues, that they were able to put incredible pressure on NYCHA, with success.

Under the leadership of Ray, LSA and Manhattan Together's biggest victory was winning a 2013 lawsuit against the New York City Housing Authority. In partnership with the Natural Resources Defense Council and the National Center for Law and Economic Justice, they achieved a landmark federal court settlement with the Housing Authority, *Baez v. NYCHA*. The settlement resulted in policy changes that compelled the city to repair leaks, eliminate mold, and address related issues in public housing buildings, and to prevent them from recurring. This was a huge victory for LSA and East Harlem, received major media coverage, and today is one of the brightest spots in the agency's history.

Victories like these have been crucial to the trust that LSA has earned in the neighborhood. Whether the changes affected individual families or hundreds of people living in public housing, families in East Harlem feel and experience something real from the LSA staff. As one mother said of first getting to know the staff at LSA and enrolling in their programs, "I was naïve . . . I actually didn't want it. I was more like, you know, 'That's a waste of my time, just people in my life.' But I'm glad it happened, you know. I grew up, I realized that this was something that was worth it, and it's such great people to have. It really is. They really work hard, they help you, and they get the job done."[72]

Ray said he has always tried not only to design programs that help individual families but also to take time to "examine the root causes of problems, and put forth some effort to address it." In one of our conversations, Ray also admitted that he was surprised to learn over the years that this is what the early Little Sisters of the Assumption founders also had in mind. When he talked about getting lawyers to come to LSA to listen to the stories of East Harlem residents to make sure their voices were present for the judge, or the fact that LSA volunteers come from all sectors of the city, he said it was "like the bringing of different classes together that the founders had in mind so long ago—a hundred and twenty years ago in Paris. That just made me think like, 'Wow, that's so cutting edge. It was happening so long ago.'"[73]

If the concept of mutuality entered the lexicon because of Sister Margaret, training offered by the Industrial Areas Foundation helped staff see how the concept could be translated into community organizing. "The idea," as Ray has explained, "is to not just deliver a family-level intervention or an individual-level intervention, but to always think about the systemic issues." There are countless examples; the lawsuit against the New York City Housing Authority was just the most famous, but there have been many neighborhood victories.

At LSA, mutuality is central to the more personal work of cultivating connection and confidence of the young mothers in the PCD program *and* is the foundation of the more overtly political work of wielding grassroots power. These are two different, related ways that relationships have led to transformation.

Achievements like the NYCHA settlement have brought the agency attention and publicity. But so many other victories accomplished with families have been smaller, quieter. We might think of a difference it made for every single family Ray helped deal with sleeplessness, stress, and terror of bedbugs, as the neighborhood "vampire slayer" described by the *New York Times*. Once Gail described success as watching a young mother who was formerly detached and overwhelmed loosen up enough to smile at her baby and play peekaboo with him. As Sister Judy wrote in an article in 1995, success also has to be "measured in inches."[74]

Conclusion

Faded photographs from the 1980s tucked away in boxes at the convent on 115th Street show a daisy painted on the façade of the old brownstone on East 119th Street. Today we see lots of daisies on LSA literature because it's their logo. The mission handbook, all public-facing literature, and LSA tote bags all feature the daisy. At the 2010 retreat, the closing ritual involved silently passing around rocks painted with daisies.

Daisies appear simple, sweet, and harmless. But perhaps there is more to it. Flowers have long symbolized life, vitality, and beauty. They indicate that there is something beyond the gritty reality of the day-to-day, beyond trauma, loss, and poverty, even beyond politics. Over the years, thousands and thousands of people have streamed in and out of LSA's building and were greeted by that daisy: mothers with HIV; middle school girls seeking mentoring; families who just crossed the border and are isolated and afraid; parents trying to figure out why their children have respiratory problems, or what a child's diagnosis means; families needing food; indigenous mothers eager to cook with ingredients from home; grandmothers from the neighborhood; nuns; nurses; social workers.

The daisy reminds them all of beauty, joy, and possibility, elements whose value and results are not so easily quantified or measured. The daisy reminds staff that the daily grind—changing bandages, filing reports, reading another grant rejection, helping a mother potty-train her kids, running a neighborhood meeting, making flyers—can be powerful, even sacred.

As Sister Judy and Sister Susanne said in a 1988 letter to supporters and staff, "The challenge is to keep hope alive. Our hope, the community's hope, every family's hope." The hope at LSA, the daisy, is always grounded in reality (the world as it is) while working to imagine better possibilities (the world as it could be).

"There is a clear sense that 'the system,' the way things are connected in our society, is hostile to the interests of the poor," the letter continues.

"But our hope is not without reasons. There is the strong commitment and mutual support that we feel every day, working with our extraordinary staff. There is the strength and determination of parents and grandparents who will not give up, and the promise in their children's eyes. There is the knowledge that we are part of an energetic and city-wide and neighborhood network of coalitions, and institutions, professionals and volunteers, ad-hoc groups and long-standing organizations who are the same dream, and the same struggle."[75]

It has not always been easy to persevere—funding comes and goes; government grants push the agency toward short-term measurable results that steer staff away from the longer-term, softer goals, like leadership development, cooking classes for indigenous families, and retreats. It is more straightforward to secure funding to show clear, quick measurables, like the number of children tutored, the number of families fed at the food bank. LSA does programming like this. But the longer-term projects centered on mutuality that cultivate leadership at the grassroots level and build intangibles like community, confidence, healing—this is what makes up LSA's distinctive spirit.

Today, it can feel as if the "old days" were a time of greater creativity. On some days, stopping into the LSA building, it seems quieter than we might imagine it was in those days of early experimentation. Of course, the poverty and health issues that stem from lack of resources, the racialized systems of inequality that made the work of LSA so needed, persist in East Harlem. In many ways, they seem worse. The wealth gap has skyrocketed in New York City. The rise of xenophobia and anti-immigrant sentiment has made the lives of many East Harlem residents more precarious than ever. On Christmas Day 2020 during COVID, one staff member's husband was picked up by ICE and detained. The systems that support migrants are at the breaking point, with asylum seekers bussed into the city, sometimes right to LSA where staff, under-resourced and overworked, scramble to help them.

But the spirit of that mission of mutuality is still present at LSA, flowing first in its earliest form with a group of nuns coming from Paris in 1896, and up to East Harlem in 1958. Mutuality was made more real when families in East Harlem came on board as leaders and staff, the early abuelas, the mothers from the neighborhood like Melina, Inginia, Norma, along with people like Gail, Ray, Trish, Sister Susanne, Mónica, and so many more. These staff and community leaders put structures of mutuality in place that pulled mothers like those featured in chapters 2 and 3 out of isolation and into community to make their lives better. The stories of these women are not individual achievements but depend on relationships and connections that were intentionally cultivated with purposeful programming and structure. The programs for collaboration between staff and mothers were central, but so were the larger, institutional collaborations that connected families to resources beyond the capacity of LSA. This includes LSA's relationships with Mount Sinai Hospital, Manhattan Together, or the National Center for Law and Economic Justice that led to the landmark legal victory against NYCHA. Relationships, partnership, and mutuality were key at every turn.

Mutuality points to a core set of values and ideals that, because they are often intangible, are more fragile in our contemporary funding landscape. But mutuality is still very much alive.

If one were to come into the building of LSA today, for instance, one would likely see Mónica Sánchez, who currently directs the agency's mental health services, running up and down the stairs at the agency. She heads the Building Bridges program, which Inginia García started in 2000. Mónica is a dedicated art therapist who works with children and parents who experience profound traumas while crossing the border. Her programs focus on using the power of the arts to heal from and process these traumas. On display at LSA one sees beautiful things Mónica has made with the women and teens in her programs over the years: black-and-white self-portrait photography, weavings, dolls, miniature boxes, all connected to some aspect of healing. This artistic work recalls elements from "the old days" at LSA: the rocks painted with daisies passed around silently at a 2011 retreat, a colorful banner sewn by neighborhood mothers that Lucia Russett organized for the 2011 *Juntos Mejoramos el Barrio* protest, countless cakes and raffles and garden parties. These creative elements instill a certain sensibility at LSA that is key to the uniqueness so many families describe. LSA is a special home where you can be *en familia*.

Mónica knows the serious work of healing that creativity provides. In a coauthored book chapter recently published, she explains, "The immigrant community of East Harlem, New York, is filled with survivors of extreme trauma who have braved inhumane atrocities to bring themselves and their families to safety in the United States. They are strong, proud, and in need of services to help facilitate the processing of trauma and the assimilation that will assist them in living in this culture. Art therapy is a way of providing access to therapy that transcends language barriers, cultural differences, and trauma symptoms."[76] In 2022, Mónica's Building Bridges arts-based program was awarded a grant from the New York Academy of Medicine for the best community organizations working for the youth of

Figure 23. Mónica Sánchez's art therapy program in 2019. Mónica is at the end of the table, surrounded by participants and art therapy interns. (Photo courtesy of Little Sisters of the Assumption Family Health Service)

East Harlem. The Museum of the City of New York recently displayed Mónica's "Spirit Traveler" exhibition, featuring the art and writing of participants in her art therapy program. On a rainy Saturday in April 2023, the museum was packed with people celebrating and honoring Mónica's work with East Harlem residents.

Staff like Mónica insist that beauty and creativity—those dimensions of human experience that are not easily quantified—belong in East Harlem too, and they are necessary to process traumas. They are just as important as the concrete political work of poverty alleviation, asthma remediation, better schools, safer buildings. A quote written on an old retreat planning page in LSA's archive says "Food is not enough. There must be soul food." This coming together—*convivencia*—is the soul food that LSA brings to its community in East Harlem.

Other aspects of LSA's spirit of mutuality are also alive and well. There are community health workers at the agency currently involved in an organizing campaign to help a group of undocumented neighborhood residents who were hospitalized from carbon monoxide poisoning in 2022. The landlord had not bothered to make the building safer. LSA staff, under Ray's leadership, is helping the neighbors join with residents of the landlord's other buildings to amass more power in numbers. LSA partnered with a legal team to learn about their rights as tenants, and they are preparing to launch a lawsuit against the landlord.

This work is reminiscent of East Harlem Interfaith in the 1970s and '80s, even though many of those original leaders are no longer in East Harlem. Sister Margaret lives in Boston. Peg and Norm Eddy died. But the spirit of organizing residents to reclaim their collective power is alive. There is a direct link from projects like the 100 Worst Buildings in the 1960s, to the Adopt a Building initiatives in the 1970s, to Ray's successful lawsuit with Manhattan Interfaith against New York City Housing Authority in 2015, to the work with East Harlem tenants living in unsafe housing today.

That these larger partnerships take place alongside a commitment to mutuality in a more personal sense—one focused on growth in the lives of vulnerable neighborhood families at every level—is what keeps the agency connected to the vision of the founders. As Trish once said, LSA "has a certain orientation because of its founding, and a spirit. And that really motivates the work. It's true."[77]

Much has been written on New York City's elite power brokers who have shaped the hierarchical structures of the city—people like Robert Moses, the Vanderbilts, and the archbishops. Our book shows how the little people, the Little Sisters, the young mothers of East Harlem, the immigrants and neighborhood leaders and staff have come together to summon alternative networks of empowerment and care. There have been losses, sicknesses, death, sorrow, but there have been considerable victories too.

The writer Krista Tippett says that humans have a bias to be more interested in what "is dysfunctional and catastrophic and frightening and failing more seriously than what works well and what is quietly flourishing."[78] Our brains are mobilized by threat or fear. We are less likely to ask questions about what is generative in our society, what is quietly flourishing. In the preceding chapters, we asked questions about flourishing, care, and solidarity. The answers to those questions turned us to the ongoing experiments that have been quietly taking place in East Harlem for over sixty-five years.

EPILOGUE

On Sister Susanne's Passing and the Shadow Side

IN A 2022 INTERVIEW, Ocean Vuong, the Vietnamese American writer, describes the refugee experience, the trauma of exile, and the human capacity for storytelling: "When we think of the refugee, we often think of a passive, needful, and pandering subject. There's this perennial victimhood that is reductive to the identity of people who are very complex." Instead, he prefers "to reorient how we see refugees as people who are incredibly creative and innovative and have to make life-saving decisions not only for themselves but for the people they love. I saw that right away with the women in my family in the stories they decided to tell."[1] Vuong and his family came to the United States from Vietnam in 1990 when he was two years old, and the women raised him on countless narratives of home. Their storytelling, according to Vuong, was inventive, decisive work: "The mind can only hold so much, so what do you remember? What do you leave behind?" Vuong ranks the innovative women storytellers of his family among his literary influences along with James Baldwin and Toni Morrison.[2]

For Vuong, stories provide a powerful way to keep the memory of the storyteller alive. "The root of the word 'narrative,'" he writes, "is 'gnarus,' Latin for knowledge. As such, all stories are first and foremost the translation of knowledge. But not only that, they are the transmission of energy." Vuong adds, "and . . . energy cannot die. . . . To read a few lines of *Gilgamesh* or *The Iliad* or the *Tale of Kiều*, is to receive the linguistic energy of a mind working up to over four thousand years ago. . . . I do believe that language, despite major developments in medicine and science, is still our most advanced technology."[3] Writing on the occasion of the death of a spiritual teacher, Vuong describes how the circulation of narratives about his life and teachings reminds us that "Yes, energy, and even people, do not truly die."[4]

In writing this book, initially we saw our focus on storytelling in the first way Vuong describes. The stories we heard from migrant mothers, from women like Melina, from nuns and staff at LSA revealed complexities all too often flattened by soundbites and stereotypes. By focusing on the stories that have flowed through the webs of relationships in East Harlem, we see strength, resistance, humor, creativity, and—most urgently—humanity.

Eventually, we came to see the stories we tell here in this second way Vuong describes as well: commemorating the energy and spirit of storytellers who have passed. On Christmas Day, 2022, we learned that Sister Susanne Lachapelle had died. Her rapid decline shocked us all. To share Susanne's story—that of her life and the stories she shared of the families she loved—is to invite readers to connect with her energy, so that her own sense of care, attention, tenderness, and mutuality remains. The spirit of mutuality surrounded Sister Susanne in her passing and as the community grieved her loss. It is a privilege to share this final story.

Despite her eighty-four years, Sister Susanne was vibrant, active, and sharp. In early November, less than two months before her death, Carey met Sister Susanne at LSA's offices to go over archival documents. That afternoon, she was to see a doctor about a fall that she had recently suffered on the one-block walk from her convent on 115th Street to the agency. In our meeting, she barely mentioned her discomfort. She happily chatted and worked, occasionally rearranging the pillow in her small office chair. That morning, she'd walked the block from the convent to the agency as she'd done for years. As Carey went through archival material, Susanne recounted a story about a homeless man whom she'd helped many years before. He'd shown up at the agency with a wound on his leg that she treated and dressed. He did not want her to call the hospital. He was worried about law enforcement. But she helped. And off he went. She told stories like this as if they were unremarkable. In her retelling, Susanne didn't question the man's integrity, or wonder aloud about what might have prevented him from seeking help. Beneath the story was a sense that whatever kept this man from getting the medical attention he needed was valid and likely pointed to larger structural issues. Her persistence and drive to enact justice together with the families in the neighborhood were, to her, unexceptional.

Figure 24. Sister Susanne Lachapelle, Melina Gonzalez, and Sister Annette Allain at a November 19, 2021, celebration in memory of Dolorita Wallace, a longtime supporter and volunteer at LSA. (Photo by Brenna Moore)

Figure 25. Sister Margaret Leonard, April 8, 2014. (Photo courtesy of Sister Annette Allain)

Less than a month later, we met Sister Margaret at the convent to get some feedback on earlier drafts of this book. Susanne was in the hospital by then and Margaret, who now lives in Boston, had come to New York to be with her. We talked about recipes for soups that Susanne might enjoy. There was optimism in the air, a sense that Susanne was going to get better. She just needed to rest.

But her fall had triggered a domino effect on her health, and as new complications arose in the hospital, Susanne started eating less and less. She wasn't improving. Sister Annette Allain oversaw her care. Annette is a remarkable religious sister and on the leadership team of LSA, coordinating the Unites States territory. She lives with Sister Margaret in Boston. In the hospital bed, Susanne was frail and soft-spoken. But on one of Brenna's last visits, she was surprised that Susanne, weighing ninety pounds and often asleep, could still joke around when she was alert. One afternoon, a priest came to administer communion to Sister Susanne in her hospital bed. We all made eyes as he talked nonstop over her and explained things we already knew. When he left, Brenna laughed and asked Susanne what she does when people like that come in. Sister Susanne said she was good at pretending to fall asleep mid-conversation, and showed Brenna: chin down, head sideways, softly snoring. We all laughed. Brenna remembered how Susanne had once said that she doesn't want to emphasize the "sad stuff" in East Harlem, because there's a "lot of funny stuff" too: cute stories about kids, families she grew close with who made her laugh. The laughter reminded Brenna of Susanne's own humanity, even at the hospital, and of the humanity she always emphasized in her work with East Harlem families.

In the hospital, over the early weeks of December, Sister Susanne's heath declined quickly and she stopped eating altogether. As Christmas approached, Sisters Annette and Margaret moved her to hospice care. On December 23, the new CEO of LSA, Jonah Gensler, visited, joining Gail Gordon and other dear friends of Susanne. A Jesuit priest and close friend came to anoint Susanne. When Jonah told the priest he was Jewish, the priest replied, "That's ok, Jesus was a Jew!" Later, the Little Sisters of the Assumption community shared this story with joy and gratitude, that two Jewish people, Jonah and Gail, along with Catholic friends, helped anoint Susanne in her last days.

On Christmas Eve, Sisters Margaret, Annette, and Deysi Martínez, an LSA sister who works at the agency, gathered around Susanne and renewed their vows in the hospice room. On Christmas morning, Sister Susanne Lachapelle died.

Right away, women whose lives Susanne had touched began the work of mourning. Rosario Jimenez and Norma, both of whom have been employed by LSA in different capacities, helped lead a three-day rosary, gathering nightly at 7 p.m., a grieving practice common in the Spanish-speaking community of East Harlem. Trish hung flyers in the neighborhood inviting residents to join in the mourning and celebration of a neighborhood icon. Sisters Annette and Margaret worked with Susanne's family and friends on the funeral, sharing photos and countless stories that we were eager to circulate as we grieved her sudden passing.

Impasse and the Shadow Side

Sister Susanne's funeral was celebrated on the Upper East Side at the majestic Church of St. Monica. The bilingual service included prayers to end injustices around the world, especially the plight of refugees, and the war in Ukraine. The church was packed with Susanne's family and friends, neighborhood families, and LSA staff and families. It was both a celebration of her outstanding accomplishments and an acknowledgement of a great loss for the LSA community. In that way, it mirrored the work of the Little Sisters, which, despite the focus on bettering conditions through growth and structural change, never ignores the inevitability of misfortune present in their work. We glimpsed this when Lucia Russett, a former LSA staff person who worked with Susanne for twenty years, read a passage from the Prophet Isaiah at the funeral. Isaiah speaks of the light given to those who suffer, those "those who live in darkness," who "walk in darkness" and "live in a land of great shadow."[5]

These words echo a persistent theme we recognized in the work of the Little Sisters. They have never been afraid to linger over and be present for parts of life in East Harlem that are more resistant to programs and plans. Their work, which often inspires changes large and small, also acknowledges that hoped-for progress does not always occur. People get sick and die. Children get sent to foster care. We tend to keep death, poverty, sickness, and abuse at bay. But the Little Sisters and the staff at the agency, when they enter the lives and homes of those on the margins, live close to these somber, immutable sides of life. They hold this acceptance of the melancholic alongside their extraordinary efforts at change and empowerment. We have celebrated the extraordinary transformation of so many of the women described throughout the book. But not all families have experienced such transformation. There have been many traumas.

Acknowledging this, being present for this, is also part of mutuality. Presence even in the times of darkness and pain with no promise of victory is central to mutuality, central to *convivencia*.

The theologian Constance FitzGerald, whom Sister Margaret once recommended to Brenna, writes in her essay "Impasse and Dark Night": "As Americans we are not educated for impasse, for the experience of human limitation and darkness that will not yield to hard work, studies, statistics, rational analysis, and well-planned programs. We stand helpless, confused, and guilty before the insurmountable problems of our world. We dare not let the full import of the impasse even come to complete consciousness. It is just too painful."[6]

Even as our American optimism and can-do spirit are inclined to lift up the agency's stories of empowerment and change, impasse is present in so much of LSA's work. Staff do not obscure these stories of death and pain in East Harlem. In the early 1970s Sister Margaret gave a talk titled "Disciples in the Shadow Side of God." "We need to discover the shadow side of humanity, those qualities and capacities of the human that have been repressed in our unconscious and unclaimed depths or relegated to the private space of our world," she says. Referring to the thirty-three million people living below the poverty line at the time (now the number is closer to forty-four million), Sister Margaret asserts that "statistics mask their humanity and fail to break their silence."[7]

Many of the stories we heard point to these moments of impasse. Once in conversation with Brenna, Sister Susanne recalled a story so disturbing, Brenna was certain she had misheard. But in researching it later, Brenna learned that Susanne was right in every detail. On the afternoon of October 10, 1981, a nun from another religious order who worked part-time as an administrator at LSA's office was alone in the convent when two young men climbed in through an open window. She handed over the money they came looking for. They proceeded to assault and rape her. The assailants carved twenty-seven crosses into her skin and then fled. The sister managed to get to a phone and call Sister Susanne, who came with another member of her congregation to help. When the ambulance arrived, they rode with her to the hospital and somehow, she lived. She left the religious order.

The story was on the news; television cameras were outside the convent all the time, especially during the grand jury proceedings. Susanne spoke only quietly and briefly about the event. But she recalled that there had been rumors that the neighborhood mafia would find the assailants and kill them.

The men were found in Chicago and eventually turned themselves in. A group of self-styled Guardian Angels, local neighborhood protectors who looked out for people in the most dangerous parts of the city, areas the police had abandoned, kept watch over the convent. Eventually, the sisters had to visit churches throughout East Harlem and urge nonviolence, imploring neighbors not to respond to violence with more violence. In the face of senseless violence, the sisters summoned patience, forgiveness, and peace.

Indeed, through their work in East Harlem, the Little Sisters nuns, lay staff, and volunteers have encountered the full spectrum of human experience. Unbelievable trauma and irreparable loss came along with the gifts of being a part of countless families' healing and development. The staff loved seeing children grow up, living life with their neighbors, and being a part of neighborhood transformation. Sometimes the sorrow and the joy were hard to separate. Sister Judy Garson, who served as executive director of LSA for twenty-five years, described a story in an unpublished essay she wrote on January 14, 1994, about a young girl and Sister Susanne:

> Natalie died on Christmas day. She was six years old. She wasn't expected to reach her first birthday, or her second; after that the doctors stopped making predictions, because she was a child who loved life and who wasn't going to give up easily!
>
> Her last outing was on December 9th, when her family brought her to the LSA holiday party. If people there noticed the tiny child with enormous eyes, with the portable oxygen tank hooked up, the child who looked as though she were three years old, not six, the only sign of special attention was that more people came to help, to bring food to their table, to make sure that "Barney" came over for a picture-taking session. Natalie smiled and laughed; she loved a party.
>
> Natalie died at home, in her grandmother's big bed that had been her bed, too, her whole life. She had been so sick during her last hospitalization that she might easily have stayed in the hospital, but her grandmother was adamant that she wanted her at home, and that nothing extraordinary was done to keep her alive when the end came. So Natalie was allowed to come home, with her oxygen and her IVs and her multiple medical problems, because LSA nurses would come daily to check on her, and were also ready to stay as long as necessary if (when) there was a crisis. Her older brothers (both healthy) also wanted her home.
>
> When Sr. Eve, Natalie's primary nurse, stopped by on Christmas Eve, Natalie was excited about the presents under the tree, hoping there was a "Barney" among them. She had a bad night and her

> grandmother saw a change, but at 6:30 Christmas morning she told her brothers to bring her presents into her bed so that she could open them. (Barney was there, of course: she held him as long as she could, and he was buried with her.) While they were doing this, she lost the power to speak or move.
>
> Then came the panic-stricken call to Sr. Susanne, the LSA nurse who lives nearby, who knew she would be home on Christmas, and who had given the family her home number for emergencies. In fact, every nurse on the LSA staff had had a turn in caring for Natalie over the years, since she had been our patient from infancy, when HIV infection was diagnosed.
>
> For five hours, Susanne stayed at Natalie's side as life slipped away, making her as comfortable as she could be, reassuring the other children that it wasn't their fault that Natalie was dying, calming the adult relatives who had lived their lives around this child for so long, staying in touch by phone with Natalie's doctor. About 2pm, the end came. Late that afternoon, Eve joined Susanne. She knew that she would have a very special role with Natalie's grandmother in the coming months, to help her begin to address her own health needs—long neglected while all her attention went to the sick child—and to hear the other children's fears and worries. "Am I in a family where everyone dies?" This from a 14 year old cousin who had been very close to Natalie's mother who died three years ago. "Was it my fault, because I didn't always get things fast enough for her, because I used to get mad at her?" "Am I going to get sick?" . . .
>
> Like everybody else who works in health care, LSA staff have to deal with very complicated bureaucracies; we spend too much time filling out forms and moving paper around. But that is all worthwhile when it enables us to be where we are supposed to be, with the Natalies of East Harlem and their families.[8]

Sister Judy's reflections about Natalie and Susanne recall the shadow side or impasse that Sister Margaret describes. The theology of accompaniment ("We grieved with them, we wept with them") holds fast to an idea that simple presence is just as important as the impressive results that leadership development, political advocacy, empowerment, and community health programs might yield.

We see this with Mónica's art therapy class, where women process the traumas of crossing the border. We see this in the Zoom ceremony Lucia, Susanne, Rosario, and others held during COVID, where people in the neighborhood shared photos of loved ones they had lost to the pandemic. Families took turns sharing the names of those who had died and of those for whose recovery they were praying. Susanne recalled, "Some families had lost five people. I mean, it was unbelievable, the sorrow that these people were carrying with them."

Sister Susanne's passing came at a time when LSA was emerging from its own institutional impasse. Over the course of the interviews we conducted, in addition to learning about the remarkable work LSA has done with families in East Harlem, we also sensed that in recent years the agency has sometimes struggled to foreground its efforts in practices of mutuality. A member of our research team, Carlos Rojas, a graduate student at Fordham's School of Social Work, picked up on it when he said in his final research presentation, "There is a nostalgia with the people I spoke with, a longing for the old days." The other students nodded. Some staff were there to hear the presentations, and some of them nodded too. We heard bits here and there from people who sensed, with some regret, that the agency had strayed from its mission.

Cecilia, one of the mothers we interviewed, shared her perspective: "Before it was different than now at Little Sisters. Before, I don't know, Little Sisters gave everything to families. Now, I don't know if there aren't as many programs, or as much funding. I really don't know, but before families were the priority." For Cecilia, the agency's hands-on engagement was directly connected to the presence of nuns: "Before there were more nuns working in every department. Now, nuns, there are hardly any."

Fewer nuns, according to Ray, also meant a change in fundraising at the agency. "The nuns used to just bring their stories, and be themselves, and funding would come in," Ray explained. As the presence of nuns decreased, the agency's pocketbook suffered. Its identity changed. Norma's comment that "the nuns take risks" echoes Cecilia's feelings of loss and nostalgia for a time when families' needs were more centered.

As Lina, the mother of four whose granddaughter recently started participating in programming at LSA, noted, "What I regret the most is how much they've changed, because I know they've changed their system. What they had before helped me . . . for example, before there were opportunities for people without documents. You could go work there, or at least help out. And now you can't. I guess you have to be legal in order to be there. And that's a shame, because you learn to grow a lot there."

This sense of longing for a lost community coincided, for Melina, with her transfer to LSA's advocacy department. She described feeling unsettled at the time, not just because of her own personal circumstance, but due to larger shifts at the agency. "I didn't want to participate in staff meetings and lots of things because I saw all the changes that were happening," Melina explained of that period in LSA's history. "It wasn't a lot of the mission that we wanted to be part of. We were preaching outside, but inside we were falling apart."

Many of the staff we interviewed described the agency in the 2010s as increasingly acquiescing to corporate models of nonprofit management where the nuanced, individualized attention families received sometimes got lost.

LSA's trajectory here tracks with larger trends in the nonprofit sector, where scholars in institutional theory have defined a move toward "coercive isomorphism," a process by which organizations become increasingly homogeneous without necessarily improving their effectiveness.[9] This increased uniformity is a response to external pressures, such as government regulations or a competitive market for resources like grants.[10] Scholars warn that such changes can have negative effects on organizations, which find it more and more challenging to center their mission or attend to local circumstances. Political scientists Bryan Evans, Ted Richmond, and John Shields underscore the grave effects of neoliberal economic models on the nonprofit sector. They explain, "The imposition of neoliberal governance structures on nonprofit service providers has served to compromise their autonomy and advocacy function, while commercialising nonprofit operations and imposing burdens that have strained organisational capacity. Market-based regulation has moved many nonprofit service organisations away from their community oriented focus and towards a 'business model.'"[11]

Clearly, a corporate model that demanded measurables and demonstrated its intolerance of impasse clashed with LSA's philosophy and its roots in mutuality. Older staff members, families, and volunteers alike remembered when the spirit of the agency was more open-ended, when many of the successes could not be easily quantified. Sister Margaret's prescient comment that "statistics mask humanity" underscores a looser spirit of creativity and less pressure to attend to short-term goals. Melina echoed this idea when she said, "I think the mission is that people are not numbers. You cannot measure the growth of a family or a child with numbers."

The incompatibility between LSA's local, small-scale mission, driven by relational mutuality, and the numbers-bound ways of organizing that had begun to take over came to a head around the same time we were doing our research. Some of this was due to the traumatic changes wrought by the COVID-19 pandemic. Right away, in the spring of 2020, the agency did a remarkable job: scrambling to get cash assistance for the most vulnerable families in the neighborhood during lockdown; turning what had been a little food bank into a massive source of essential groceries for neighborhood residents who were sick or out of work; moving parenting classes online; and continuing home nursing in the midst of even the scariest days of the pandemic, through each variant of the virus, before the vaccines.[12] But the staff was burned out. Most were living in, and all were working in one of the neighborhoods in New York City that was hardest hit by COVID. The morgue on 116th Street, just a block from the agency, was so full that in April 2020 it had to rent U-haul, Ryder, and Penske trucks, and refrigeration trucks, to store and transport bodies. These trucks were double-parked in front of the funeral home. Everyone knew what they were for.[13] Within this context, in 2021, the board and the executive director went their separate ways.

Indeed, many LSA staff and families we spoke with over the course of the two years we researched this book longed for the past. They felt exhausted and traumatized in the present, and deeply uncertain about the future. While the agency needed to do something to emerge from its institutional impasse, everyone was nervous and cautious about new leadership.

In September 2022, Jonah Gensler began his tenure as LSA's chief executive officer. He brings to the job direct experience as a bilingual nonprofit leader and strategic thinker. But crucially, he also recognizes the value of local, personalized, community-based work. On September 6, 2022, one week before assuming his new post, Jonah shared a video via email introducing himself to the LSA community. In it, he appears on camera with his family. His wife and three children speak of the importance of language and culture to their family. In fact, the video was sent in English and Spanish, a demonstration of his family's lived commitment to values shared with the LSA community. Jonah talked about his previous experience and his excitement to join the LSA family. "This is not about me, it's about we," he said, underscoring the importance of listening and learning from staff who have been doing decades of good work at LSA.

Jonah's hands-on, nonhierarchical approach came through when he mentioned his desire to get to know staff by joining them in their work—going on a home nursing visit or helping bring boxes into the building for the food pantry. He also emphasized the importance of family, saying that if colleagues find him late in the office too frequently, they should send him home to his wife and kids. This emphasis on family life is reminiscent of the visit Sister Judy Garson paid to Melina to give her a saint's pin after she had been told her pregnancy was high risk. For Melina, one of the things that has been missing in recent years is the space for people to appreciate flourishing, healthy family lives. "I think it's not the same thing to work with religious people who believe that family is a priority, and even your own family is a priority, [as] working with what I would consider regular people who need numbers, who need a statistic, who want to have change but also have deadlines," Melina explained. "Sometimes, they don't have the same concept of what a worker needs. One of the things that actually impacted me at the beginning when I started work with Little Sisters was the commitment of our executive director, who was a religious person, to the worker."

By centering family and personal relationships, Jonah signaled that perhaps he could help revitalize the essential personal, relational aspects that define LSA. In early September, Sister Susanne shared Jonah's video with Carey, beaming as we watched together, exhibiting renewed hope for a future that focuses the agency's core values of relationships and mutuality.

It is this dual emphasis on personal relationships *and* structural change that is LSA's center of gravity. LSA has always used the term "family" to signal its relational emphasis. This means seeing neighbors in the context of their own families, but also in the sense of chosen family, created family, especially for those in East Harlem uprooted from traditional family structures. Examples abound: the *abuelas* hired to mimic extended family systems of support in the neighborhood; Norma moving back to East Harlem to be close to the agency who were like family; or longtime board member Ralph Siciliano bringing his elderly mother to LSA's fundraiser gala, where she was welcomed as family. Jonah promoted Melina to a new role as community and individual engagement manager, where she is thriving as a leader today.

The founding spirituality of the Little Sisters congregation, the agency's foundation, animates the agency's ongoing emphasis on relationships. Its recent General Chapter explained, "This universe that God dreams of is an incredible web of relationships because the Creator is a web of loving relationships. Together we have the responsibility to weave this communion between us and the whole of humanity."[14] In recognizing the relationships that structure each of our lives, we commit to creating new modes of relationality, sociality, and care. As Sister Susanne once said, "The suffering and challenges of God's poor people, are a channel of life in me. We are together as we reshape the world so everyone has a place to call home."[15] Reconstituting the world through new relationships is what is taking place in East Harlem: between religious sisters and laypeople, mothers and children, senior citizens and young mothers, English speakers and Spanish speakers, tenants, neighbors. Within this concentration of relational power, stories circulate communally. The stories we have told in *Mutuality in El Barrio* do not illustrate the individual achievements of the self-reliant individual. They highlight how mutual connection can be the starting point for the transformation of entire communities.

In the summer of 2022, several weeks before Jonah took up his new post, Brenna spent several weeks working at LSA's offices. One day, she parked her car a couple of blocks up from the agency near the Little Sisters convent, a little brownstone building next to Our Lady of Mount Carmel Church. Brenna called Sister Susanne so they could walk to the agency together. Susanne steadied herself while pushing a roller cart that held her tote bag and assorted work items. Susanne knew she was too frail for home visits. "I wish I could," she said, but the walk-up apartments were too hard for her. At the time, Susanne was working in the office, helping with the nursing program. Brenna recalls a sweltering heat—when it's hot in New York City, it feels hotter in East Harlem, where trees and shade are scarce. But walking down the block that morning with Sister Susanne, Brenna got to see the neighborhood from her perspective. Everyone said hello to Sister Susanne, she had lived and worked there for so long. A young couple was walking with their young boy pushing a scooter, with his Minecraft backpack and water bottle, probably on their way to a summer program in the neighborhood. When they passed, Susanne whispered to Brenna, "What a cute, sweet, good family." She had seen the little boy grow up since he was a baby. "Just don't ask me what his name is. I've gotten so bad with names," she laughed. It was clear she did not see a mass of "the poor" in East Harlem in need of salvation, but families, friends, people with assets and strengths. She loved telling stories about all of them. Susanne witnessed a lot of tough things, but she always said she considered herself fortunate to live there. It's clear how differently Sister Susanne saw the neighborhood, how differently we could all see it because of people like her. Until the very end, she continued teaching us how to see, too.

ACKNOWLEDGMENTS

THIS BOOK IS the result of deep, sustained collaborations. From its inception as a small research project to its fruition as a book, our work has relied on the generosity and knowledge of capable, insightful and hard-working partners at Fordham University and within the LSA community. First and foremost, nothing we said here would have been possible without the honesty, commitment, and trust of the eighteen mothers we interviewed. They gifted us with their most precious stories, sitting with us on Zoom, sometimes for hours, and patiently responding as we followed up, often multiple times, to get the contours of their stories just right. Without the staff and collaborators from LSA Family Health Service and LSA Family in Mission, we never would have gained access to these women's stories at all. Because of the transformative, steady, and loving work of LSA over the course of decades, these women trusted us. Special thanks to Inginia García, who first saw value in following up with mothers who had worked with LSA to track their family stories. Inginia put together the list of former LSA clients that led to our interviews. Her tireless work with mothers and children in LSA's early childhood program laid the groundwork, decades ago, for our research. Jacqueline Shannon and Tracy Dewart developed a comprehensive survey that became the jumping-off point for our interviews. The LSA community made itself available to us for interviews, emails, phone calls, and endless questions. Sisters Margaret Leonard, Annette Allain, and the late Susanne Lachapelle were particularly generous with their time, in person, on Zoom, and over the phone. They spent countless hours telling us their remarkable stories, helping us fact check, tracking down details, finding old photos, checking in on our progress. We are so grateful for everything they shared. Thank you also to Maryalice Spencer, who opened the Little Sisters of the Assumption archives and helped orient us in innumerable ways. Special thanks to Lucía Aguilar, Tracey Dewart, Norma Benitez Sánchez, Inginia García, Jonah Gensler, Melina Gonzalez, Gail Gordon, Trish Gough, Sister Susanne Lachapelle, Sister Margaret Leonard, Sister Annette Allain, Sister Jean McCormack, Ray López, Joshua Nowrangilall, Mónica Sánchez, Jacqueline Shannon, Ralph Siciliano, and Lorraine Tierney. These remarkable individuals worked with us every step of the way—sharing articles and press material, unpacking the history, mission, and philosophy of the organization, sitting for interviews, providing key contacts, supplying photographs, analyzing data, and reading drafts of the manuscript. This book would not have been possible without their partnership. We are especially grateful for the thoughtful comments on an earlier draft of the book by Gail, Mónica, Sister Margaret, and Trish. Thank you also to the chairperson of LSA's board, Ted Hopper, who has worked so hard to keep the agency thriving amid a tumultuous few years as we worked on this book. Thanks to Jonah Gensler, LSA's CEO, for conversations about and support of this research project, and for his careful reading of the manuscript.

When the Fordham team came together in September 2020 to start this project, we embarked on a journey without knowing where it would take us. Faculty, graduate students, and undergraduates alike showed up, did the work, and were ultimately touched by the work of LSA. Dr. Larry Farmer was an essential partner at the information-gathering stage of this work. He helped us navigate the IRB process and oriented our entire team in carrying out qualitative data analysis. The remarkable team of Fordham graduate and undergraduate student researchers—Caroline Albacete, Rosaana Conforme, Dita Dobroshi, Malinda Eberly, Camila Gomez, Maddie Hilf, Carlos Orbegoso, Carlos Rojas—were key contributors, particularly in the interview stage of this project. They conducted and translated interviews and helped us identify salient points that ended up shaping the way this book is organized and the larger story it tells. At the same time, they shared personal insights, often related to their own experiences as immigrants or children of immigrants, about how much LSA's mission and work resonated for them. This project was never simply a research project. It touched each of the researchers in unique, personal ways. Christopher Méndez joined as a student researcher to help us organize data and material—his contributions were key for compiling our appendix.

Our research and writing were generously supported by several grants. Our sincere thanks to Jonathan VanAntwerpen of the Henry Luce Foundation for generous support of our project that was critical to our progress. We are also especially grateful to Julie Gafney from Fordham's Center for Community Engaged Learning along with Mick McCarthy, Fordham's former VP of Mission Integration. Mick and Julie's initial financial support got the project off the ground. Thank you also to Fordham's Center for Ethics Education, whose generous Ethics, Social Justice and Health Equity Grant was also a wonderful source of support. Thanks also to the Department of Theology and the Hunt Women, Faith, and Feminism Grant for their generosity. Our thanks also to George Hong from Fordham's Office of Research. In providing funding for our work, these organizations recognized the importance of this unique collaboration, and we are so grateful for their sharing of precious resources with us.

At Fordham, we are also especially grateful to our colleague Jim McCartin and Fordham's Office of Mission Integration for supporting our faculty immersion trips to the US/Mexico border. These experiences transformed our thinking on many of the issues we discuss in the book. Brenna especially thanks her colleague Leo Guardado for his remarkable leadership on her trip.

Of course, writing never happens in a vacuum, and we have certainly benefited from generous friends and colleagues who have read and commented on our work. Our collaborators in Fordham's Community Engaged Scholarship Writing Group—Gregory Acevedo, Gregory Donovan, Liz Gil, Leo Guardado, Liz Raposo and Angelina Tallaj—helped us think through key ideas and structural issues. They also provided a space of intellectual exchange. Thanks to Julie Gafney and Mick McCarthy for establishing the structural support for our writing group, and in general for promoting scholarly engagement with community work. We are grateful to other friends and colleagues—Michael Ossorgin VIII, Keasha Palmer, Brenna's mom—who read and commented on our work. Brenna also offers her thanks to her many friends in Hastings on Hudson and at Fordham who have supported LSA over the years, contributing donations, attending events, listening to stories, offering feedback, with special thanks here to Maureen O'Connell and Natalia Imperatori-Lee. Thank you especially to Mónica Sánchez for sharing your work at LSA with so many of Brenna's friends and family.

Thank you to Fred Nachbaur of Fordham University Press for his support of our book, and to Fordham's Editorial Board for their insightful suggestions on our draft. We are especially grateful to Fred for connecting us with the generous scholars Alyshia Gálvez and Angel García, who read the manuscript draft in full as reviewers and offered detailed, smart, and incisive feedback. Their scholarship on New York serves as a model for us. We are so appreciative for the time they took with our work, and we learned so much from their suggestions. We are also very grateful for the editorial expertise of Constance Rosenblum and Nancy Basmajian, who sharpened and clarified our prose.

Of course, none of this would have been possible without our families' generosity in giving us the space and time to research and write this book. From Carey: Felix and Tobias, I know how hard it was in the era of Zoom school and endless quarantines to resist knocking on the office door when I was in a meeting or an interview. Thank you for that gift. Jared, thanks for keeping the kids on track, for understanding the value of this work and for giving me the space and time to write. From Brenna: My love and deep gratitude to John, Tavia, and Jonah, who have been with me every step of the way with LSA. Their own volunteering and insightful discussions have enriched my experience of LSA so much. While LSA feels very connected to our family, I thank John, Tavia, and Jonah for supporting me in the solitude I needed to finally write down these stories.

APPENDIX: DATA ON MOTHERS INTERVIEWED

Name	*Birth year*	*Birthplace (state in Mexico)*	*Number of children*	*Birth years of children (names included when specifically mentioned in chapters)*	*Year of arrival in NYC*
Mercedes	1981	Guerrero	4	2000 2003 2005 2011	1999
Evelyn	1973	Guerrero	4	1992 1996 2003 2007	1990
Josefina	1979	Puebla	2	2000 2003 (Begoña)	1999
Estrella	1978	Puebla	3	1998 2001 2009	1997
Clara	1973	Guerrero	5	1992 1995 2004 2005 2008	1989
Roberta	1973	Guerrero	4	1992 1996 2002 2006	2000

(continued on next page)

Name	*Birth year*	*Birthplace (state in Mexico)*	*Number of children*	*Birth years of children (names included when specifically mentioned in chapters)*	*Year of arrival in NYC*
Emilia	1975	Puebla	6	1994 1995 2000 2004 2012 2014	—
Rosario	1978	Oaxaca	2	1999 (Andrew) 2007–2015 (Genoveva)	1998
Mónica	1975	Puebla	3	1992 1994 1998	1989
Leonila	1975	Puebla	3	1995 (Ryan) 2001 (Ana) 2004	1990
Cecilia	1967	Guerrero	2	1996 1999	1991
Andrea	1970	Puebla	1	2000	1998
Lina	1974	Mexico City	4	1994 1997 2004 2007	1998
Raquel	1981	Guerrero	4	2001 (Mayra) 2004 2007 2009 (Hugo)	1998
Estefanía	1971	Oaxaca	2	1997 (Elsa) 2006 (Gabriel)	1995
Paloma	1984	Guerrero	2	2004 2009	2002
Melina	1975	Mexico City	3	1993 (Ricardo) 1995 (Mila) 2008	1989
Yolanda	1975	Puebla	2	1995 1998 (David)	1994

*All of the mothers' names have been changed except for Melina's and Yolanda's. All of the children's names listed here have been changed.

NOTES

Introduction. Humanizing Stories: Relationships and Beginnings

1. Todd J. Scribner, "'Not Because They Are Catholic, but Because We Are Catholic': The Bishops' Engagement with the Migration Issue in Twentieth-Century America," *Catholic Historical Review* 101, no. 1 (2015): 74.

2. "Servants of the Poor Recruited from the Wealthy: Titled Women among Members of Order Which Shows Remarkable Growth Despite Great Self Sacrifices Involved," *The Sun and New York Herald*, August 29, 1920.

3. Margaret A. Leonard, "Mutuality as a Catalytic Power for Growth," *Social Casework* 53, no. 2 (Feb. 1972): 67–72.

4. See for example the transcript of the panel discussion by Jay Pearson, Aliyah Abdur-Rahman, Lorena Andrade, and Danielle Spurlock held at Duke University, "Research Justice: Shifting from Extractive Study to Humanized Relationship," last accessed March 20, 2023, https://wfpc.sanford.duke.edu/resources/research-justice-shifting-from-extractive-study-to-humanized-relationship/.

5. LSA Family Health Service website, https://littlesistersfamily.org/mission/.

6. LSA Family Health Service website, https://littlesistersfamily.org/mission/.

7. "ICE Launches Raids Targeting Migrant Families," *New York Times*, July 14, 2019, https://www.nytimes.com/2019/07/14/us/ice-immigration-raids.html.

8. We use the word "Hispanic" throughout the book, as opposed to Latinx, Latine, or Latino, because that is how LSA's community refers to itself. A 2020 Pew Research poll points to the fact that just 3 percent of Hispanics in the United States use the term Latinx, and while the poll indicates that around a quarter of Hispanics are familiar with the term, "awareness of the term Latinx does not necessarily translate into use." Luis Noe-Bustamente, Lauren Mora, and Mark Hugo Lopez, "About One-in-Four U.S. Hispanics Have Heard of Latinx, but Just 3% Use It" (Pew Research Center, August 2020).

9. This presentation was recorded and is available publicly: https://www.youtube.com/watch?v=Zm9fVhEEPIo.

10. Recorded February 13, 2023, https://www.youtube.com/watch?v=Au6rNrEm8tA.

11. Doris Sommer, *The Work of Art in the World: Civic Agency and Public Humanities* (Durham, NC: Duke University Press, 2014), 5.

12. Sommer, 3.

13. We have included our own translation of Luiselli's text, as the published translation fails to convey the importance of documenting and telling stories. The original Spanish text reads as follows: "quizá, la única manera de empezar a entender estos años tan oscuros para los migrantes que cruzan las fronteras de Centroamérica, México y Estados Unidos sea registrar la mayor cantidad de historias individuales posibles. Escucharlas una y otra vez. Escribirlas, una y otra vez. Para que no sean olvidadas, para que queden en los anales de nuestra historia compartida y en lo hondo de nuestra conciencia" (*Los niños perdidos: Un ensayo en cuarenta preguntas* [México: Sexto Piso, 2016], 32). The published translation is included here: "Perhaps the only way to grant any justice—were that even possible—is by hearing and recording those stories over and over again so that they come back, always, to haunt and shame us" (Valeria Luiselli, *Tell Me How It Ends: An Essay in Forty Questions* [Minneapolis: Coffee House, 2017], 31).

14. Tobin Hansen and María Engracia Robles Robles, eds., *Voices of the Border:* Testimonios *of Migration, Deportation, and Asylum* (Washington, DC: Georgetown University Press, 2021), 16. John Beverley explains the complicated encounters that take place in testimonio literature, where race, class, gender, and language are often performed through interview, editing, and publishing processes that involve both a narrator and a interlocutor: "Was testimonio an authentic subaltern voice, or, to use one characterization, a 'mediated' narrative in which a literary simulacrum of that voice was being staged, in the form of what Spivak called a 'domesticated Other' for the reader, whose own position of relative authority and privilege was left uncontested in the process?" (John Beverley, *Testimonio: On the Politics of Truth* [Minneapolis: University of Minnesota Press, 2004], xvi).

15. Beverley, xvi.

Chapter 1. "The Power of Growth Is in Relationship": The History of the Little Sisters of the Assumption Nuns in East Harlem, 1865–1970

1. Sister Susanne Lachapelle, interview by Brenna Moore, June 3, 2022.

2. Susanne Lachapelle, private writings shared with the authors in 2021.

3. Paragraph 2, "Justice in the World," the World Synod of Bishops, 1971, https://www.cctwincities.org/wp-content/uploads/2015/10/Justicia-in-Mundo.pdf.

4. Sister Margaret Leonard, interview by Brenna Moore, March 1, 2021.

5. Sonia Singh, interview by Brenna Moore, September 2, 2021.

6. Trish Gough, interview by Brenna Moore, December 9, 2021.

7. Singh, interview.

8. Margaret McGuinness, *Called to Serve: A History of Nuns in America* (New York: New York University Press, 2015).

9. There is surprisingly little academic work on the US region of the Little Sisters of the Assumption. LSA Family Health Service published a short digitized history, "Celebrating 60 Years," accessed May 1, 2022, https://littlesistersfamily.org/celebrating-60-years/. There are resources in French on the origins of the Little Sisters of the Assumption congregation; see

Les Petites-Soeurs de l'Assomption, in *L'Oeuvre des tracts* series (Montreal, Canada) no. 306, December 1944, 1–15 (author unknown). For a thorough biography of the founding figures, Sister Antoinette Fage and Father Pernet, see Frédérique de Watrigant, *Passionnés de Jésus Christ: Etienne Pernet et Antoinette Fage, fondateurs des Petites Soeurs de l'Assomption* (Paris: Desclée de Brouwer, 2013). In English there is an extensive and well-researched history of the congregation of the Little Sisters in Ireland that includes some of the shared history in the United States; see Carol Dorgan's *To Tell Our Story Is to Praise God: A History of the Little Sisters of the Assumption in Ireland* (Dublin: LSA, 2016). See also T. Taaffe (1907), "Little Sisters of the Assumption," in *The Catholic Encyclopedia* (New York: Robert Appleton), retrieved June 4, 2022, from *New Advent*, http://www.newadvent.org/cathen/02005d.htm. For an excellent history of the larger Assumptionist community in the United States (that includes the Little Sisters community along with several others), see Henry Moquin and Richard Richards, *Assumptionists in the United States* (Worcester, MA: Assumptionist Communications, 1994). The bulk of the story we tell draws on interviews and archival holdings maintained in the Little Sisters of the Assumption archive on 115th Street in East Harlem. We are grateful to have had access to unpublished time lines and rough drafts of histories completed by former LSA archivists at different periods in the order's history.

10. Rachel G. Fuchs, *Poor and Pregnant in Paris: Strategies for Survival in the Nineteenth Century* (New Brunswick, NJ: Rutgers University Press, 1992), 9.

11. *Mère Marie de Jésus: Foundress of the Little Sisters of the Assumption, Nursing Sisters of the Poor in Their Own Homes*, translation from French, author and translator unknown (London: Longmans, Green, 1917), 4.

12. Steven M. Beaudoin, "'Without Belonging to Public Service': Charities, the State, and Civil Society in Third Republic Bordeaux, 1870–1914," *Journal of Social History* 31, no. 3 (1998). Also Katherine Lynch, "Social Provisions and the Life of Civil Society in Europe: Rethinking Public and Private," *Journal of Urban History* 36, no. 3 (2010); Richard Wilson and Richard D. Brown, *Humanitarianism and Suffering: The Mobilization of Empathy* (Cambridge: Cambridge University Press, 2008).

13. Thomas Max Safley, *The Reformation of Charity: The Secular and Religious in Early Modern Poor Relief* (Boston: Brill, 2003), 176–92.

14. Quoted in *Mère Marie de Jésus*, 28.

15. *Mère Marie de Jésus*. See also the description in "Little Sisters of Assumption Mark Centenary," *Catholic Standard and Times*, June 11, 1965, 8.

16. Fr. Pernet's words quoted in *Mère Marie de Jésus*, 29.

17. "Guide for the Nursing Sisters," from chapter 12 of the Commentaries of Our Venerated Founders (1962), unpublished, LSA archive, East Harlem. Sister Gisèle Marchand, "Little Sisters of the Assumption," in *Origins of the Assumption Family: Founders and Foundresses, Foundations and Intuitions, Relations and Disagreements*, Acts of the Inter-Assumption Colloquium, Paris (January 6–10, 2004), 142–66.

18. "To Nurse the Sick Poor: Little Sisters of the Assumption Coming Here from France," *The Sun*, April 19, 1891.

19. *Mère Marie de Jésus*, 73.

20. Marchand, "Little Sisters of the Assumption," 151.

21. "Servants of the Poor Recruited from the Wealthy," *The Sun and New York Herald*, August 29, 1920.

22. *Mère Marie de Jésus*, 75.

23. *Les Petites-Soeurs de l'Assomption*, 2.

24. Thank you for correspondence with Sister Jean McCormack on the clarification of these issues.

25. *Mère Marie de Jésus*, 65.

26. The first Rule was approved in 1875, and in 1896, "he made this Rule more specific by writing the Constitutions (approved in 1901) and the Directory." Marchand, "Little Sisters of the Assumption," 142.

27. Marchand, 239.

28. Quoted in Marchand, 240.

29. See also "Guide for the Nursing Sisters."

30. *Mère Marie de Jésus*, 92.

31. Marchand, "Little Sisters of the Assumption," 148.

32. *Mère Marie de Jésus*, 54.

33. *Mère Marie de Jésus*, 117.

34. Affiliation promise of the Lady Servants of the Assumption, in Marchand, "Little Sisters of the Assumption," 148.

35. Talk by Fr. Pernet to the Lady Servants of the Poor, July 4, 1882, quoted in Marchand, "Little Sisters of the Assumption," 159.

36. Talk by Fr. Pernet to the Lady Servants of the Poor.

37. "To Nurse Poverty's Sick," *Catholic Telegraph* 59, no. 13, 27 March 1890.

38. "To Nurse the Sick Poor: Little Sisters of the Assumption Coming Here from France," *The Sun*, April 19, 1891.

39. "To Nurse the Sick Poor."

40. "Reclaiming Black Spaces," The Tenement Museum Lower East Side Tour, accessed May 25, 2023, https://www.tenement.org/reclaiming-black-spaces/. See also "Tenement Museum Makes Room for Black History," *New York Times*, June 9, 2021, https://www.nytimes.com/2021/06/09/arts/design/tenement-museum-black-history.html?mc_cid=bb1bc48b23&mc_eid=bef73da296.

41. Sister Marie-Mercedes's notebooks were translated from French into English by Ida Mary Smalley and published in a slim volume, *Little Sister Missionary: The Life of Sister Marie-Mercedes of the Little Sisters of the Assumption* (Chicago: Benzinger Brothers, 1932). Copy from LSA archive.

42. "Obituary," *The Sun*, June 5, 1891.

43. Letter from Marie de Christ to LSA Mother Superior and Fr. Pernet in Paris, undated, LSA archive, box 1.

44. Unpublished notebook, LSA archive, box 1.

45. Letter to the editor, *New York Times*, June 26, 1891.

46. Unpublished time line in "The Congregation in New York" folder, LSA archive, box 3.

47. "A Fair in Aid of the Little Sisters of the Assumption," *The Sun*, December 15, 1896.

48. Notice posted in *the Evening World*, December 15, 1894, 8.

49. "Musicale for Charity: Well-Known Artists to Sing in Aid of the Little Sisters of the Assumption," *The Sun*, February 15, 1898.

50. Unpublished notebooks in "The Congregation in New York" folder, LSA archive, box 3.

51. For more on the relationship between diocesan charities and those of more independent orders and the laity, see Mary Oates, *The Catholic Philanthropic Tradition in America* (Bloomington: Indiana University Press, 1995).

52. "Little Sisters of the Assumption to Be Aided May 14," *New York Times*, May 2, 1932.

53. "The Little Sisters of the Assumption," *Catholic News Service*, October 10, 1950.

54. Unpublished notebook in "The Congregation in New York" folder, LSA archive, box 3.

55. "Servants of the Poor Recruited from the Wealthy."

56. "Servants of the Poor Recruited from the Wealthy." By 1920, the Little Sisters of the Assumption were embodying what many Catholics in the United States were aiming to do. At the turn of the century, Bishop John Ireland put forward a vision of a distinctly Catholic way of doing charity in a Protestant majority country: "We do not fulfill our duty by paying a tax to the State or by sending to a committee an annual subscription, leaving to the State or the committee to stand proxy for us, and neglecting to come, ourselves, into contact with the poor. Charity is love for the victim of sorrow, and love demands personal attention." Catholic philanthropy, at the time, held out the ideal of personal involvement, whether poor, working class, or wealthy, and the Little Sisters of the Assumption provided these opportunities. Oates, *Catholic Philanthropic Tradition*, 168.

57. "Servants of the Poor Who Labor in the Slums: Members of an Order Who Live Up to the Title of Their Organization: How They Command Respect from All Classes with Whom They Come in Contact," *New York Times*, August 30, 1903, 33.

58. Matt Moran, "Irish Missionary Nun Who Nursed Pope Francis as a Baby," *Independent Catholic News Service*, January 8, 2019.

59. "LSA Family Health Service Welcomes Pope Francis to East Harlem," September 3, 2015, https://littlesistersfamily.org/lsa-welcomes-pope-francis/.

60. Box 3, folder 8, LSA archive, East Harlem.

61. "Project Hope: An Interview with Sr. Margaret Leonard," *America*, November 2, 1996, 10–14.

62. Oates, *Catholic Philanthropic Tradition*, 168.

63. For an excellent discussion of issues of race and segregation in the religious communities of nuns who ran schools and hospitals, see McGuinness, *Called to Serve*, chapters 3 and 4.

64. "Assumption Sisters Receive First Negro Girl," *Catholic Standard and Times* 61, no. 32, May 4, 1956.

65. "Little Sisters of Assumption Hold Investiture in Haverford," *Catholic Standard and Times* 64, no. 35, May 22, 1959.

66. *Gaudium et spes* [Pastoral Constitution of the Church in the Modern World, 1965], https://www.vatican.va/archive/hist_councils/ii_vatican_council/documents/vat-ii_const_19651207_gaudium-et-spes_en.html.

67. The best historical overview of this transformation for women religious is in McGuinness, *Called to Serve*, chapter 7.

68. Heather McGhee, *The Sum of Us: What Racism Costs Everyone and How We Can Prosper Together* (New York: One World, 2021).

69. Sister Margaret Leonard, interview by Brenna Moore, March 1, 2021.

70. Elizabeth Walker, "What Hope Looks Like," a profile of Sister Margaret Leonard, *Assumption College Magazine*, Winter 2008, 12–15.

71. Leonard, interview, March 1, 2021.

72. Sister Margaret Leonard's written notes given to the author.

73. Christopher Bell, *East Harlem Remembered: Oral Histories of Community and Diversity* (New York: McFarland, 2008), 120.

74. For a fuller portrait of Puerto Rican and Hispanic history in New York City, see Arlene Dávila, *Barrio Dreams* (Berkeley: University of California Press, 2004).

75. Bell, *East Harlem Remembered*, 120.

76. Piri Thomas, *Down These Mean Streets* (New York: Vintage, 1997), 105.

77. Thomas, 313–14.

78. Bell, *East Harlem Remembered*, 120–37.

79. Oates, *Catholic Philanthropic Tradition*, 88.

80. Lachappelle, interview.

81. As the Little Sisters like Margaret were settling into the neighborhood, there were other Catholics also interested in East Harlem's cultural vitality. Dan Wakefield published a book in 1959 on Spanish Harlem called *Island in the City*. Not long after, he moved into the Catholic Worker Movement with Dorothy Day as a volunteer. In 1971, the archdiocesan magazine *The Catholic Transcript* published an excerpt of the New York University sociologist Patricia Cayo Sexton's 1965 book, *Spanish Harlem: An Anatomy of Poverty*. The book gives a vivid feel of the people, colors, sounds, and smells of East Harlem, showcasing the neighborhood's vitality along with the well-documented poverty and need:

> East Harlem is a busy place, night and day, filled with the joyous troubled lives of residents—rather than the heavy commercial traffic of mid-Manhattan. . . . East Harlem is the poorest spot in one of the richest areas of the world, Manhattan. Across its southern border is the glitter of the east side gold coast, home of some of the world's richest and most celebrated people. On its west flank is another fabled area, Negro Central Harlem, off-and-on home of Adam Clayton Powell, A. Philip Randolph, James Baldwin, Malcolm X. In contrast to such celebrities, East Harlem is plain Jane. If it is "exotic," as advertising for middle-income housing claims, that is because of the Spanish flavor below 125th Street. Almost half of its population speaks Spanish. As one of the world's largest Spanish communities, it has been a port of entry for the vast migration that has shuttled back and forth by air express from San Juan to New York for two decades. The spirited Latin music of East Harlem pouring out from open tenement windows in every block, is Puerto Rican.

82. Leonard, interview, March 1, 2021.

83. Lachappelle, interview.

84. Leonard, interview, March 1, 2021.

85. Leonard, interview, March 1, 2021.

86. Lachapelle, interview.

87. *Hearings, Reports and Prints of the Senate Select Committee on Nutrition and Human Needs* (Washington, DC: U.S. Government Printing Office, 1970).

88. The Washington Consulting Group, *Uplift: What People Themselves Can Do* (Salt Lake City: Olympus, 1974).

89. Lachapelle, interview.

90. Sister Margaret Leonard, private papers shared with authors.

91. 1969 LSA Annual Report, LSA archive, East Harlem.

92. Margaret Leonard, "Mutuality as a Catalytic Power for Growth," *Families in Society: The Journal of Contemporary Social Services* 52, no. 2 (February 1972).

93. 1969 LSA Annual Report.

94. 1969 LSA Annual Report.

95. Notes from 1969 retreat on the theme of mutuality, LSA archive.

96. Also quoted in 1969 LSA Annual Report.

97. Singh, interview.

98. Singh, interview.

99. Michael Joyce, "Assignment: East Harlem," *American Journal of Nursing* 69, no. 7 (1969): 1497–502.

100. Leonard, "Mutuality."

Chapter 2. "LSA Is Like a Second Home": The Story of Melina Gonzalez

1. United States Department of State Bureau of Consular Affairs, "Visa Bulletin for February 2022," *The Visa Bulletin* 10, no. 62, January 7, 2022, https://travel.state.gov/content/travel/en/legal/visa-lawo/visa-bulletin/2022/visa-bulletin-for-february-2022.html.

2. "Mexicans who were legalized during the late 1980s through IRCA received permanent residency or U.S. citizenship in the early 1990s. . . . Once they obtained this status, they could apply to sponsor the immigration of family members living in Mexico, which, not surprisingly, led to a big increase in the migration of Mexican children to New York in the 1990s." Robert Courtney Smith, "Mexicans: Civic Engagement, Education, and Progress Achieved and Inhibited," in *One Out of Three: Immigrant New York in the Twenty-First Century*, ed. Nancy Foner (New York: Columbia University Press, 2013), 248. Other factors such as NAFTA or the 1994 devaluation of the peso also influenced Mexican migration to the United States in the 1990s.

3. Elisa Gootman, "Small Schools Show Concern over Proposal to Swap Land," *New York Times*, June 28, 2006.

4. Ann Cook, "The Transformation of One Large Urban High School: The Julia Richman Education Complex," in *Creating New Schools: How Small Schools Are Changing American Education* (New York: Teachers College Press, 2000), 106.

5. Gootman, "Small Schools."

6. This was part of a larger movement to eradicate large underperforming urban schools known for violence and replace them with numerous smaller schools that would be more attentive to student needs. Several academic articles detail this process. See Annette Fuentes, "The Schoolhouse as Jailhouse," *Counterpoints* 453 (2014): 37–53; Daniel L. Duke, Thomas DeRoberto, and Sarah Trautvetter, "Reducing the Negative Effects of Large Schools" (revised),m National Clearinghouse for Educational Facilities, 2009; Linda Darling-Hammond, Jacqueline Ancess, and Susanna Wichterle Ort, "Reinventing High School: Outcomes of the Coalition Campus Schools Project," *American Educational Research Journal* 39, no. 3 (Fall 2002): 639–73.

7. Cook, "Transformation," 105.

8. Gina M. Pérez, *Citizen, Student, Soldier: Latina/o Youth, JROTC, and the American Dream* (New York: New York University Press, 2015), 153.

9. Pérez, 160–61. Pérez examines how the study and promotion of citizenship manifests for a student group of young Ohio Latinos: "Participating in JROTC . . . shapes their sense of citizenship and national belonging by providing them with the opportunity to be the kind of reliable, responsible, and other-centered people they aspire to be. In doing so, they defy characterizations that stigmatize them, their families, and their communities and become, instead, models others should emulate" (197).

10. "NJROTC," Naval Education and Training Command website, accessed February 14, 2022, https://www.netc.navy.mil/Commands/Naval-Service-Training-Command/NJROTC/Cadet-Information/.

11. Pérez, *Citizen, Student, Soldier*, 152–53.

12. Carolina Bank Muñoz, "A Dream Deferred: Undocumented Students at CUNY," *Radical Teacher* 84 (Spring 2009): 11–12. In the wake of September 11, this policy was briefly

revoked and undocumented students were again charged international student tuition rates. In-state tuition was reinstated in 2002 following a three-day student-led hunger strike in January 2002. The in-state policy remains in place today, although students currently need to prove that they've been in New York for two years, not one year. For more information, see Smith, "Mexicans," 246–66.

13. Smith, "Mexicans," 259.

14. Bank Muñoz, "Dream Deferred," 12.

15. We consciously use the term "adjust" here as that is the wording that Melina adopted. The term "to normalize one's status" is also commonly employed as a more humane way to refer to the process that others call "becoming documented" or "legalizing." It bears mention that immigration advocates have long argued that no human being is illegal. The term "illegal immigrant" is politically charged, and mobilized to portray immigrants as lawbreakers. Furthermore, the term dehumanizes, especially when coupled with the word "alien." Melina explained her use of the term "adjust," saying that she changes her language depending on her interlocutor: "It depends on the person that I'm speaking to because I have to know what level of education you have and what you can understand because if I spoke to somebody and I said, 'Do you want to adjust your status?' they're not going to understand if they have the level of education of a sixth grader. They're not going to understand what adjusting means. I have to say '¿Usted quiere arreglar sus papeles?,' or, 'You want to see what are the conditions of how you can fix your documents, or how you can become a legal permanent resident?' I have to use several different ways so they can understand what I'm talking about." When we asked Melina directly about the use of the term "normalize," she said, "Normalize would be one of the kindest words you can use." But then she laughed and said that "adjust" is an even kinder term.

16. The 245(i) provision was enacted in 1994 through the Immigration and Nationality Technical Corrections Act, which amended the 1952 law to make residency available to people previously ineligible. We include this information here to underscore how the migration process has become increasingly challenging in recent years. While provisions like 245(i) have not been eradicated, they have also not been updated. In order to qualify for status adjustment under provision 245(i), undocumented migrants would need to have submitted their application on or before April 30, 2001. Very few people qualify for 245(i), and those people would have to leave the country to have their petitions granted. Congress has the power to update this deadline anytime, but this has not happened since the April 30, 2001, deadline passed. In May 2021 the Fairness for Immigrant Families Act was introduced in Congress. It would reactivate the provisions to allow immigrants to adjust their status from within the United States for a period of five years after the legislation's adoption. Regardless, the bill has never been referred to a committee, much less put to a vote.

17. Hirokazu Yoshikawa, *Immigrants Raising Citizens: Undocumented Parents and Their Young Children* (New York: Russell Sage, 1992), 24.

18. Yoshikawa, 65–66.

19. Yoshikawa provides detailed information on Mexican families and childcare: "The Mexicans were consistently by far the lowest in their use of child care subsidies, with virtually no increases across fourteen to thirty-six months. . . . The Mexicans in our study sample were more likely than the Dominicans to state a mistrust of out-of-home care and express fears of abuse. Trusting only relatives with their children was also more common among our Mexican mothers than among the Dominican and African American mothers. And not surprisingly, Mexican mothers were returning to work across the first three years of their children's lives at lower rates than Dominican and African American mothers" (Yoshikawa, 65–66).

20. While this book does not take on the school choice debate, it has been proven that the trend toward school choice greatly benefits families who know how to navigate the system. That LSA helped empower Melina's family to learn, explore, and choose shows how it challenges the system.

21. Nicole Mader, Clara Hemphill, and Qasim Abbas with Tainá Guarda, Ana Carla Sant'anna Costa, and Melanie Quiroz, *The Paradox of Choice: How School Choice Divides New York City Elementary Schools* (New York: The New School, 2018), 12. As Elizabeth H. Park sums up in her dissertation, "Diversity in Gifted-and-Talented Programs: The Role of Family Engagement and Bureaucratic Rules" (PhD diss., Columbia University, 2021), "nearly 60 percent of students in gifted-and-talented programs across the country are White, compared to 50 percent of public school enrollment overall. In contrast, less than 30 percent of gifted-and-talented students are Black or Hispanic, although they represent 40 percent of the overall student population" (1–2).

22. Park, "Diversity in Gifted-and-Talented Programs," 2.

23. For more information, see Lei Lei and Scott J. South, "Racial and Ethnic Differences in Leaving and Returning to the Parental Home: The Role of Life Course Transitions, Socioeconomic Resources, and Family Connectivity," *Demographic Research* 34, no. 4 (January 2016): 109–42, and Jennifer Reid Keene and Christie D. Batson, "Under One Roof: A Review of Research on Intergenerational Coresidence and Multigenerational Households in the United States" *Sociology Compass* 4, no. 8 (August 2010): 642–57. "Britton (2013) found that higher rates of coresidence among minorities are not attributable to subcultural differences in attitudes toward family and marriage, but are partially explained by group differences in socioeconomic attainment and marital status" (Lei and South, 111). "Black and Mexican young adults' lower tendency to enter and to remain in college partially explains their delayed timing of home-leaving and their higher risk of home-returning relative to Whites" (Lei and South, 134). "Racially differentiated access to socioeconomic resources, reflected especially in mother's education and financial assistance received from parents, is another important part of the explanation for why White and minority young adults differ in the timing of home-leaving and returning" (Lei and South, 134).

24. Renate Belville, Debbie Indyk, Vivian Shapiro, Tracey Dewart, Jane Z. Moss, Gail Gordon, and Sister Susanne Lachapelle, "The Community as a Strategic Site for Refining High Perinatal Risk Assessments and Interventions," *Social Work in Health Care* 16, no. 1 (1991): 9.

25. Belville et al., 9.

Chapter 3. Voices from the Neighborhood: Immigrant Mothers at Little Sisters

1. The names of all mothers (except Melina's and Yolanda's) and children in this chapter have been changed.

2. Gail Gordon, "A Multidisciplinary Approach to Family Growth," *Early Child Development and Care* 22, no. 1 (1985): 39.

3. All ages reflect the age of the interviewee at the time of our interview.

4. Peter Silvern, "From Generation to Generation," *Family Resource Coalition Report* 6, no. 1 (1987): 15.

5. Gail Gordon, in conversation with the author, August 2022.

6. Given that seventeen of the eighteen interviews were conducted in Spanish, all of the interview material cited here has been translated from the original Spanish. Carey translated

all of the included quotations, relying on both the original transcription and rough translations provided by our bilingual undergraduate and graduate student researchers. At times Carey has included words or phrases in Spanish to capture a specific meaning that is hard to replicate in English or to provide the reader with some of the original rhythms of the speaker.

7. Alyshia Gálvez, *Patient Citizens, Immigrant Mothers: Mexican Women, Public Prenatal Care, and the Birth-Weight Paradox* (New Brunswick, NJ: Rutgers University Press, 2011), 17.

8. The eighteen mothers interviewed arrived in New York between 1989 and 2002, with the bulk of arrivals focused in the latter half of the 1990s. "In 2000 the Mexican-origin population in New York City, including both immigrants and native-born Mexican Americans, was 275,000 to 300,000, about half of whom were between the ages of twelve and twenty-four. This figure represents a remarkable increase from 40,000 Mexicans in 1980 and 100,000 in 1990." Robert Courtney Smith, *Mexican New York: Transnational Lives of New Immigrants* (Berkeley: University of California Press, 2006), 19.

9. Smith, 19.

10. Gálvez, *Patient Citizens*, 17.

11. Parker and Pederizini's 2000 World Bank report on gender and education in Mexico reveals that by age twelve, a gender gap in school attendance emerges, indicating that more girls than boys end their education at the primary school level (19). Their work also shows that the gender gap is more significant in rural areas (20). Furthermore, overall school attendance for boys and girls is further decreased for families with lower income levels (21). Susan Wendy Parker and Carla Pederizini, "Gender Differences in Education in Mexico," Report for World Bank, August 2000.

12. Gálvez, *Patient Citizens*, 22.

13. Gálvez, *Patient Citizens*, 25.

14. Jessica P. Cerdeña, *Pressing Onward: The Imperative Resilience of Latina Migrant Mothers* (Oakland: University of California Press, 2023), 143.

15. Raja Sakrani traces how *convivencia*—beyond scholars' application of the term in medieval Spain—appears in contemporary usage. She cites Pope Francis's use of the term in Sarajevo in 2015 to echo the religious pluralism the term invokes (Sakrani, "Convivencia: Reflections about Its "Kulturbedeutung" and Rereading the Normative Histories of Living Together," Max Planck Institute for European Legal History Research Paper Series, no. 2016-02, last revised February 15, 2020, 10–11). Pablo M. Jasis and Rosario Ordoñez-Jasis's article on the effects of parent empowerment in advocating for children's schooling documents the importance of *convivencia* in the parental mobilization. They define *convivencia* in the following terms: "The flowing moments of collective creation and solidarity, the bonding that developed from a joint, emerging moral quest against the backdrop of experiential sharing" (Jasis and Ordóñez-Jasis, "Latino Parent Involvement: Examining Commitment and Empowerment in Schools," *Urban Education* 47, no. 1 [January 2012]: 35). Jasis and Ordoñez-Jasis document how through convivencia families were inspired to work together and became more committed to organizing efforts to better their kids' schooling.

16. Hirokazu Yoshikawa, *Immigrants Raising Citizens: Undocumented Parents and Their Young Children* (New York: Russell Sage, 1992), 60.

17. Gabrielle Oliveira, *Motherhood across Borders: Immigrants and Their Children in Mexico and New York* (New York: New York University Press, 2018), 74.

18. Diane Whitmore Schanzenbach and Lauren Bauer, "*The Long-Term Impact of the Head Start Program*," Brookings Institution, August 19, 2016, 3, https://www.brookings.edu/articles/the-long-term-impact-of-the-head-start-program/.

Chapter 4. Mutuality for a New Era

1. Daniel Kaufman and Ross Perlin, "Indigenous Latin American Languages in NYC: A Report to the NYC Department of Health," July 1, 2019, https://54.80.248.249/wp-content/uploads/2021/12/Surveying-Indigenous-Latin-American-Languages-in-NYC.pdf. See also NYC Health Department, *Epi Research Report: Health of Indigenous Peoples of the Americas Living in New York City,* December 2021, https://www.nyc.gov/assets/doh/downloads/pdf/episrv/indigenous-peoples-health-2021.pdf.

2. Mixteco mother quoted in "Promoting the Health of Indigenous People Living in New York City through Culture, Food, and Language," report from collaboration between Endangered Language Association, LSA, and the NYC Department of Health and Mental Hygiene, April 2020, https://content.endangeredlanguagealliance.org/wp-content/uploads/2020/04/Xilonen.pdf.

3. Margaret Leonard and Carol Ann Joyce, "Two Worlds United," *American Journal of Nursing* 71, no. 6 (1971): 1152–55. See also Margaret Leonard, "The Older Non-Professional in Community Service: Four Professional Viewpoints," *National Council on Aging*, 1971.

4. Leonard and Joyce, "Two Worlds United," 1152.

5. Leonard and Joyce, 1152.

6. "Grandmother Program Project," submitted to Ford Foundation by Little Sisters of the Assumption Family Health Service, Inc., LSA archive, East Harlem, box 12.

7. "Grandmother Program Project."

8. Leonard and Joyce, "Two Worlds United," 1152.

9. Leonard and Joyce, 1152.

10. "East Harlem's 'Grandmothers' Aid 2 Generations," *New York Times*, February 10, 1985, 55.

11. Lorna G. Canlas, "Issues of Health Care Mistrust in East Harlem," *Mount Sinai Journal of Medicine* 66, no. 4 (September 1999): 257–58.

12. Ken Auletta, "The Underclass," *New Yorker*, November 16, 1981, 57.

13. Marybeth Shinn and Margaret Rosario, "The Extended Family Program," *Community Psychologist* 19, no. 1 (1985): 5.

14. Marybeth Shinn, "Expanding Community Psychology's Domain," *American Journal of Community Psychology* 15, no. 5 (1987): 563.

15. Jere Van Dyk and Joseph Rodriguez, "Growing Up in East Harlem," *National Geographic* 177, no. 5 (May 1990): 52–75.

16. "Celebrating 60 Years: Our History," *Little Sisters of the Assumption* website, accessed March 3, 2022, https://www.littlesisters.org/history.php.

17. Office of the Inspector General, "Services Integration for Families and Children in Crisis," *Report on Little Sisters of the Assumption Family Health Service*, January 1991, 21–23.

18. Described in Gail Gordon, "A Multidisciplinary Approach to Family Growth," *Early Childhood Development and Care* 1, no. 22 (1985): 37–52.

19. VHS film, "World of Families, Little Sisters of the Assumption Family Health Service," 1989, LSA archive.

20. Described in Gordon, "Multidisciplinary Approach to Family Growth," 37–52.

21. "East Harlem's 'Grandmothers,'" 55.

22. Gordon, "Multidisciplinary Approach to Family Growth," 50.

23. Gail Gordon, interview by Brenna Moore, February 10, 2022.

24. VHS film, "World of Families."

25. Inginia García, interview by Brenna Moore, June 20, 2023.

26. García, interview.

27. "Laughter Workshop Brings Smiles to HBS Families," LSA website, February 12, 2015, https://littlesistersfamily.org/laughter-workshop-brings-smiles-to-hbs-families/.

28. Alfredo Lopez, *The Puerto Rican Papers: Notes on the Re-emergence of a Nation* (Indianapolis: Bobbs-Merrill, 1973), 222–23.

29. Norma Benítez Sánchez, interview by Brenna Moore, December 10, 2021.

30. Benítez Sánchez, interview.

31. Benítez Sánchez, interview.

32. Conversation with Melina Gonzalez, November 19, 2021.

33. "Nursing Order Aids Harlem Families: Little Sisters Assist Health Agencies," *The Anchor*, January 3, 1974, 10. An excellent book exploring this (sometimes uneven) transition from Catholic hierarchical, old-fashioned models of power to more transparency in hiring, recruitment, asset management, and so on within the Society of Jesus is Peter McDonough and Eugene C. Bianchi, *Passionate Uncertainty: Inside the American Jesuits* (Berkeley: University of California Press, 2003).

34. Benítez Sánchez, interview.

35. Trish Gough, interview by Brenna Moore, December 4, 2021.

36. Gough, interview.

37. Martha Andrade, interview by Brenna Moore, December 9, 2021.

38. "Small Charities Fear Impact of National Service," *AP News Service*, October 8, 1993, 17.

39. Gough, interview.

40. Ralph Siciliano, interview by Malinda Eberly, October 16, 2020.

41. Trish Gough, quoted in "Wishing Sister Judy Farewell," LSA website, August 15, 2017, https://littlesistersfamily.org/wishing-sr-judy-farewell/.

42. Siciliano, interview.

43. Gordon, interview.

44. Gough, interview.

45. Some of this material is in LSA folder 8, in LSA archive; other items are in the personal work papers of Ray López, shared with the authors. Ray has held on to old LSA files, knowing that someday they would be important for telling LSA's story, and we thank him for sharing these materials with us.

46. Papers of Ray López, shared with the authors.

47. Gordon, interview.

48. VHS film, "World of Families."

49. VHS film, "World of Families."

50. Gordon, interview.

51. Gordon, "Multidisciplinary Approach to Family Growth," 37–52.

52. Gordon, interview.

53. "Little Sisters of the Assumption," *Services Integration for Families and Children in Crisis*, report by the Department of Health and Human Services, Office of Inspector General, January 1991.

54. "Little Sisters of the Assumption."

55. "Little Sisters of the Assumption."

56. Gordon, interview.

57. Julia Martin, "Gathering Spot: Little Sisters' East Harlem Thrift Shop Is a Place of Good Prices, Good Will," *Catholic New York*, July 19, 1999.

58. Gordon, interview.

59. George Anderson, "Of Many Things," *America*, December 9, 2002.

60. LSA retreat planning and meeting notes shared by Ray López with the authors.

61. John Freeman Gill, "Ray Lopez vs. the Critters of the Night," *New York Times*, October 1, 2006, https://www.nytimes.com/2006/10/01/nyregion/thecity/01bedb.html.

62. Gill, "Ray Lopez."

63. Gill, "Ray Lopez."

64. Ray López, interview by Brenna Moore, February 16, 2021.

65. López, interview.

66. From that point on, Ray said that he not only has always tried to design programs that help individual families, but takes time to "examine the root causes of problems, and put forth some effort to address it."

67. "Collaborating with Community Organizers for Social Justice: An Interview with Michael Stanley and Ray Lopez," Law firm's "Proskauer for Good" Blog, August 3, 2020, https://www.proskauer.com/blog/collaborating-with-community-organizers-for-social-justice-an-interview-with-michael-stanley-and-ray-lopez.

68. Arnold Mann, "When Mold Takes Hold," *USA Weekend*, July 19–21, 2002.

69. López, interview.

70. Edward T. Chambers, *The Power of Relational Action* (Chicago: ACTA Publications, 2016), 18.

71. López, interview.

72. East Harlem mother of four, quoted in "A Community Health Worker Model to Address Childhood Asthma: Perspectives of Program Participants," by Lillian Jin, Ivan Marquez, Ray López, Lindsey Realmuto, Anne Bozack, Matthew Perzanowski, and Linda Weiss, *New York Academy of Medicine* (New York), August 2017, 2, available online at National Library of Medicine, https://collections.nlm.nih.gov/catalog/nlm:nlmuid-101715497-pdf.

73. López, interview.

74. Anderson, "Of Many Things."

75. LSA Newsletter, 1988, LSA archive.

76. Rachel Brandoff and Mónica Sánchez, "Art Therapy with Latin-American Women," *Exploring the Benefit of Creative Arts Therapies for Children, Adolescents, and Adults*, ed. Nava R. Silton (Hershey, PA: IGI Global, 2023), 43.

77. Gough, interview.

78. Clay Skipper, "Hope Is a Muscle: Why Krista Tippett Wants You to Keep the Faith," *GQ*, July 21, 2022, https://www.gq.com/story/krista-tippett-on-being-interview.

Epilogue. On Sister Susanne's Passing and the Shadow Side

1. Ocean Vuong, "Poet Ocean Vuong on the Creativity of Refugees," *Tricycle: The Buddhist Review*, May 4, 2022, https://tricycle.org/article/ocean-vuong-time-is-a-mother/.

2. Vuong, "Poet Ocean Vuong."

3. Ocean Vuong, "A 'Love Letter' for Our Community," written to the Plum Village monastic and lay community on the occasion of the death of Buddhist teacher Thich Nhat Hanh, Thich Nhat Hahn Foundation website, February 17, 2022, https://thichnhathanhfoundation.org/blog/2022/2/17/a-love-letter-for-our-community-by-ocean-vuong.

4. Ocean Vuong, "'Love Letter' for Our Community."

5. Isaiah 9:2.

6. Constance FitzGerald, "Impasse and Dark Night," in *Desire, Darkness, and Hope: Theology in a Time of Impasse*, ed. Laurie Cassidy and M. Shawn Copeland (Collegeville, MN: Liturgical, 2021), 113.

7. Margaret Leonard, "Disciples in the Shadow Side of God" (1–11), unpublished talk shared with authors. Undated, but likely early 1970s.

8. Sister Judy Garson, notes. Personal papers of Susanne Lachapelle, shared with authors.

9. Paul J. DiMaggio and Walter W. Powell, "The Iron Cage Revisited: Institutional Isomorphism and Collective Rationality in Organizational Fields," *American Sociological Review* 48, no. 2 (April 1983): 147–60.

10. As scholars Lauren Taylor and Elena Byhoff explain in relation to how the field of health care interacts with CBOs, "Within a resource-scarce environment, changes are successful in increasing viability to the extent that they signal legitimacy to those audiences who can provide the resources necessary for survival." Lauren A. Taylor and Elena Byhoff, "Money Moves the Mare: The Response of Community-Based Organizations to Health Care's Embrace of Social Determinants," *Milbank Quarterly* 99, no. 1 (March 2021): 173.

11. Bryan Evans, Ted Richmond, and John Shields, "Structuring Neoliberal Governance: The Nonprofit Sector, Emerging New Modes of Control and the Marketisation of Service Delivery," *Policy and Society* 24, no. 1 (2005): 74.

12. LSA food pantry visits nearly doubled in the months after the beginning of the pandemic and have continued to climb steadily since then. For example, in September 2020, there was a 65 percent increase in food pantry visits as compared to the same month the previous year. In December 2020, this number climbed to a 75 percent increase over the previous year. These increases have generally continued, although more modestly, throughout 2021 and 2022, with a general increase of 82 percent from 2019 to 2022. This percentage is likely even higher, given that the agency collected no data on the many food pantry recipients from March 2020 to August 2020 who were not regular LSA clients. This information is based on analysis generously supplied to us by Joshua Nowrangilall, who works as a data quality and reporting specialist at LSA.

13. Yoav Gonen and Ben Fractenberg, "Moving Trucks Carry the Dead as Funeral Homes Get Slammed, *The City*, April 30, 2020, https://www.thecity.nyc/coronavirus/2020/4/30/21247104/moving-trucks-carry-the-dead-as-funeral-homes-get-slammed.

14. Sabine Puhl, "Synthesis of Companions of Hope in Times of Fragility—Spiritual Journey," from 2023 General Chapter of the Little Sisters of the Assumption, unpublished document given to Brenna Moore, April 18, 2023.

15. Quoted in "The Passing of Sr. Susanne Lachapelle," LSA Family Health Service News, January 3, 2023, https://littlesistersfamily.org/the-passing-of-sr-susanne-lachapelle/.

INDEX

*Page numbers in **bold** refer to figures.*

Carey Kasten is an associate professor of Spanish language and literature at Fordham University. She researches contemporary Spanish culture and Spanish-speaking communities in New York City. She is the author of *The Cultural Politics of Twentieth-Century Spanish Theater: Representing the Auto Sacramental* (Bucknell, 2012). Dr. Kasten works with the Kino Border Initiative to take students to the Arizona-Mexico border and learn about the complex realities of migration. In 2021, she curated "Hostile Terrain 94," an art installation that depicts the loss of migrant life in the Sonoran desert, at Fordham University's Lipani Gallery.

Brenna Moore is a professor of theology at Fordham University. She is a specialist in the area of modern Christianity, with a focus on Catholic intellectual and cultural history in twentieth-century Europe. Her most recent book is *Kindred Spirits: Friendship and Resistance at the Edges of Modern Catholicism* (Chicago, 2021), in which she explores a community of Catholic artists and thinkers who responded creatively to the far-right surges of xenophobia and nationalism in the mid-twentieth century. She is a longtime volunteer at the Little Sisters of the Assumption Family Health Service and serves on their board of directors.

EMPIRE STATE EDITIONS

SELECT TITLES FROM EMPIRE STATE EDITIONS

Salvatore Basile, *Fifth Avenue Famous: The Extraordinary Story of Music at St. Patrick's Cathedral*. Foreword by Most Reverend Timothy M. Dolan, Archbishop of New York

William Seraile, *Angels of Mercy: White Women and the History of New York's Colored Orphan Asylum*

Andrew J. Sparberg, *From a Nickel to a Token: The Journey from Board of Transportation to MTA*

Anthony D. Andreassi, C.O., *Teach Me to Be Generous: The First Century of Regis High School in New York City*. Foreword by Timothy Michael Cardinal Dolan, Archbishop of New York

Daniel Campo, *The Accidental Playground: Brooklyn Waterfront Narratives of the Undesigned and Unplanned*

Gerard R. Wolfe, *The Synagogues of New York's Lower East Side: A Retrospective and Contemporary View, Second Edition*. Photographs by Jo Renée Fine and Norman Borden, Foreword by Joseph Berger

Joseph B. Raskin, *The Routes Not Taken: A Trip Through New York City's Unbuilt Subway System*

Stephen Miller, *Walking New York: Reflections of American Writers from Walt Whitman to Teju Cole*

Tom Glynn, *Reading Publics: New York City's Public Libraries, 1754–1911*

R. Scott Hanson, *City of Gods: Religious Freedom, Immigration, and Pluralism in Flushing, Queens*. Foreword by Martin E. Marty

Dorothy Day and the Catholic Worker: The Miracle of Our Continuance. Edited, with an Introduction and Additional Text by Kate Hennessy, Photographs by Vivian Cherry, Text by Dorothy Day

Mark Naison and Bob Gumbs, *Before the Fires: An Oral History of African American Life in the Bronx from the 1930s to the 1960s*

Sharon Egretta Sutton, *When Ivory Towers Were Black: A Story about Race in America's Cities and Universities*

Pamela Hanlon, *A Wordly Affair: New York, the United Nations, and the Story Behind Their Unlikely Bond*

David J. Goodwin, *Left Bank of the Hudson: Jersey City and the Artists of 111 1st Street*. Foreword by DW Gibson

Nandini Bagchee, *Counter Institution: Activist Estates of the Lower East Side*

Susan Celia Greenfield (ed.), *Sacred Shelter: Thirteen Journeys of Homelessness and Healing*

Elizabeth Macaulay-Lewis and Matthew M. McGowan (eds.), *Classical New York: Discovering Greece and Rome in Gotham*

Susan Opotow and Zachary Baron Shemtob (eds.), *New York after 9/11*

Colin Davey with Thomas A. Lesser, *The American Museum of Natural History and How It Got That Way*. Forewords by Neil deGrasse Tyson and Kermit Roosevelt III

Wendy Jean Katz, *Humbug: The Politics of Art Criticism in New York City's Penny Press*

Lolita Buckner Inniss, *The Princeton Fugitive Slave: The Trials of James Collins Johnson*

Angel Garcia, *The Kingdom Began in Puerto Rico: Neil Connolly's Priesthood in the South Bronx*

Jim Mackin, *Notable New Yorkers of Manhattan's Upper West Side: Bloomingdale–Morningside Heights*

Matthew Spady, *The Neighborhood Manhattan Forgot: Audubon Park and the Families Who Shaped It*

Robert O. Binnewies, *Palisades: 100,000 Acres in 100 Years*

Marilyn S. Greenwald and Yun Li, *Eunice Hunton Carter: A Lifelong Fight for Social Justice*

Jeffrey A. Kroessler, *Sunnyside Gardens: Planning and Preservation in a Historic Garden Suburb*

Elizabeth Macaulay-Lewis, *Antiquity in Gotham: The Ancient Architecture of New York City*

Ron Howell, *King Al: How Sharpton Took the Throne*

Phil Rosenzweig, "12 Angry Men": *Reginald Rose and the Making of an American Classic*

Jean Arrington with Cynthia S. LaValle, *From Factories to Palaces: Architect Charles B. J. Snyder and the New York City Public Schools*. Foreword by Peg Breen

Boukary Sawadogo, *Africans in Harlem: An Untold New York Story*

Alvin Eng, *Our Laundry, Our Town: My Chinese American Life from Flushing to the Downtown Stage and Beyond*

Stephanie Azzarone, *Heaven on the Hudson: Mansions, Monuments, and Marvels of Riverside Park*

Peter Quinn, *Cross Bronx: A Writing Life*

Mark Bulik, *Ambush at Central Park: When the IRA Came to New York*

Matt Dallos, *In the Adirondacks: Dispatches from the Largest Park in the Lower 48*

Brandon Dean Lamson, *Caged: A Teacher's Journey Through Rikers, or How I Beheaded the Minotaur*

Raj Tawney, *Colorful Palate: Savored Stories from a Mixed Life*

Edward Cahill, *Disorderly Men*

Joseph Heathcott, *Global Queens: An Urban Mosaic*

Francis R. Kowsky with Lucille Gordon, *Hell on Color, Sweet on Song: Jacob Wrey Mould and the Artful Beauty of Central Park*

Jill Jonnes, *South Bronx Rising: The Rise, Fall, and Resurrection of an American City*, Third Edition

Barbara G. Mensch, *A Falling-Off Place: The Transformation of Lower Manhattan*

David J. Goodwin, *Midnight Rambles: H. P. Lovecraft in Gotham*

Felipe Luciano, *Flesh and Spirit: Confessions of a Young Lord*

Maximo G. Martinez, *Sojourners in the Capital of the World: Garifuna Immigrants*

Jennifer Baum, *Just City: Growing Up on the Upper West Side When Housing Was a Human Righ*

Davida Siwisa James, *Hamilton Heights and Sugar Hill: Alexander Hamilton's Old Harlem Neighborhood Through the Centuries*

Annik LaFarge, *On the High Line: The Definitive Guide*, Third Edition. Foreword by Rick Dark

Marie Carter, *Mortimer and the Witches: A History of Nineteenth-Century Fortune Tellers*

Alice Sparberg Alexiou, *Devil's Mile: The Rich, Gritty History of the Bowery*. Foreword by Peter Quinn

Kimberly A. Orcutt, *The American Art-Union: Utopia and Skepticism in the Antebellum Era*

For a complete list, visit www.fordhampress.com/empire-state-editions.

